Urban Warfare in the Twenty-First Century

Urban Warfare in the Twenty-First Century

Anthony King

polity

First published in 2021 by Polity Press

Polity Press
65 Bridge Street
Cambridge CB2 1UR, UK

Polity Press
101 Station Landing
Suite 300
Medford, MA 02155, USA

ISBN-13: 978-1-5095-4365-6
ISBN-13: 978-1-5095-4366-3 (pb)

A catalogue record for this book is available from the British Library.

Library of Congress Cataloging-in-Publication Data
Names: King, Anthony, 1967- author.
Title: Urban warfare in the twenty-first century / Anthony King.
Description: Cambridge, UK ; Medford, MA : Polity Press, 2021. | Includes bibliographical references and index. | Summary: "An outstanding interdisciplinary introduction to urban warfare in the contemporary world"-- Provided by publisher.
Identifiers: LCCN 2020053371 (print) | LCCN 2020053372 (ebook) | ISBN 9781509543656 (hardback) | ISBN 9781509543663 (paperback) | ISBN 9781509543670 (epub)
Subjects: LCSH: Urban warfare--History--21st century. | Metropolitan areas--Strategic aspects. | Siege warfare--History.
Classification: LCC U167.5.S7 K56 2021 (print) | LCC U167.5.S7 (ebook) | DDC 355.4/26--dc23
LC record available at https://lccn.loc.gov/2020053371
LC ebook record available at https://lccn.loc.gov/2020053372

Typeset in 10.75 on 13 Adobe Janson by
Servis Filmsetting Ltd, Stockport, Cheshire

The publisher has used its best endeavours to ensure that the URLs for external websites referred to in this book are correct and active at the time of going to press. However, the publisher has no responsibility for the websites and can make no guarantee that a site will remain live or that the content is or will remain appropriate.

Every effort has been made to trace all copyright holders, but if any have been overlooked the publisher will be pleased to include any necessary credits in any subsequent reprint or edition. The author and publisher would like to thank the following for permission to use copyright material: Figure 3.1 from *Castle, The Journal of the Royal Anglian Regiment*; Map 1.1 and Map 5.3 from the Institute for the Study of War; Map 2.3 from The Map Archive; Map 3.1 from *Geografski vestnik*; Map 11.1 from Army University Press; and Map 2.2 and Map 8.1 from *Cobra II: The Inside Story of the Invasion and Occupation of Iraq* by Michael R. Gordon, copyright © 2006, 2007 by Michael R. Gordon and Bernard E. Trainor. Used by permission of Pantheon Books, an imprint of the Knopf Doubleday Publishing Group, a division of Penguin Random House LLC. All rights reserved.

For further information on Polity, visit our website: politybooks.com

Contents

Maps, Figures and Tables

Tables

Preface

I cannot remember precisely when it was. It may have been in 2001 or 2002, or it might have been in 2004 or 2005, after I had already started to work on the armed forces. However, the memory itself remains quite distinct. In my first years at Exeter University my office was directly opposite that of Barry Barnes, who held the professorial chair of the department. I was very lucky. Our proximity in the department was congenial and instructive for me. As an eminent sociologist, Barry was a very fine mentor and friend. I met Barry frequently, as a result, and we talked about many things, including sociology and social theory. In one of those conversations, as was common, he invited me into his room and, as we chatted, he showed me a small, yellow booklet, the reading list from an old course on 'Social Order' which he had taught at Edinburgh. On the cover of this booklet was the photocopy of an engraving of a late fifteenth- or early sixteenth-century siege, in which cannon had breached a wall, while soldiers attacked a gate as defenders poured burning oil upon them. Barry motioned excitedly at the image and cried: 'Look at all the social stuff going on there.' His point was, of course, that once humans were able to form social groups and cooperate with each other, there was almost no limit to their powers – for good or ill.

I would like to say that, from the moment I saw that image, I decided to take Barry up on his challenge and to write a sociology of urban warfare. Yet, that would not be true. I remembered the image and Barry's exhortation as a general lesson about sociological analysis, not as an injunction to write a particular book. The idea of a book on urban warfare only came much later as I was finishing my book on command in 2018. At this point, British and American and, indeed, Western armed forces generally were beginning to think seriously about urban operations. Their concerns about the increasing likelihood of urban operations, as well as their intense experience of them over the previous decade or more, attracted my interest. I had, in fact, written about urban tactics in *The Combat Soldier*, published in 2013. However, Barry's image of that early modern siege became increasingly significant to me as I researched urban warfare. So in the end, this book might be read as a circuitous answer to Barry's challenge. It is a sociology of urban warfare; it is an attempt to show how the changing size and density of military forces and cities, as social groups, have reconfigured the urban battle in the twenty-first century. I do not mention the work of Émile Durkheim in this book anywhere. Yet, for anyone who knows his work, its influence on my thinking about urban warfare past, present and future should be obvious.

As always, many friends and colleagues helped me with this book. I am grateful to them all. I offer special thanks to the following. I could not have conducted the military research I have without the support of the British Army and the Royal Marines, and especially 40 and 45 Commando Royal Marines. I am personally grateful to: Ben Baker, James Bashall, Jules Buczacki, Matt Cansdale, Alec Case, Innes Caton, James Cook, Kevin Copsey, Mike Cornwell, Gerry Ewart-Brookes, Adam Fraser-Hitchen, Paddy Ginn, Stephen Greenberg (USMC), Paul Hammett, Sigolene Hobson, Rupert Jones, James Martin, Nick McGinley, Charles 'Jack' Nicholson, Nick Perry, Jamie Powell, Dan Reeve, Clo O'Neill, Dom Rogers, Simon Rogers, Dickie Sernberg, Jolyon Simpson, Al Speedie, Zac Stenning, Johnny Stringer, Andrew Stuart and Matt Taylor. Stephen Bowns, Peter Dixon, Robert Goodin and the Royal Anglian Regiment were extremely generous in their support for my research on Belfast in 1972 and the permission to use some images. I would also like to thank Ben Barry, Virginia Comolli and Antonio Sampaio at the International Institute for Strategic Studies; Marcus Geisser at the International Committee of the Red Cross; and James Denselow at Save the Children. At Warwick, Jon Coaffee and Stuart Elden provided very useful guidance, as did Randall Collins, Russell Glenn, Patrick Finnegan and Jeremy Black.

The US Army was no less helpful. At West Point, the Modern Warfare Institute has provided invaluable support, especially John Spencer (who has been particularly kind), John Amble, Liam Collins and Noel Siosson. I am indebted to Doug Winton not only for some fascinating conversations but also for allowing me pre-emptively to read his excellent doctoral dissertation on urban warfare, which I look forward to seeing in print and which I would recommend to everyone interested in the topic. I am very grateful also to Sean MacFarland, Joseph Martin, Joe O'Callaghan and Danilo Pamonag (Filipino Army) for their time and insights. At NATO, Jeff Biddiscombe, Frode Rieger, Simon Thomsett and Jan van der Werf were very helpful.

At Polity, I am very grateful to John Thompson, who initially saw potential in the project; Louise Knight, who has been a brilliant editor; Inès Boxman for her assistance; and Sarah Dancy. Will Crosby helped check the references. As always, I am indebted to those who read and commented on the manuscript. Charles Heath-Saunders and Patrick Jackson at the MOD confirmed that the book did not breach operational or personal security and provided useful comments. The feedback from Christopher Dandeker, Chris Torchia and two anonymous reviewers at Polity was very helpful indeed. I am particularly grateful here to Patrick Owen, an excellent student from my first cohort at Warwick. Finally, as always, Patrick Bury provided perceptive and very pertinent guidance about how to improve the manuscript.

1

Gomorrah

Mosul

On 16 July 2018, the last bombs fell on Mosul. A battle, which some American generals described as 'the most significant urban combat since World War Two', was over.[1] After nine months of bitter fighting, ISIS was defeated, but the city was also destroyed. Homes, government and commercial buildings, factories, shops, mosques and hospitals had been ruined; the streets were choked with rubble and the detritus of war. The civil infrastructure – water, electricity, sewage – had collapsed. The fighting had been truly terrible. One of the American commanders of the operation, General Stephen Townsend, recalled: 'The battle of Mosul was the most disorganized, chaotic, debris-littered place I've ever seen. Large swathes of the city were damaged. Some parts, especially the west side, were completely levelled – entire neighbourhoods destroyed.'[2] Other US officers, closer to the combat, were shocked: 'You can't replicate how stressful it was: how bad the slaughter was in Mosul.'[3]

It was a scene worthy of the Old Testament. Indeed, the battle of Mosul had a strange historical parallel. More than 2,500 years before, in 612 BCE, the capital of the Assyrian Empire, Nineveh, located on the east bank of the Tigris in modern Mosul, had been sacked by Babylonian forces. Excavations at the Halzi Gate discovered the remains of men, children and even a baby, killed by arrows as they tried to escape the burning city. Then, the last king of Assyria, Sin-shar-ishkun, had perished in the flames with his possessions, his eunuchs and his concubines.[4] Like their Assyrian predecessors, ISIS too had chosen to die in the ruins of Mosul.

In June 2014, ISIS advanced on Mosul. The city of over 1.5 million, the second biggest in Iraq, was a major strategic prize. Although Mosul was defended by an American-equipped Iraqi division of some 20,000 soldiers, the entire force fled in the face of a bold advance by only 1,500 ISIS fighters. The ISIS force, mounted in Toyota trucks, entered the city all but unopposed. With the capture of Mosul, the ISIS leader, Abu Bakr Al-Baghdadi, declared the creation of the caliphate. For more than two years, ISIS imposed a reign of terror on their territory in eastern Syria and northern Iraq. Remarkably, they were able to unite the entire international community against them. The war against ISIS converged inexorably on Mosul.

On 16 October 2016, the Iraqi Security Forces, under the supervision of a US Combined Joint Task Force based in Baghdad, began its campaign to retake Mosul with a force of 94,000 Iraqi soldiers.[5] Initially, the Iraqi 1st Infantry and 9th Infantry Divisions attacked the eastern part of the city from the east and south-east, though the Iraqi Counter-Terrorist Service, an elite special forces formation of about 10,000 soldiers, led most of the attacks. The Iraqi Security Forces were accompanied by about 1,000 American advisers with a further 2,000 supporting them.[6] They were opposed by an ISIS force of some 5,000–8,000 active fighters, supported by locally recruited young militants; ISIS probably fielded a force of about 12,000 in the city.

From October 2016, Iraqi Security Forces began to advance on and into eastern Mosul (see Map 1.1). Iraqi forces faced intense resistance. Mosul consisted of some 200,000 buildings and 3,000 kilometres of road; millions of rooms and thousands of square metres of terrain had to be cleared. Organized into small squads of perhaps five fighters, ISIS defended the city fanatically from their prepared strongpoints, engaging in frequent counterattack, often using subterranean passages to infiltrate Iraqi lines.

Of course, improvised explosive devices (IEDs) – mines and booby-traps – played a central role in the ISIS defence plan. ISIS laid belts of IEDs across roads and avenues of advance, hiding them in the rubble and ruined buildings. However, their most feared and effective weapon was the suicide vehicle-borne improvised explosive device (SVBIED). ISIS had prepared hundreds of armoured vehicles before the Iraqi attack; many were camouflaged to look like civilian vehicles.[7] Whenever the Iraqi Army mounted an assault, ISIS launched suicide fleets against Iraqi lines. Having observed the Iraqi dispositions from

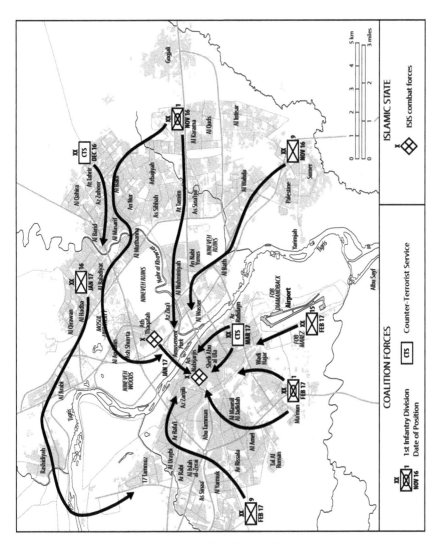

Map 1.1: The battle of Mosul, 2016–17
Source: Map courtesy of the Institute for the Study of War:
http://www.understandingwar.org/map/map-mosul. Modifications based on
Thomas D. Arnold and Nicolas Fiore, 'Five operational lessons from the
battle for Mosul', *Military Review*, Army University Press, January–February
2019, 63: https://www.armyupress.army.mil/Portals/7/military-review/
Archives/English/JF-19/Arnold-Fiore-Lessons-Mosul.pdf.

remotely controlled drones, ISIS commanders directed the vehicles along routes to inflict maximum damage and casualties. In all, ISIS mounted 482 suicide vehicle attacks in Mosul.[8] Eventually, the Iraqi Army developed effective countermeasures, blocking side roads with tanks, barricades or craters created by bombs dropped by US aircraft. Thwarted by these obstacles, ISIS loaded their armoured vehicles with squads of suicide bombers. Once the vehicles reached Iraqi lines, the individual bombers burst out of the trucks and charged towards the Iraqis detonating themselves in hellish scenes.

The fight for Mosul was desperate, especially once Iraqi forces crossed the Tigris into western Mosul and the Old Town. In a strange echo of Assyrian siege techniques from the seventh century BCE, bull-dozers led the way clearing the rubble so that Iraqi troops, tanks and armoured vehicles could advance. From the rear, artillery, mortars and rocket launchers fired heavy bombardments onto identified targets, while attack helicopters, drones, gunships and jet and propellered air-craft monitored the city and struck targets with cannon fire, Hellfire missiles and precision bombs.

The final acts of the battle were worthy of Stalingrad itself. The last ISIS fighters were trapped in fighting positions in a shrinking pocket near the west bank of the Tigris. As they refused to surrender, the Iraqi forces eventually bulldozed over their positions, eliminating any final resistance with grenades. 'It reminded me of something you would watch on a World War II video of Iwo Jima; marines burying Japanese die-hard defenders on Iwo Jima. I never thought I'd see that.'[9] Although some escaped, most of the ISIS fighters were killed. Officially, 1,400 Iraqi soldiers were killed and 7,000 wounded, but casualties were probably much higher.[10] Although thousands left Mosul before the battle, estimates of civilian deaths vary wildly. The lowest suggest that 3,000 died, the highest 25,000. Any figure within this range seems possible.

The Urban Revolution

Mosul may, indeed, have been one of the greatest urban battles of the twenty-first century, but it was far from unique. On the contrary, urban warfare has become normal, even the norm, today: 'Warfare, like everything else, is being urbanized.'[11] Of course, since the early 2000s, there has been extensive fighting in rural and mountainous areas in conflicts in Sudan, Afghanistan, Mali, Nigeria, Ethiopia and Eritrea, and in Kashmir and Ladakh. By contrast, in Iraq, Syria, Libya, Georgia,

Yemen, Israel, Libya and the Ukraine, populations have been over-whelmingly caught up in the fighting; in these theatres, wars have taken place inside urban areas.

The rise of urban warfare in the early twenty-first century now has a well-recognized chronology. In October 1993, US Special Operations Forces and Rangers were trapped inside Mogadishu for twelve hours after an attempt to seize a Somali warlord had failed. In stark contrast to the Gulf War, when US Abrams tanks were able to engage Iraqi T-72s in the open desert from several kilometres before the Iraqis had even detected them, the canyons of Mogadishu became a killing zone; two Black Hawk helicopters were shot down and in running gun battles with local militia that lasted for more than twelve hours, eighteen US soldiers were killed and seventy-three wounded.

The battle of Grozny a year later was an even more sobering portent of the urban future. In December 1994, in response to the declara-tion of Chechen independence by President Dudayev, Russian Army forces advanced into the capital Grozny in order to reassert Moscow's authority. The Chechen rebels allowed Russian armoured columns to penetrate deep into the city. The 131st Mechanized Rifle Brigade, under Major-General Politovsky, reached the central station, where some conscripts, thinking the conflict was over, even bought rail tick-ets home.[12] Yet, the war had only just begun. A brigade commander, Colonel Stavin, later claimed that he heard the words, 'Welcome to hell', over his radio. At that moment, with complete surprise, Chechen hunter-killer teams ambushed the Russian columns from high-rise buildings, destroying numerous armoured vehicles and tanks, and kill-ing many soldiers, before moving through cellars and sewers to new positions. In the end, the Russians had to mount a systematic clearance of the city, destroying much of it, before the uprising was suppressed in February 1995. Even so, a second bitter battle occurred over the city in 1999–2000, as Russian forces seized Grozny from the rebels once again.

In 1984, Sarajevo was the site of a very successful Winter Olympic Games. However, only a decade later, Sarajevo came to haunt public imagination as symbol of ethnic war. From May 1992 to December 1995, Serbian forces besieged and bombarded the city as part of its war in Bosnia-Herzegovina. The blockade, watched across Europe on nightly news programmes, inflicted terrible suffering on the citizens of Sarajevo, who had to endure constant sniper and artillery fire. There were some notorious incidents, including the Serbian mortaring of Markale marketplace on 28 August 1995, which killed forty-three civil-ians and injured seventy-five more.

By the late 1990s, Sarajevo, Mogadishu and Grozny were being interpreted not just as significant incidents in themselves, but as the start of a trend. They denoted an epochal turn to urban warfare. The past couple of decades have only affirmed this trajectory. Since 2000, urban warfare has been almost continuous. During the 2003 invasion of Iraq, for instance, a few engagements took place outside urban areas, but the battles inside Iraqi cities were far more significant. The battle of Nasiriyah on 23–24 March 2003 was notorious. There were other major battles: in Baghdad, Samawah and Najaf.

The Iraqi invasion was rapid, but it established the tone for the rest of the campaign. From 2003 to 2008, US-led forces were engaged in an urban counterinsurgency campaign against Al Qaeda terrorists, and Sunni and Shia militias. The most intense urban battles occurred in November 2004 with the second battle of Fallujah and, in March to May 2008, when Shia militias were finally suppressed in Sadr City and in Basra. Yet, the US also conducted major operations in Tal Afar in 2005 and Ramadi in 2006. Most of the campaign took place in the towns and cities of Iraq, with US coalition forces fighting to control the streets. Sometimes the situation was relatively benign. In Basra, British troops wore berets on patrol until 2004, but, for the most part, coalition forces wore helmets and body armour and moved in protected vehicles because of the threat from IEDs, rocket-propelled grenades and small arms fire. It was a high-intensity urban guerrilla war, with Ramadi, Fallujah, Mosul and Baghdad the sites of extreme violence and, sometimes, grotesque atrocity.

Other recent conflicts in the Middle East only reaffirm the point. The Syrian civil war is the most important case here. It began as a series of urban protests in the towns and cities of eastern Syria, beginning in Dar'a in February 2011. However, in the face of extreme repression, antiregime elements formed increasingly effective local militias and began to fight Assad's troops. Between 2011 and 2016, fighting took place in most Syrian cities and towns. Major battles took place in Homs, Damascus, Aleppo, Ghouta, Idlib, Latakia, Hama and many other towns and cities. In addition to indiscriminate artillery and air bombardment, the regime periodically employed gas to kill civilian opponents. Local and international reportage has captured the horror of these sieges.

ISIS's rise and fall is a case study in urban warfare. In early 2014, ISIS began to ally itself with tribal groups in eastern and southern Syria, in Deir Ezzor, Hasaka, Raqqa and Dar'a. As a result, ISIS took control of Deir Ezzor in July 2014 and from there began to expand its caliphate.

ISIS inserted Sunni sleeper cells into towns and cities across the region. These cells mobilized the local Sunni population in support of ISIS's imminent assaults, and provided intelligence and mounted attacks on the opposition forces holding the towns. As a result, ISIS took Raqqa, al-Bab, Fallujah and Mosul in a 'lightning push' in 2014, the towns falling in quick succession, often without significant fighting. Once established in an urban hub, ISIS was then able to dominate the surrounding area.

Almost all ISIS's offensive operations were urban, then. The eventual defeat of the group took precisely the same form; most of the fighting took place in cities. The caliphate was destroyed as the US-led coalition reversed ISIS's own urban gains, retaking Iraqi and Syrian cities in turn. As a British officer noted:

> The campaign for the liberation from IS was a series of urban battles. There was no front line. It was just the cities and then the manoeuvre to them. If you looked at the campaign map, it consisted of spots: the fights were in cities and towns. In the Soviet era, there were large fronts, you don't have those forces now. You are going to go from point to point.[13]

Both the Libyan and the Yemen civil wars have also been heavily urbanized. Following Gaddafi's fall in 2011, Libya quickly descended into a struggle between General Haftar's Libyan National Army and the Government of National Accord based in Tripoli. They fought major battles for control of Benghazi in 2012 and Sirte in 2016 – and continue to do so. Similarly, the Yemen civil war has been highly urbanized with a major battle over control of Sana'a between Houthi rebels and government forces.

The West has been involved in the wars in Iraq, Syria, Libya and Yemen. Elsewhere, war has also migrated into cities. The experiences of Israel reflect this process. During the Six Day War in 1967, Israeli paratroopers retook Jerusalem, but in that conflict and the subsequent Yom Kippur War of 1973, the Israeli Defence Force (IDF) was primarily engaged in open manoeuvre war in the Sinai desert or on the Golan Heights. The first phase of the invasion of Lebanon in 1982 was also predominantly characterized by manoeuvre warfare. However, since then, IDF operations have become increasingly urban. Ironically, even during the Second Lebanon War of 2006, many of the most intense engagements occurred in the towns of south Lebanon. Despite the fact that this region consists of rural, rocky hills and scrubland, 'most of the fighting took place in built-up areas'.[14] Circumstances have forced the IDF to urbanize.[15]

Russia had also experienced an urban revolution by the mid-1990s; the battles of Grozny in 1994–5 and 1999–2000 suggested that something profound had changed. Russian conflicts since the Chechen wars have only affirmed the point. Since 2000, Russia has fought wars in Georgia in 2008 and Ukraine from 2014. After years of tension, in August 2008, Georgia deployed a force to suppress Russian-supporting Ossetian separatists who had been shelling Georgia. On this pretext, President Putin initiated a large operation to regain control of South Ossetia and drive out the Georgian troops. The fighting in the 2008 Russo-Georgian War concentrated on Gori and Tskhinvali. Similarly, in the Donbas, most of the fighting took place in urban areas. Donetsk Airport, for in instance, was the site of a major six-month battle in 2014 and 2015. The airport was eventually taken by the Donetsk People's Republic Army in January 2015, when Russian special forces blew up the terminal building and its Ukrainian defenders. In early 2016, there was a renewed bout of fighting, which again focused on three urbanized areas: Avdiivka, a Ukrainian controlled industrial town with large coke and chemical plants, the major railway junction of Yasinovata, and Horlivka.[16] In each case, the Ukrainian and Donetsk Peoples' Republic forces have tried to seize – or hold – key industrial or transport nodes in cities and towns.

Across Eurasia and the Middle East, then, warfare has urbanized. However, the urbanization of warfare is a truly global phenomenon. In India, on 26 November 2008, ten terrorists from the Lashkar-e-Taiba group arrived secretly by boat into Mumbai. Armed with automatic rifles, grenades and suicide vests, they rampaged through some of the most prominent landmarks of the city, including the Taj Hotel, for four days, killing 174 civilians and security personnel. The 2008 Mumbai attack has highlighted the vulnerability of Indian cities to attacks. The Indian Army is currently concerned about improving its capacity to mount urban operations. In the Philippines in recent years, the armed forces have been engaged in two major urban battles against Islamicist jihadists: in Zamboanga in 2013 and in Marawi in 2017. The battle of Marawi was a brutal and intense engagement, when local militants from the Maute group reinforced ISIS jihadists led by Isnilon Hapilon to seize control of the main buildings in the centre of the town. The jihadists were eliminated only after bitter fighting against the Filipino Army, led by the special forces.

Mosul may, then, stand alone as the Stalingrad of the early twenty-first century. For Western forces, it was certainly the largest and most intense urban campaign of the past two decades. Yet, despite its scale,

Mosul was not an aberration. Urban combat has become a central, maybe even the defining, form of warfare in the twenty-first century. In the twentieth century, armies prepared to fight in the field. Today, it seems all but inevitable that they will fight in cities.

Urban Origins

The rise of urban warfare is deeply troubling. The scale of human suffering and the destruction it has inflicted have often been terrible. Nevertheless, it would be quite wrong to suggest that urban warfare itself is new. Urban warfare was a regular occurrence in antiquity. Indeed, the siege and the sacking of cities were central themes in classical literature, as the *Iliad* and the *Odyssey* demonstrate. Roman literature is also replete with depictions of urban warfare. Unlike the *Iliad*, Virgil's *Aeneid* was not a primarily a poem about battle. Yet, some of its most powerful passages describe the sacking of Troy, the most famous siege of all:

> There we found the fighting so heavy that it seemed there were no battles anywhere else, that this was the only place in the city where men were dying. We saw Mars, the irresistible God of War, Greeks rushing to the palace, men with shields locked over their backs packing the threshold, ladders hooked to the walls and men struggling to climb them right against the doorposts, thrusting up their shields on their left arms to protect themselves while their right hands gripped the top of the walls.[17]

Virgil took his imagery from Roman siege techniques; his observation of the details of the escalade are striking. His moving depiction of the destruction of Troy seems to be a subtle interrogation of the hypocrisies of Roman imperialism.

Yet, written between 29 and 19 BCE during Augustus's Principate, Virgil's account of urban warfare was anything but new, even then. On the contrary, by the first century BCE, siege warfare was a prominent, even primary, form of warfare. The Old Testament, composed between about 1200 and 165 BCE, records the sacking of many cities, including Nineveh, and, of course, Jericho: 'And they utterly destroyed all that was in the city, both man and woman, young and old, and ox, and sheep, and ass, with the edge of the sword.'[18] Archaeology affirms the literary evidence. According to the archaeological research, humans first started to inhabit urban settlements at the beginning of the Neolithic period, about 10,000 years ago; Jericho has been dated

Figure 1.1: The ancient walls of Jericho
Source: Daniel Case / Wikimedia Commons / CC BY-SA
(https://creativecommons.org/licenses/by-sa/3.0).

to 9000 BCE. Similarly, in Anatolia, Çatalhöyük seems to have been inhabited from 7500 to 5700 BCE.[19] Both display signs of militarization. Jericho was surrounded by rock-cut ditch and three-foot-thick walls (see Figure 1.1).[20] The original Jericho was destroyed in *c.* 5000 BCE. Although Çatalhöyük is not so obviously fortified, it was plainly a stronghold. The settlement consists of a series of tightly packed, baked mud houses, accessible only through the roof by means of a ladder, and with blank exterior walls (see Figure 1.2). Moreover, wall paintings of what may have been a warrior have been discovered inside the settlement.[21]

Fortified settlements may have predated agriculture and the state. However, the first true cities emerged in Mesopotamia around 3000 BCE. The first city-states appeared in Sumer, an area that is now southern Iraq but was then a coastal, estuarine area bordering the Gulf. Ur, for instance, was founded about 2100 BCE; at its peak, it had 35,000

Figure 1.2: Çatalhöyük
Source: Çatalhöyük Research Project (http://www.catalhoyuk.com/).

inhabitants.[22] There were approximately twenty other rival city-states in existence at this time. The subsequent history of Bronze Age Mesopotamia consisted of the cyclical rise and fall of agrarian empires, centred on the cities of Akkad, Sumer, Babylon, Assyria and Elam. Warfare – and above all siege warfare – was a central element of the almost constant conflict between these empires.

The Assyrian Empire of the seventh century BCE illustrates this process. Between 711 and 627 BCE, Assyria attained dominance in the region under a succession of powerful kings: Sennacherib, Esarhaddon and Ashurbanipal. The recent battle of Mosul raged around their palaces in Nineveh. From the late eighth century, Assyrian kings engaged in a series of successful campaigns against their Elamite and Babylonian rivals, defeating them in battle and sacking their cities. The extraordinary murals in Ashurbanipal's palace include detailed depictions of successful sieges. Having taken Babylon, Ashurbanipal attacked Elam and eventually besieged and took the royal city of Hamanu. One of the friezes shows Assyrian soldiers climbing ladders, while others, protecting themselves with shields, undermine the walls. The corpses of Elamite soldiers sink in the river.[23]

Siege warfare and urban fortification reached a very high level of development in the Mesopotamian Bronze and Iron Ages, then. Similar developments are observable in other major pristine civilizations of the

Americas, China and India. All agrarian city-states were able to generate hitherto unachievable concentrations of military power. They built
and fortified very large cities, but were also able to besiege, assault and
sack their enemies' cities. Later, around the fourth century BCE, states
developed sophisticated siege engines and catapults. The power of the
Roman Empire, for instance, rested not primarily in the superiority
of the Roman legions in open battle but in their unique ability to
build fortifications in the field and to take apparently impregnable fortresses like Alesia, Maiden Castle and Masada. Urban warfare certainly
reached a higher level of sophistication and intensity in the era of great
ancient agrarian empires in the Middle East and Mediterranean from
3000 BCE to the fall of Rome in 476 CE. However, urban warfare was
already established, when the Greeks and Romans perfected the art of
siege warfare.

Urban warfare is, then, as old as cities themselves. The sad conclusion must be that from the moment humans, as aggressive, intelligent
and highly social primates, began to live in urban settlements, they
also began to fight each other for them and to kill each other in them.
Indeed, while it might be comforting to preserve a pacific vision of
early human urban evolution, evidence suggests that warfare was in fact
always an integral part of city life. From the outset, urban settlements
were primarily defined by the wall that surrounded them and protected
their inhabitants. The city may well have been the cradle of civilization;
but it was also the crucible of war.

Understanding Contemporary Urban Warfare

Urban warfare is ancient. Its long provenance is widely recognized by
commentators today. Yet it has, once again, come to prominence in
the early twenty-first century. Clearly, the reappearance of the urban
battle has engendered deep concern, not only among the armed forces
who have to fight in this dangerous and difficult terrain, but also among
politicians, political leaders, humanitarian agencies and, of course, citizens themselves. Many towns and cities have been destroyed – often
irrevocably – in recent decades; huge numbers of civilians have been
killed, wounded or displaced. The suffering has been truly terrible.
There seems little doubt that urban conflict and warfare will continue to
proliferate in the coming decades. It will remain a global issue, affecting
the lives of millions, threatening major political, economic and cultural
centres. If the political and social implications of the rise of urban
warfare are so profound, it cannot be dismissed as a technical military

issue. On the contrary, precisely because urban warfare always involves large civilian populations, it is imperative that policymakers, scholars, humanitarians, commentators and the general public all understand the realities of such conflicts.

How is it possible to understand urban warfare today, though? This is very difficult. Urban warfare is a complex and diverse phenomenon. No two battles are exactly alike; each one is bewildering in itself. As a general phenomenon, it is even harder to capture the character of urban warfare today with any fidelity. It is a prodigious political, social, military and intellectual challenge. Nevertheless, whatever the obstacles, it is necessary to try at least to comprehend the anatomy of the urban battle.

Contemporary scholarship on urban warfare is the best place to start. Two broad schools of thought are observable in the literature today and it is useful to look at each of them in turn. On the one hand, some scholars and military professionals emphasize the novelty of urban conflict today. They believe that a profound military transformation – even an urban revolution – has occurred, altering the very character of contemporary military operations in cities. Disturbed by the vast metropolises in which forces now operate, they declare that urban military challenge is without precedent. Richard Norton's 2003 article, 'Feral Cities', might be taken as a seminal moment in this catastrophic vision of the urban future:

> Imagine a great metropolis covering hundreds of square miles. Once a vital component in a national economy, this sprawling urban environment is now a vast collection of blighted buildings, an immense Petri dish of both ancient and new diseases, a territory where the rule of law has long been replaced by near anarchy in which the only security available is that which is attained through brute power. Such cities have been routinely imagined in apocalyptic movies and in certain science-fiction genres.[24]

For Norton, the feral city of the future presents the armed forces with a totally new predicament. Since military forces might have to fight in human settlements of a size never seen before, future urban operations will be without historic parallel. Norton is not alone in having such thoughts. On the contrary, the claim of originality is, perhaps, most apparent in recent discussions about war in megacities of 10 million inhabitants or more: 'While urban combat operations are not new, a megacity presents old challenges at a previously unimaginable scale and complexity.'[25] Here, mere quantity gains a quality all of its own. Others have confirmed the sheer difficulty of operating in large urban areas. They claim that the urban environment has become the hardest of all theatres.[26] For these scholars and practitioners, the sheer scale and complexity of cities in the early twenty-first century has revolutionized urban operations. For them, urban warfare today is a radical historic departure. While the siege might indeed be old, the twenty-first-century urban battle is fundamentally new.

Other scholars claim precisely the opposite: they reject novelty altogether. In a joint article, for instance, war studies scholar David Betz and British Army officer Hugh Stanford-Tuck maintained that 'nothing fundamental has changed' in urban warfare. For them, the basic features of urban warfare endure across the decades, centuries and, indeed, millennia: 'Even the challenges that might seem new, such as the prevalence of the media, are only superficially different or, at most, an amplified echo of the past.'[27] They argue that many of the practices employed by Titus in the siege of Jerusalem in 70 CE are immediately observable today. For instance, in the second week of the siege, Titus made a small breach in the second wall and sought to enter it with about 1,000 legionnaires. However, because the breach was too small and the Jewish resistance fanatical, there was a serious risk that the assault force, which could not easily retreat, would be massacred. So Titus stationed 'his archers at the end of the streets and taking post himself where the enemy was in greatest force, he kept them at bay with missiles'. Betz and Stanford-Tuck translate this action into modern vernacular:

> That this battle involved swords and clubs rather than M-4s and AK-47s matters little – just replace 'archers' and 'arrows' with 'close combat attack' and 'armed aviation' and the scene has an obvious contemporary resonance. Moreover, the tactics of the Jewish rebels differed little from those of, say, Islamic State insurgents in the months-long battle for Mosul in Iraq.

Their point is that urban battles of the twenty-first century are not remotely new; they have all been seen before. Similarly, the British scholar Alice Hills has claimed that 'city fighting remains essentially unchanged at this level of intensity, regardless of whether conventional or irregular forces are involved'.[28]

This scepticism is valid. It is all too easy to presume that urban warfare itself is objectively new. The armed forces are themselves vulnerable here. Soldiers have sometimes assumed that, because they are experiencing urban warfare for the first time, it must be a genuinely new phenomenon in itself. Their understandable shock at the horrors of urban combat has induced historical myopia. Some correction may be appropriate. Yet, while it is entirely cogent for leading scholars like David Betz or Alice Hills to argue that there is some continuity in weaponry and tactics, it is less sustainable to claim that there is nothing distinctive about contemporary urban warfare at all. While arrows might suppress defenders like bullets, and bulldozers might knock down walls like battering rams, it is not true that recent urban battles have been conducted in the same way as they ever were. Although certain features of urban combat endure, the physiology of urban warfare has changed. At this point, these commentators may conflate urban tactics with urban warfare itself. Urban tactics are certainly a valid object of analysis. However, to understand urban warfare, it is insufficient to focus on specific weapons or individual techniques; it is, rather, necessary to consider the urban battle as a whole. The moment the focus of analysis moves up to the level of the urban battle, it becomes difficult to ignore a military transformation in the twenty-first century. Urban combat may not be entirely new, but urban warfare today certainly has a *distinctive* anatomy.

It is possible to identify its special topography by taking a wider view of the urban battle. While the details of each battle are different, urban warfare consists of three fundamental elements: cities, weaponry and forces. Urban warfare is defined by the scale and geography of the urban settlements in which fighting occurs, the weaponry available to the combatants and the size of military forces – and their type. These three factors – cities, weaponry and forces – constitute the atomic elements of urban warfare. Together, they generate a recognizable 'battlescape'.[29] Each historical era has its own characteristic battlescape.

The interplay of these three factors is key to understanding urban warfare. Scholars must try to show how the physical and social topographies of cities interact with military forces and the weapons they use to generate a particular kind of battle. This is challenging. It is difficult to hold all these factors in mind at the same time and to see how they manifest themselves in the urban battle. Moreover, in order to understand urban warfare, it is necessary to transcend disciplinary boundaries. Anthropology, history, geography, politics and sociology are all immediately relevant; indeed, each is indispensable. However, and this is where the true difficulty lies, it is also necessary to have an understanding of military science and security studies, as well as detailed knowledge of military tactics, doctrine and organization. Furthermore, it is important to comprehend the city as a social space, and also to understand how the armed forces organize themselves for warfare. It is often the case that academic scholarship has little apprehension of the armed forces, while military scientists have an inadequate appreciation of cities. This book seeks to transcend these disciplinary limitations by analysing the interplay between cities, weaponry and forces in order to unite social and military sciences. As a result, the analysis is intended to be helpful both to scholars and to students in the social and political sciences as well as to urban policymakers, humanitarians and military professionals themselves.

The central argument of the book is simple. Up to now scholars and practitioners have explained the rise of urban warfare by reference to the global explosion of the urban population. They believe that the expansion of cities has both made urban warfare more likely and also determined its character. In fact, in order to understand urban warfare today, a better approach may, ironically, be to begin not with cities, but with the armed forces themselves. Moreover, it may be best to begin with an apparently banal fact about them, concerning their size. Since the late twentieth century, state armed forces almost everywhere have shrunk radically. This reduction has had profound implications for urban warfare. It has not only made urban warfare more likely, because armies, no longer big enough to form fronts, have been dragged into cities, but it has also transformed the anatomy of the urban battle itself. Urban battles in the twentieth century encompassed entire cities. Mass armies swamped cities, forming large fronts around and through them. Even inside cities, twentieth-century forces typically fought across the entire urban area.

Today, cities envelop the armed forces. Armies are simply not big enough to surround whole cities. Battles for cities now take place inside cities themselves, as contracted forces converge on decisive points. Because forces have shrunk, the urban battle has coalesced into a series of localized micro-sieges in which combatants struggle over buildings, streets and districts. Instead of battle-lines bisecting an entire city, sieges explode at particular locations. The urban battle is punctuated by localized fights.

It is important to understand the character of today's localized sieges. These sieges do not just involve passive encirclement and blockade; they are not completely static. They also involve massive strikes and aggressive assaults. Is it still legitimate to call them sieges at all, then? The term 'siege' refers literally to a military operation in which a city is surrounded and its inhabitants forced to surrender.[30] On this account, a siege involves no assault. Yet, in everyday usage, 'siege' is normally applied in a looser sense. A siege refers not just to encirclement, but also to positional warfare in general. In a war of position, there is little genuine manoeuvre because combatants struggle for heavily fortified positions. Yet, there are many attacks. On this definition, the siege certainly includes a partial or temporary blockade, but it also involves limited attacks on fortified positions. The inner-urban sieges of the twenty-first century have taken this second form. They involve a local blockade, encirclement and contravallation of enemy positions within the city itself. Yet, they have also included intense, attritional fights over fortified positions.

Inner-urban sieges of the twenty-first century are violent and gruelling. As Mosul has shown, they involve bitter fighting at close quarters between troops, tanks, armoured vehicles and bulldozers. Yet, they are highly complex, involving conventional, hybrid, irregular forces on the ground and aerial platforms flying high above the city. Precision artillery, deployed miles outside the city, information and cyber operations, collaboration with local militias and civil agencies have all become critical to the outcome. Consequently, the urban battle has localized onto specific sites within the city, but it has simultaneously extended out across the global urban archipelago by means of social media and information networks. Peoples across the world are now implicated in the fight as audiences, supporters and sometimes even participants. The anatomy of urban warfare in the twenty-first century has evolved, then. Even while ancient practices endure in the bitter close fight, the urban battlespace has been redesigned. Its topography has both contracted within the city, and also expanded outwards across the world. This book adopts a transdisciplinary approach to describe the architecture of this new battlescape.

There are a number of ways to analyse contemporary urban warfare. It would be possible to examine a single major urban battle and extrapolate the main features of urban warfare from that one event. Or, it would be possible to analyse and compare several urban battles. This book employs a different method. I do not tell the history of one battle, like Mosul, or several battles comparatively. Rather, I examine a suite of contemporary examples in order to identify the general anatomy of urban warfare today. Consequently, the book proceeds thematically, dissecting the urban battle to explore each of its constitutive elements in turn. I begin with an analysis of the rise of urban warfare, arguing for the importance of numbers to both interstate and insurgent urban warfare. We will then look at how reduced military forces have been compelled to change the way they fight in cities, as they are increasingly committed to localised micro-sieges. I will show how fortification, airpower, firepower, armour, partnering with local forces and information operations have become vital in these battles, reconfiguring their topographies. Each of these themes will be discussed in turn to provide a comprehensive picture of the urban battle of the twenty-first century. The book concludes with a discussion of the likely future of urban warfare over the next two decades. It considers how the micro-siege that we have seen since the early years of this century might develop in the next two decades. Will we be fighting in megacities in the 2020s and 2030s? Will robots take over? Or will cities be destroyed by mass conventional or nuclear strikes?

2

Numbers

Defining Urban Warfare

Everyone knows an urban battle when they see one. It only takes a moment to look at footage of Mosul, Aleppo or Donetsk to know that these were urban battles. Yet, despite its apparent obviousness, urban warfare is difficult to define precisely. In particular, as the human population thins and disperses, it often becomes hard to identify exactly what constitutes a town or city and, therefore, when field campaigns become urban operations. Yet, although there is no absolute divide, it is necessary to have some at least pragmatic classification. In a celebrated essay, the twentieth-century sociologist, Louis Wirth, defined the city according to three characteristics; size, density and heterogeneity.[1] Cities consist of large, dense and heterogeneous populations. Urban warfare occurs, therefore, in large, dense and diverse human settlements.

It is, in fact, possible to be more precise about how large and how dense a settlement needs to be before it is defined as urban. Traditionally, a city has been defined as a population of 100,000 or more. Below 100,000, and a settlement has been defined as a town. This number seems beyond dispute. The problem of definition arises at the lower end of the scale. How small does a town need to be before it is no longer urban at all? When does it become a village? With 50,000, 20,000 or 10,000 inhabitants? The last figure is plausible. However, a settlement of 10,000 inhabitants is still a large conglomeration and, prior to the modern era, it would have constituted a very significant habitation.

From a military perspective, a town of 10,000 people represents a major objective. Military doctrine is actually useful here. For instance, current US Army and US Marine urban operations doctrine define an urban area as comprising 'villages of fewer than 3,000 to large cities of over 100,000'.[2] A plausible boundary seems to be about 3,000 inhabitants. When the population reaches 3,000, an urban threshold has been met.

Of course, an urban environment is not just defined by its size. As Wirth emphasized, density is very important here. A population of 3,000 people spread over a large area is not urban, as Afghanistan shows. Urbanization requires density. Again, as with the figure of 3,000, there is some arbitrariness about the density required before a settlement can be defined as urban. On the basis of a variety of national demographics, the UN and the World Bank employ a figure of 400 people per square kilometre. Consequently, a settlement can be defined as urban if it consists of 3,000 people, at a population density of 400 people per square kilometre, and, therefore, concentrated in an area of no more than 7.5 square kilometres. Military operations become urban when forces begin to fight in densely populated areas that consist of at least 7.5 square kilometres of continuous human habitation and associated structures. It might, perhaps, be useful to round up the figures for mnemonic purposes, suggesting that urban warfare begins in settlements of 3,000, at a density of 500 inhabitants per square kilometre and, therefore, covering 6 square kilometres. Of course, an urban area can expand far beyond these figures, as recent battles of shown. They have been regularly fought in cities with populations of hundreds of thousands or millions, extending over hundreds of square kilometres. Yet, the figures of 3,000 people at a density of no fewer than 400 per square kilometre provide a useful threshold for urban warfare.

As the Western campaign in Afghanistan has shown, troops can certainly operate in settlements below this size and density. These actions may certainly feel urban to the platoons and companies conducting them. Below the level of 3,000, forces can be involved in 'fighting in built-up areas' and the immediate tactical problems are often exclusively urban for them. Squads and platoons can be engaged in urban combat. However, although individual combat can certainly be urban, the operation – the battle – is simply not urban. The congested, multidimensional challenges of urban operations do not pertain below a dense population of 3,000.

It is possible to set a numerical threshold for urban operations but it is also useful to identify a spectrum of conflict along which urban warfare is located. In *On War*, Clausewitz famously proposed that 'war is merely the continuation of policy by other means'.[3] War is an act of organized violence aimed at achieving a political goal:

> War is nothing but a duel on a larger scale. Countless duels go to make up war, but a picture of it as a whole can be formed by imagining a pair of wrestlers. Each tries through physical force to compel the other to do his will; his immediate aim is to throw his opponent in order to make him incapable of further resistance. War is thus an act of force to compel our enemy to do our will.[4]

Defined in this way, it becomes easy to define urban warfare when the fighting is intense. When the armies of two states attack each other in a densely populated settlement of more than 3,000 inhabitants, it is self-evidently urban warfare. In the twenty-first century, states have rarely fought each other within cities; the norm, rather, has been for state actors to fight nonstate insurgents. However, even here, the combat has become intense enough to describe the subsequent engagements as urban warfare without difficulty; Mogadishu, Grozny, Mosul, Aleppo and Marawi were all manifestly high-intensity battles.

As with the density and size of settlements, the problem of definition comes at the lower end of the spectrum, when violence is infrequent and small-scale. Urban violence takes many forms. Protestors, terrorists and criminals are all potentially violent; they can all compromise civic order. Yet, it would be wrong to describe lawlessness and criminality as warfare, disturbing though they might be to authorities or citizens. When exactly can protest, crime and terrorism, as forms of urban violence, be defined as urban warfare?

There are some useful statistics here that are typically employed by academics and analysts to categorize conflict and war. While a conflict is defined as active if either protagonist suffers 25 battle deaths in a year, war requires at least 1,000 or more combat-related deaths in a year. It is an arbitrary but useful number. Consequently, although the line is blurred, urban warfare begins when 1,000 combatants or civilians are killed in politically motivated attacks by recognizable, antagonistic groupings inside in the city. Gang warfare, terrorism and public protests are certainly not as obvious as a form of urban warfare as interstate conflict, but there is a threshold at which criminality or political violence can begin to be defined as war. In Brazil today, one in five citizens lives in a *favela* (slum) on the peripheries of major cities; in these areas, every year, there are 200 murders per 100,000 people, which is comparable to the death rate in Iraq in 2003 or the Balkans in the 1990s. The Brazilian state has contributed significantly to these figures: 676 people were killed by the security forces alone in 2019. The conflicts in these areas are not wars in a traditional sense. Yet, it would also seem incorrect to dismiss them as mere criminality.

Yet, while numbers are important, they are not sufficient to define urban conflict as war. Political motivation is, of course, very important here. In a large city, it might be possible that 1,000 citizens could be killed in quite random, unconnected murders. Public order would be severely compromised in this situation, but it would not be war. Crime descends into warfare when the objectives of criminals become explicitly political – when criminals are not simply robbing civilians or disputing drugs deals, but are actively contesting terrain and the application of the law against the state, compelling their enemies to do their will. Similarly, at a certain point, terrorist attacks escalate into a serious challenge to the state when they start to kill enough people.

While urban warfare is most obvious in a battle like Mosul, there is no reason to limit the analysis of contemporary warfare in cities to high-intensity conflict. On the contrary, to have a full appreciation of the diversity and complexity of urban warfare in the twenty-first century, it is pertinent to include lower levels of conflict in the analysis. Gang warfare, terrorism and protests have often taken place alongside genuine urban warfare; they are part of the phenomenon. Although Brazilian *favelas* might typically be relatively peaceful for most of their inhabitants, not only do they have very high murder rates, but they are periodically the scene of intense gun battles between rival gangs, and between gangs and the police. 'In 2018, this violent territoriality was reflected in 83 instances of gunfights lasting two hours or more.'[5] At such times, *favelas* are rightly described as warzones. The actions of police and gangs in these clashes provide useful additional evidence about the character of urban warfare today, and should not be ignored simply because no official war has been declared or recognized between them.

Demography and Asymmetry

It is now universally acknowledged that the principle reason for the rise of urban warfare is demographic. There are simply so many people now living in cities that conflict has necessarily converged on urban areas. In 1960, the world population was 3.5 billion, of whom 0.5 billion lived in cities. In 2020, the world population was 7 billion, of whom 3.3 billion lived in cities.[6] As early as 1996, commentators began to notice this urban turn. Russell Glenn, one of the first urban experts, rightly noted the military implications of this demographic revolution: 'Demographics ensure that cities will become future battlegrounds.'[7] At the same time, a prominent US Army officer, Ralph Peters, made the same point: 'We declare that only fools fight in cities and shut our eyes against the future. But in the next century, in an uncontrollably urbanizing world, we will not be able to avoid urban deployments.'[8] Their predictions have been vindicated. Commentators from across the spectrum have been all but unanimous about the prime cause of the rise of urban warfare in the twenty-first century:[9] 'The rise of urbanization – and all of the complexity it entails – increases the likelihood that at least some future conflicts will take place in cities.'[10] Similarly, the US Army's publication, *Megacities and the United States Army*, noted that the rise in the number of huge urban conurbations has increased the likelihood of fighting in cities. Since more people live in cities today than in the past, in often desperate conditions, it is inevitable, on this account, that conflict has and will become more metropolitan. Urbanization, in and of itself, has forced war into cities:

> The nexus between globalization, urbanization and rapid demographic growth in the 'global South' of the developing world appears to be changing the character of warfare. We appear to be on the cusp of an 'urban century' dominated by burgeoning megacities with a growing potential for violent implosions capable of causing major political crises.[11]

Demographics are plainly important. However, in addition to urbanization, scholars have also emphasized the asymmetric advantages of fighting in cities for weaker, nonstate insurgents. Cities offset the advanced weaponry that states possess, while maximizing the utility of suicide attacks and IEDs. Plainly, cities have always offered major defensive advantages. However, scholars have claimed that, against technologically superior state forces, contemporary cities – especially ones with rapidly growing slums – now offer the best opportunities for evasion, concealment, ambush and counterattack.[12] By operating in cities, insurgent groups also enhance the protection afforded by the laws of armed conflict and international humanitarian law. Knowing that Western powers, in particular, will seek to minimize civilian casualties, insurgents have actively sought to operate among the people.[13] Indeed, the city offers such advantages that some have claimed that urban insurgency has constituted the major military challenge of the early twenty-first century.[14]

Interstate War

When scholars invoke demographics and asymmetry, they have been mainly concerned with explaining urban insurgencies and civil conflict.[15] This is not unreasonable; most urban battles this century have occurred as part of civil conflicts. Nevertheless, these scholars have also assumed that their explanations of those civil conflicts apply equally well to interstate wars. For instance, at the beginning of his work on the history of the US Army's urban battles, Alec Wahlman argues that demography and asymmetry have been the decisive variables in determining contemporary urban warfare.[16] He then goes on to analyse the battles of Aachen, Manila, Seoul and Hué. In each case, including Hué, these were battles between state forces – not between insurgents. The implication is clear. Given urban demography and asymmetry, the US Army should expect to operate in cities against peer opponents in the future, just as much as against insurgents. The same reasoning is evident in the work of Alice Hills and David Kilcullen.[17] States will also fight against each other in cities because of urban demographics and the protection that cities offer against even the most advanced weaponry.

Clearly, although interstate and civil wars have merged in the last decade into a form of hybrid conflict, some clarification is required here. Both interstate urban warfare and civil urban conflict require explanation. Yet, for the sake of clarity, it is necessary to discuss them separately. It is convenient to discuss the question of interstate warfare first and to consider why it has tended, and is increasingly likely, to converge on cities. Because scholars have focused primarily on insurgencies, they have prioritized demography and weaponry to the exclusion of all other factors. They presume that because cities have become so large, they are almost unavoidable in any future campaign. In addition, the development of advanced surveillance technologies and precision munitions will encourage even heavy state forces to take refuge within urban areas. There is no denying the importance of urban demographics and weaponry to urban warfare. They have always played a constitutive role in this kind of warfare and are likely to do so in the future. However, there is an obvious gap in the current literature.

Historically, urban warfare has also been constituted by a third factor: the size of military forces themselves. Yet, in the contemporary literature, there is almost no discussion of the size of military forces today. This factor has fleetingly been acknowledged, but never systematically investigated.[18] Perhaps, because force size seems such a banal fact, its potential significance to the urbanization of interstate war has been ignored. However, by highlighting the importance of force size – numbers – it may be possible to improve on existing explanations of interstate urban warfare.

Force Size

Force size has, of course, long been recognized as an important determinant of warfare in any era. Many military scholars have been fully aware of the significance of numbers. Hans Delbrück, the German historian, is highly pertinent here. At the beginning of his celebrated work on politics and military history, he asserted that the best starting point for the analysis of warfare was always the size of military forces. 'Wherever the sources permit, a military-historical study does best to start with the army strengths ... Without a definite concept of the size of the armies, therefore, a critical treatment of the historical accounts, as of the events themselves, is impossible.'[19] Delbrück's four-volume work on military history is not a quantitative study of armies; it is a critical study of military operations, their political purposes and effects. Yet, throughout the study, he uses numbers to illustrate the special problems of campaigning and to demolish specious claims in the historiography.

For example, in the first volume, he comprehensively destroyed the notion that Xerxes could have led a 2-million-man army when he tried to invade Greece in 480 BCE; the march column would have been 420 miles long.[20] The army would still have been leaving Susa when its head arrived in Greece. Delbrück also concluded, against Herodotus, that the Persian Army at Marathon in 490 BCE must have been smaller than the Greek force of 12,000, given the quality of Persian troops and the size of the actual battlefield (in the Brana Valley, not its attributed location).[21] For Delbrück, numbers became a critical tool for interrogating military history. He was able to deduce the character of military operations merely on the basis of the size of the armies involved. Indeed, mere size had serious political repercussions.

Delbrück's analysis is highly perceptive. However, he did not specifically discuss the relationship between force numbers and urban warfare. In order to appreciate the almost direct historical correlation between force size and urban combat, it is necessary to turn to the work of other military historians. Christopher Duffy is immediately relevant here. In his seminal analysis of the early modern fortress, he explicitly highlighted the relationship between force size and urban warfare. Duffy has shown how the *trace italienne* (bastion fort) was developed in response to the rise of artillery and how these forts, in turn, changed the character of both states and armies at that time. From 1500 to the mid-eighteenth century, the fortress and the siege played a critical role in military operations. Indeed, it might even be claimed that the siege – not the battle – was the defining characteristic of warfare at this time. However, Duffy notes that there was a decline in siege warfare in the course of the eighteenth century.

Crucially, this decline had little to with improvements in armaments. Although new methods of forging artillery were discovered, which facilitated the production of lighter field guns, ballistic capabilities were not radically changed, especially in the case of siege guns. Early modern fortifications were, consequently, preserved until the 1850s. The decisive factor in the decline of siege warfare in the late eighteenth century was organizational. From the middle of the eighteenth century and especially during the era of the revolutionary wars, armies grew prodigiously. Napoleon's *Grande Armée* of 1812 consisted of 1 million men; but his enemies also began to expand their forces in response. The implications for early modern fortification were profound: 'Fortresses were also predominant because, according to a rough rule of thumb, we find the smaller the forces engaged on a theatre of war, the more importance attaches to the available strongpoints.'[22] As armies grew in size at the end of the Age of Enlightenment, they were able to bypass fortresses or fortified towns, the garrisons within which were simply too small to threaten them or their lines of communication.[23] Fortresses and cities could be enveloped or overwhelmed by increasingly large hosts.[24] The implication of Duffy's thesis is quite radical. On this account, in any era, campaign geometry is substantially a function of the size of the armies involved. The weaponry available to Napoleonic armies was better, but not radically different from that fielded by General John Churchill, 1st Duke of Marlborough, at the battle of Blenheim in 1708. Yet, siege warfare had become less important. Written in response to the revolutionary and Napoleonic wars, Clausewitz's *On War* demonstrates this shift very clearly. It is striking that, although he wrote an entire book on the 'Engagement' (battle), he devoted only three chapters of *On War* to fortresses and none specifically to cities and siege warfare. Eleven pages of a 600-page treatise referred to urban warfare.[25]

Duffy suggests that the operational significance of urban warfare in the early modern period was dependent on the size of armies. This is a deeply significant claim. If the early modern period is taken as indicative, it is possible to propose a wider hypothesis about urban warfare.

In any historical era, the smaller the armies, the more important cities become; urban warfare attains priority as military forces contract. By contrast, the larger the armies, the more likely that open warfare in the field will predominate over siege-craft. As forces expand, cities become less operationally significant. The frequency and importance of urban warfare is, therefore, substantially a function of the size of military forces.

The Decline of Mass Armies

Duffy's thesis about numbers is particularly pertinent to the question of urban warfare in the early twenty-first century because military forces are smaller now than they have been for centuries. Since the 1970s – and especially in more recent decades – large, state, Western forces have all but disappeared; the mass citizen army, which was the norm during the twentieth century, has been displaced by smaller all-volunteer forces. Military scholars began to note this important transformation of Western armed forces in the 1970s. By that point, some Western forces had already begun to abolish conscription.[26] Following the Cold War, conscription and the mass army became increasingly obsolete, so that by the 2010s, all major Western powers had abolished national service. As a result, Western forces have declined to about half or a third of their Cold War size (see Table 2.1). After the end of the Cold War, the active-duty US Army, for instance, contracted from 700,000 to 480,000 personnel and it is set to contract further. It is true that some European countries, such as Sweden, have recently reintroduced

Table 2.1: Army size (active service personnel), 1991–2019

Country	1991	2019	% reduction
US	731,700	481,750	–35
UK	149,600	83,500	–46
Germany	335,000/*566,000**	62,150	–77/89
France	280,300	114,850	–61
Soviet Union/Russia	1,400,000	280,000	–80
PLA (China)	2,300,000	975,000	–58
Iraq	350,000	180,000	–48
Syria	300,000	130,000	–43
Israel	104,000	126,000	+21

*The italicised figure includes the DDR's *Nationale Volksarmee*
Source: International Institute for Strategic Studies, *The Military Balance 1991*; International Institute for Strategic Studies, *The Military Balance 2019*.

limited conscription, but these selective drafts in no way reverse the general trend.

American and European commentators have often worried about this reduction of state forces. Yet, in fact, the trend is global. China and Russia have both displayed the same pattern. Indeed, with the collapse of the Soviet Union, Russia's Army is now proportionately far smaller than its Western rivals. In 1991, the Soviet Army consisted of 1.4 million active soldiers and a reserve of a further 2.75 million. Today, the Russian Army fields 280,000 personnel, of whom 195,000 are regular professionals; it is approximately 20 per cent of its Cold War size.

Because of the objective decline in troop numbers, states have necessarily deployed much smaller forces on recent operations than in the twentieth century. They simply cannot mount mass operations anymore. This is even true for the IDF. Although the IDF remains a large conscript force, which has apparently maintained its size since 1991, only small elements of it were ever deployed on Israel's recent campaigns.[27] During the First Lebanon War of 1982, 78,000 troops were deployed. By contrast, 10,000 Israeli troops fought in the Second Lebanon War of 2006; only in the very last few days of the war, after a series of defeats, did the IDF increase the deployment to 30,000.[28] Similarly, Operation Cast Lead against Hamas in Gaza in 2008 also involved a relatively small ground deployment of about 10,000 troops. If Duffy's thesis is correct, then the reduction of combat densities on the battlefield should be expected in and of itself to increase the frequency of urban fighting. Reduced state forces necessarily converge on cities and towns.

Fronts: Twentieth-Century Warfare

In order to understand the significance of declining force sizes to urban warfare today, it is useful to consider the twentieth century, as both comparison and contrast. Urban warfare was, of course, by no means irrelevant during this period. In the First and Second World Wars, armies sometimes fought directly for possession of major and capital cities such as Antwerp, Leningrad, Moscow, Stalingrad, Manila, Warsaw and Berlin, as well as a host of smaller towns and cities such as Brest and Aachen. The grand strategic aim of the protagonists in both wars was to defeat their opponents' field armies and to occupy their capitals. Cities were typically the operational and strategic objectives and, sometimes, serious fighting took place in them.[29]

However, throughout the twentieth century, armies were so big that they campaigned in the field. In the First World War, Russia, France,

Germany, Britain and the United States raised, respectively, armies of 12 million, 8 million, 11 million, 8 million and 4 million. In the Second World War, they fielded armies of 12 million, 5 million, 10 million, 4 million and 8 million respectively. In each major land campaign, the mass citizen armies of these nations formed fronts. There were three reasons for this. Fronts allowed armies to bring all their combat power to bear. It was also necessary to form a front in order to avoid being outflanked by the huge hosts that opposed them. Finally, but no less importantly, mass armies could be supported logistically only if they spread out across a large rail and road system; fronts protected their rear areas. The implications for urban warfare were profound. Because armies gathered on large fronts, twentieth-century armies predominantly fought for cities, outside them.

Perhaps the best example of the distinctive topography of twentieth-century warfare is provided by the most famous urban battle of the Second World War: Stalingrad. Stalingrad has rightly fascinated and appalled military historians and novelists alike. Not only was it one of the most savage engagements of the war, but it is plausibly held as the turning point of the conflict in Europe. Much of the historiography of Stalingrad has focused on the urban combat between August and November 1942. This is totally understandable. The fighting that took place inside the city was among the most intense of all the urban battles that took place during the Second World War. It was the first time that mass industrial armies, fully equipped with modern weaponry of machine guns, tanks, artillery and airpower, had been involved in a sustained battle against each other inside a city.

Stalingrad has been taken as the avatar of modern urban warfare, then. At the tactical level, this may be true. Yet, the Stalingrad campaign also exemplified the wider geometry of twentieth-century warfare. While they were the most intense and important actions, Sixth Army's operations in Stalingrad were only part of much wider German Army campaign on this front. Sixth Army was part of the Wehrmacht's redesignated Army Group B (formerly Army Group South), which orchestrated a wide-ranging campaign across a front, hundreds of miles north and south of Stalingrad. Stalingrad itself was not a particularly large city; in July 1941 it had a population of 900,000.[30] Most of the Wehrmacht's Army Group B, which consisted of the Fourth Hungarian, Third Rumanian, Fourth Rumanian, Eighth Italian, Fourth Panzer, Second and Sixth Armies (1.5 million men), was deployed not into Stalingrad, but into the field around it.[31] Army Group B comprised seventy-four divisions in total. Only the twenty-seven divisions of the Sixth Army and Fourth Panzer Army were ever committed to the fight in and around Stalingrad itself. The rest were deployed on the Russian steppes.[32] The Sixth Army was responsible for taking the city. It consisted of seventy divisions organized into four corps.[33] Even at the climax of the battle in November 1942, during the assault on the Barrikady Gun and Red October factories, only LI Army Corps' eight divisions (389 Infantry, 305 Infantry, 14 Panzer, 79 Infantry, 100 Jäger, 295 Infantry, 24 Panzer and 71 Infantry) were directly committed to urban combat at any one time, while the other divisions were deployed well outside the city defending German lines to the north.[34] The Red Army's deployment was similar. Only the Sixty-Second Army under General Vasili Chuikov fought in the city itself. In the course of the battle, Chuikov commanded thirteen divisions and some additional brigades; it was a very large force but constituted only about 15 per cent of the Red Army's total forces in the theatre.[35] Eight Soviet Armies, consisting of more than sixty divisions, eventually executed Operation Uranus in November 1942, encircling the Sixth Army. While the most intense fighting certainly took place in Stalingrad itself, where combat forces were most highly concentrated, the majority of German and Soviet troops were never deployed into the city. On the contrary, the battle in Stalingrad was part of a larger campaign fought along a front in the field (see Map 2.1).

It might be thought that Stalingrad was unique. Yet, this would be wrong. Allied campaigns in this period assumed a similar geometry. For instance, during the Normandy Campaign of 1944, Caen constituted the crucial hub of the whole theatre. The city was eventually destroyed by air bombardment. Yet, there was hardly any ground fighting in the city itself. The Allied Front enveloped Caen, which General Bernard Montgomery, the commander of the 21st Army, sought to take by a series of assaults – Operations Perch, Epsom, Charnwood and Goodwood – around its flanks in June and July.[36] It is no accident that Normandy was remembered primarily for the difficulty of fighting in the *bocage*, not for urban combat. The topography evident during the Stalingrad campaign pertained for most of the twentieth century. NATO and the Warsaw Pact prepared themselves for a lineal field campaign along the Inner German border to the very end of the Cold War.[37]

It is noticeable that military doctrine throughout the twentieth century typically recommended that armies avoid fighting in cities.[38] This has often been interpreted today as evidence of the unique difficulty of such battles, both then and now. This is not a complete misreading

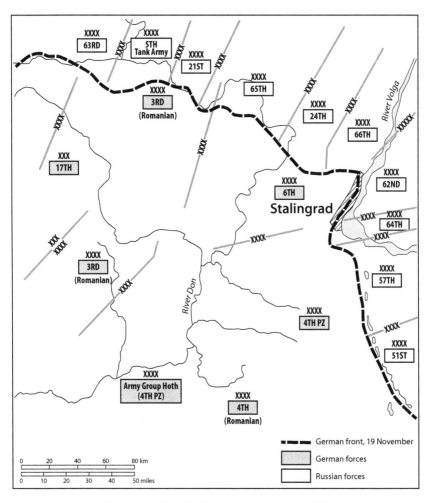

Map 2.1: The Stalingrad campaign, 1942
Source: Based on map from iMeowbot / Wikimedia Commons /
Public domain.

of military doctrine; urban fighting was demanding, and was recognized as such. However, in fact, twentieth-century military doctrine recommended avoiding cities not primarily because they were so much more impenetrable than field defences – the Western Front in the First World War showed how formidable field fortifications could be. Rather, urban fighting was to be avoided because, with mass armies deployed, the main element of the enemy's force was almost certainly to be found in the field – not in the town. It was, therefore, a mistake to commit forces to attacking a town, when the centre of gravity was elsewhere. This is why commanders were warned against it: 'Tactical doctrine stresses that urban combat operations are conducted only when required and that built-up areas are isolated and bypassed rather than risking a costly, time-consuming operation in this difficult environment.'[39] Commanders often followed the advice. At Aachen in 1945, for instance, the US Army's VII Corps assigned only two battalions to clear the city, while concentrating its forces further to the east of the city against the main element of the German Army on the Siegfried Line.[40] In the Philippines, the Japanese Army did not think that Manila should be defended at all and sought to defeat the American forces in the mountains outside it.[41] At Stalingrad, German generals catastrophically forgot the injunction.

The twentieth century seems to confirm Duffy's thesis. From 1914 to 1991, a correlation between force numbers and urban warfare is observable. Urban warfare was the subordinate form of battle. The mass armies of this era were so large that they formed fronts that encompassed cities and urban areas. Sometimes, armies conducted urban battles, but, precisely because of their immense size, most major confrontations took place in the field where combatants could deploy their full combat power against each other.

Converging on Cities: Twenty-First-Century Warfare

The military situation is now quite different. Yet, the significance of reduced forces has barely been mentioned in the current literature on urban warfare. If Delbrück and Duffy are correct, though, then it is almost certain that the radical reduction in force sizes evident in the last few decades will have been significant. Clearly, in order to demonstrate the correlation between reduced combat densities and urban warfare, empirical exemplification is necessary. This is not easy. While civil wars have proliferated, there have been few interstate wars in this century, and even fewer between advanced powers. So, the evidence is sparser. Indeed, only two recent interstate wars have involved at least one global power whose forces have been equipped with advanced weaponry: the invasion of Iraq in 2003, and the ongoing war in the Donbas.

Neither example is perfect. The Americans fought a very weak Iraqi Army in 2003; it was a mismatch that lasted only three weeks. American forces enjoyed a freedom of manoeuvre that they would certainly not be accorded against a more equal rival. So great care needs to be taken in extrapolating from it. However, Operation Iraqi Freedom also has some methodological advantages. In particular, the invasion becomes particularly pertinent as a data point when it is compared to the 1991 Gulf War. The Donbas, of course, is not officially an interstate war at all; it is a civil war between the Ukrainian government and separatist militias. However, the involvement of Russia has been so pronounced that this conflict is better understood as a hybrid war between two states. So, while significant caution needs to be exercised when extrapolating from these wars, they offer at least some evidence for testing Duffy's thesis.

Following Donald Rumsfeld's imperatives about the 'Afghan model', the US-led coalition that invaded Iraq in 2003 was small.[42] The total coalition force consisted of about 500,000 personnel, with 466,000 Americans, but the invasion force was much smaller – just 143,000 troops.[43] The Land Component consisted of five divisions (four American and one British). The US forces advanced on Baghdad on two parallel axes: the 3rd Infantry Division in the west, the 1st Marine Division in the east. The other three divisions (101st Airborne, 82nd Airborne and 1 UK Divisions) played supporting roles, clearing and holding the lines of communication in the south.

The Iraqi Army was similarly diminished. In 2003, it consisted of 350,000 troops: twenty to twenty-three Regular divisions, six Republican Guards divisions and one Special Republican Guard division.[44] Yet, most of these formations played no part in the invasion. The coalition eventually engaged a force of only four divisions, consisting of 12,000 Special Iraqi Republican Guards, 70,000 Republican Guards, supported by 15–25,000 Fedayeen fighters and a Special Security Service: around 112,000 in total.[45] The Iraqi Army deployed in a highly unusual if not idiosyncratic manner.[46] Much of Saddam's force was positioned in the north or east against the Kurds and Iran. Saddam deployed his best Republican Guard and Special Republican Guard divisions to the south of Baghdad, with a view to defending the city in a series of blocking positions outside it. In the end, these divisions fought very poorly. They suffered disastrous desertions before they were even engaged and were easily targeted by US air forces once the war started.[47] They participated in only one noteworthy encounter: the fight at al-Kaed Bridge (Objective Peach) on 2–3 April 2003, the 'single largest battle against regular Iraqi forces'.[48] In this engagement, a single US battalion – the 3rd Battalion, 69th Armor Regiment – defeated elements of the 10th Armoured Brigade of the Medina Division, the 22nd Brigade of the Nebuchadnezzar Division as well as Iraqi special forces in just three hours – without suffering a single casualty.[49] Meanwhile, Saddam deployed only the Ba'ath Party and Fedayeen into his cities, primarily to shore up his own regime, though, in the end, they did much of the fighting.

The Americans were worried that Saddam would turn his cities into fortresses.[50] Certainly, the scale of urban fighting would – and perhaps should – have been much greater in 2003 had Saddam deployed his heavy forces into his cities. For Stephen Biddle, 'perhaps the most serious Iraqi shortcoming was the systematic failure to exploit the military potential terrain'.[51] Indeed, Iraq officers were bizarrely opposed to urban fighting: 'Why would anyone fight in a city?'[52] Yet, combat was still concentrated in urban areas. The battle of Al-Kaed Bridge, notwithstanding, most of the major engagements occurred in An Nasiriyah, An Najaf, Samawah and Baghdad. For instance, An Nasiriyah was the site of a major battle because two crucial bridges over the Euphrates River and a canal on Highway 7 were located there. The bridges were strategic choke points on the US line of advance. The Iraqi Army's 11th Infantry Division, supported by Fedayeen fighters, put up a formidable defence in the city on 23 March 2003 against the US Marine Corps' Task Force Tarawa.[53] The battle was the single most costly action in the whole campaign for the US: eighteen US marines were killed in the course of the fighting.[54]

In addition, 101st Airborne Division mounted a major assault to clear An Najaf, while 82nd Airborne secured Samawah. The two battles were the largest ground combat operations in which either formation was involved. Finally, although it had been involved in a number of engagements during its advance, the 3rd Infantry Division experienced its most intense challenge when it eventually reached Baghdad during its famous 'thunder runs' into the city. The 2003 Iraq invasion was a relatively urbanized campaign, then (see Map 2.2).

How is the scale of urban fighting during the invasion to be explained? Demography was plainly not irrelevant. An Nasiriyah, An Najaf, Samawah and Baghdad each had large populations, of respectively 300,000, 400,000, 200,000 and 5.6 million.[55] Because the objective was Baghdad, the US forces had to advance through these urban areas in order to defeat the Iraqi Army and bring down the regime. It was, therefore, highly likely that there would be extensive urban fighting, especially since American weaponry was so devastating in the field. However, while demographics played a part, force numbers were very significant too. Yet, they have been overlooked. It is possible to rectify this neglect by thinking comparatively. Here, the influence of numbers on the distinctive geometry of the Iraq War can be illustrated most graphically by comparing the invasion of 2003 with the Gulf War of 1991. During the 1991 conflict, a US-led coalition sought to eject Saddam Hussein's forces from Kuwait, which he had invaded in August

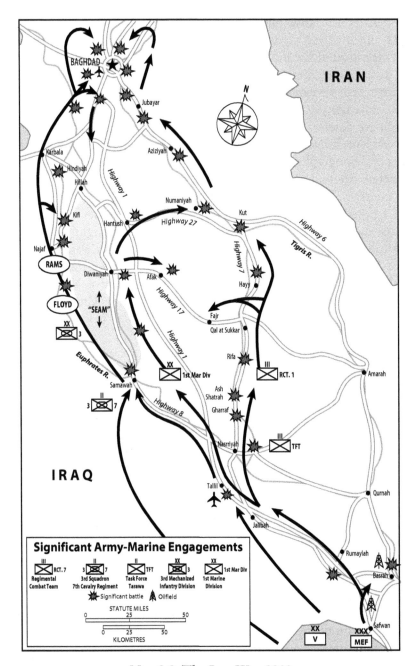

Map 2.2: The Iraq War, 2003
Source: Reproduced with permission from Michael R. Gordon and
Bernard E. Trainor, *Cobra II: The Inside Story of the Invasion and Occupation
of Iraq* (Pantheon, 2006), xviii.

1990. After a massive build-up, the Gulf War began in early January 1991 and involved six weeks of coalition air bombardment before a four-day ground battle. The Iraqi Army suffered a crushing defeat in the deserts of southern Iraq and Kuwait. There were evident parallels between the two campaigns.

Because the 1991 Gulf War was fought in Kuwait and southern Iraq, which are deserts, the lack of urban fighting has always been taken as self-evident. In fact, it was actually a rather striking fact. Indeed, on the basis of demography alone, significant urban fighting might have been expected. After all, in 1991, Kuwait was not without towns or cities. On the contrary, Kuwait's coastline was heavily urbanized: Kuwait City had a population of 1.5 million surrounded by a series of suburban towns, such as Mangaf, Abu'Fteira and Al Jafrah. It might be thought that urban warfare would have been inevitable in this war, especially since Kuwait City, located only a hundred miles from the front line on the Saudi border, was the ultimate coalition objective. Yet, the only urban battle – a small engagement – took place in Khafji, in Saudi Arabia, when Iraqi forces raided across the border before the major ground operations began.[56]

At this point, the insufficiency of the demographic argument becomes clear. While both Kuwait in 1991 and Iraq in 2003 had significant urban areas, there was one very obvious difference between the two campaigns: force size. In 1991, opposing forces were radically bigger than in 2003. For Operation Desert Storm, the US deployed 700,000 personnel as part of a multinational coalition of more than 900,000. The coalition ground force comprised 500,000 soldiers in sixteen divisions; the US Army and Marine Corps fielded 334,000 troops in almost ten divisions.[57] Iraq eventually mobilized 1,100,000 soldiers, deploying forty-three divisions, approximately 336,000 troops, to Kuwait and southern Iraq.[58] The 11th Iraqi Division defended Kuwait City, but the rest of Saddam's army was positioned along the border of Kuwait and Iraq to form a front of about 350 miles. Combat densities were very high, therefore.

Saddam's deployment requires some explanation. A number of factors influenced him. Naturally, he wanted to defend not just Kuwait City but Kuwait in its entirety. This could only be accomplished by positioning his forces on the border. In addition, following his experiences in the Iran–Iraq War, he presumed that his forces would be best able to stop the US-led coalition in the desert, where they could bring their full combat power to bear. Indeed, he boasted that his deployment would generate 'the mother of all battles'.[59] Of course,

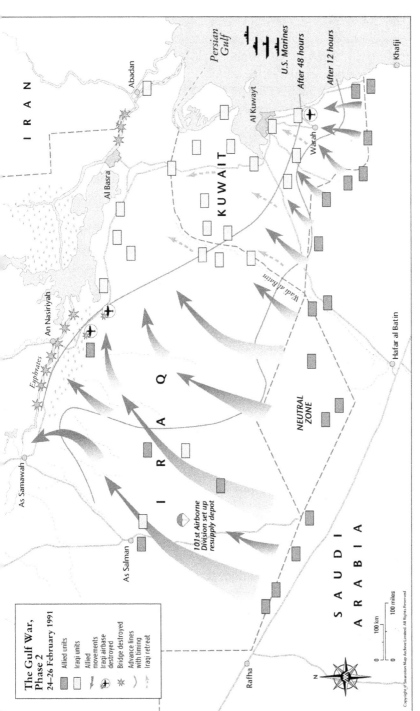

Map 2.3: The Gulf War, 1991
Source: Courtesy of The Map Archive.

The Gulf War,
Phase 2
24–26 February 1991

Allied units
Iraqi units
Allied
movements
Iraqi airbase
destroyed
Bridge destroyed
Advance lines
with timing
Iraqi retreat

Persian
Gulf

U.S. Marines

After 48 hours

After 12 hours

Khafji

Abadan

IRAN

Al Kuwayt

Al Basra

KUWAIT

Warah

Euphrates

An Nasiriyah

Wadi al Batin

I   R   A   Q

NEUTRAL
ZONE

Hafar al Batin

As Samawah

As Salman

101st Airborne
Division set up
resupply depot

SAUDI
ARABIA

Rafha

N

0   100 km

0   100 miles

Saddam disastrously underestimated coalition airpower. Nevertheless, as a result of the large forces involved and their subsequent deployment along a front, 'the battles and engagements of the first Gulf War were set-piece battles, reflective of World War II European combat'.[60] The most famous encounters, the battles of 73 Easting and Objective Norfolk, for instance, occurred in the desert miles from any human settlement (see Map 2.3).

It would be wrong to reduce the Gulf War or the invasion of Iraq to force size alone. Nevertheless, when compared with each other, it is possible to see the limitations of the demographic argument. Above all, it becomes apparent that force sizes played a significant role in generating their respective geometries. In 2003, Iraqi and American forces engaged in a few brief, one-sided encounter battles in the field, but the war was relatively heavily urbanized. Because neither side had sufficient combat forces to form major fronts in 2003, Iraqi and American forces converged on decisive operational locations: roads, bridges and other transportation nodes. These decisive points were typically located in urban areas which, then, became the foci of combat. By contrast, in 1991, even though there was significant demographic potential for urban combat in Kuwait City and its suburbs, the armies fought each other exclusively in the open desert, very substantially because of their mass. The 2003 invasion and the Gulf War seem to confirm Duffy's thesis; as armies contract, urban warfare becomes more prevalent.

Although great care needs to be taken, it may be useful to consider the 1991 Gulf War counterfactually in order to affirm this thesis. How might it have been fought if the US-led coalition and Saddam Hussein had had the forces available in 2003? If Saddam Hussein had defended Kuwait in 1991 with four divisions and some Fedayeen fighters, and the coalition had attacked with only five divisions, it seems probable that the campaign geometries would have been very different. In particular, the lineal defence Saddam actually adopted for Desert Storm along the Kuwait border would have made no sense. The five coalition attack divisions would have easily bypassed their positions on the border and driven straight on to Kuwait City. Consequently, the classic tank battles of that war might not have occurred at all. Rather, with only 112,000 troops, it seems more probable that Saddam Hussein would have been compelled to draw his forces back to Kuwait City, creating a defensive ring around that city or even inside it. Under air bombardment and ground attack, Iraqi forces might have been driven deep into urban areas. Fought with 2003 combat ratios, the mother of all battles is more likely to have taken place in and around Kuwait City, rather than in the desert. In this scenario, the Gulf War would have been an urbanized war – not primarily because of the demographics – but because of the force numbers.

Russia's war in the Donbas seems to confirm the evidence from the Iraq invasion and the Gulf War. There, force size seems to have played a significant role in defining the campaign, although precise figures are difficult to confirm. Like Saddam and the US in 2003, Russia deployed a relatively small force into the Donbas in 2014. An estimated 10,000 Russian troops augmented a local force of some 45,000.[61] The summer and winter campaign of 2015–16 subsequently involved about 36,000 Russian, Donetsk People's Army and Luhansk People's Army troops.[62] The Ukrainian regime deployed a similarly sized force of about 64,000 troops. There were probably just over 100,000 combatants operating in a theatre of 15,000 square miles. After the initial battles, the fighting descended into low-grade cross-border skirmishes along a lightly held, 300-mile, militarized frontier, the 'grey zone'.[63] However, the major battles between the Ukrainian Army and the separatist forces in 2014 and 2016 all concentrated around Luhansk and, especially, Donetsk. Indeed, some of the heaviest fighting occurred around Debal'tseve, Avdiivka, and Pisky. Some of the towns which have been the scene of battles have been quite large; Horlivka has a population of 257,000. However, most of the others are much smaller; Ilovaisk has 15,600 inhabitants, Debal'tseve 25,000, Avdiivka 35,000, and Pisky 2,000. Demographics does not seem to be the prime driver in the Donbas; it is not a heavily urbanized area. Rather, in each case, the Ukrainian and separatist forces have tried to seize – or hold – key industrial or transport nodes inside cities and towns. Reduced Ukrainian and Russian-backed separatist forces have converged on these urban locations because they were operationally important, and because neither was large enough to form a front around them.

In recent decades, scholars and military professionals have explained the rise of urban warfare by reference to demographics and asymmetry. On this account, because cities have grown so large and, therefore, offer the best protection for insurgents against advanced weaponry, it is inevitable that war has migrated and will move to urban areas. It has been assumed that interstate war will also converge on cities for the same reasons. It is understandable why scholars have been so attracted by these factors. Demography and asymmetry do seem to explain the rise of urban insurgencies. However, when it comes to interstate war, demography and asymmetry become less satisfactory as independent explanations. In understanding interstate warfare, numbers are also important. The invasion of Iraq and the war in the Donbas are suggestive here. In both scenarios, there were simply too few forces to form the massive fronts that typified twentieth-century land warfare. Combat density – the sheer number of military personnel deployed into a theatre – is likely to play an increasingly important role in the urbanization of warfare over the twenty-first century. Simply because state forces are so much smaller now than previously, it is likely that they will converge on decisive urban terrain. The war of fronts, defined by large engagements in the field, has been replaced by more dispersed operations, which converge on urban areas, where the decisive tactical and operational objectives have been located. As fronts disappear, towns and cities, having become the focus of military operations, are where the major battles now occur.

3

The Urban Guerrilla

Out of the Mountains

Interstate warfare is migrating to urban areas not only because of the growth of cities and new weaponry, but also, very substantially, because of the contraction of military forces. Reflecting the experiences of recent decades, contemporary literature on urban warfare focuses primarily on civil conflict, insurgency and terrorism, rather than on interstate war. The US Army, for instance, is troubled by the prospect of megacities, not because it will be forced to fight China or Russia in one, but because it fears it will be dragged into an urban counterinsurgency campaign, the demands of which will dwarf Ramadi or Fallujah. Leading commentators on the urban turn all prioritize urban insurgency as the most probable and most challenging operation for state forces in the future. David Kilcullen has been a proponent of this approach, claiming that insurgents have come 'out of the mountains'. Rural insurrection has been displaced by urban insurgency. For Kilcullen, four interrelated processes have led to this: population growth, urbanization, littoralization and connectedness. The result is potentially catastrophic: 'The world's cities are about to be swamped by a human tide that will force them to absorb – in just one generation – the same growth of population that occurred across the entire planet in all of recorded history up to 1960.'[1] Kilcullen is convinced that urban insurgency is the absolutely primary threat in the bloating cities of the twenty-first century.

Kilcullen has been among the most prominent commentators signposting an urban insurgent turn. He is far from alone though. For instance, current NATO doctrine asserts: 'The greatest threat faced by modern forces is facing an adversary who hides among civilians, has mobility, communications, and firepower capable of fighting a guerrilla war but has no clear military organization.'[2] The statement is surprising given the rising challenge posed by nuclear states like Russia, China and North Korea, and the proliferation of nuclear weapons in others. Yet, it is categorical evidence that the threat of the urban guerrilla has captured security debates today.

Out of the City

Kilcullen and many others claim that insurgents have come out of the mountains in recent decades. Yet, in fact, urban insurgency was already a constant feature of the twentieth century. Throughout the Cold War, Britain, France and the United States conducted a series of counter-insurgency campaigns in Africa, the Middle East and Southeast Asia, most notably in Palestine, Malaya, Kenya, Cyprus, Algeria, Oman, Yemen, Vietnam and Northern Ireland. Of course, the vast bulk of the operations mounted during these campaigns were in the field; most British, French, and American troops fought in arid mountains, dense jungles or swamps. Yet, it would be quite wrong to think that these campaigns were entirely rural. On the contrary, in almost every single case, there was a very significant urban dimension to these conflicts. A brief history of some of these campaigns proves the point.

Before the Second World War, the British Army had suppressed an Arab revolt in Palestine. Almost immediately afterwards, they were drawn back into a second conflict in the Holy Land, this time against the Jewish struggle for independence. This conflict involved extensive urban violence. In July 1946, the Irgun Gang bombed the King David Hotel in Jerusalem, used by the British regime as an administration centre; the attack killed ninety-one people. In April 1948, the Irgun mounted an assault on Jaffa, which they seized from Arab defenders. British responses were confused, but they eventually sought to regain the city in May. Irgun mounted a furious defence, which played a very significant role in Britain's decision to withdraw from Palestine and to grant Israel its independence.

Palestine was not exceptional. British campaigns in Malaya, Kenya, Cyprus and Yemen also involved urban fighting. Malaya, for instance, is rightly remembered for its jungle fighting – this is where most communist guerrillas were eventually located and, as a result, the struggle became one for the countryside and villages. Yet, after the Second

World War, the Communist Party of Malaya infiltrated villages, towns and cities. Between 1948 and 1951, they were robustly expelled from these populated areas by overwhelming force. In this period, the colonial authorities employed 40,000 British and Commonwealth troops, 67,000 police and 250,000 Home Guard against 8,000 insurgents in a country the size of England. This force was able to resettle the population and dominate urban areas through sheer weight of numbers. Only then, after 1951, when the crisis had been averted, did the insurgency become an exclusively rural phenomenon, with most of the fighting taking place in the jungle.[3]

A similar pattern is observable in Kenya. The Mau Mau had emerged as an insurgent group in the early 1950s among the Kikuyu, Meru and Embu tribes in the White Highlands. The central dispute, which precipitated the uprising, was land distribution. It was, therefore, certainly a rural rebellion mounted by the disenfranchised young men of these tribes, disadvantaged by population growth and the system of land-ownership instituted by the colonial government. Yet, although it emerged in the White Highlands, the Mau Mau fighters quickly infiltrated Nairobi and, by 1954, had numerous cells operating in the city with significant local support. Recognizing the danger of a general insurrection against the colonial authorities, British Army officer General 'Bobbie' Erskine, Commander-in-Chief, East Africa, mounted a major operation to clear the city of insurgents. On 24 April 1954, 20,000 British and Commonwealth troops, supported by police and Home Guard units, flooded the city as part of Operation Anvil.[4] In the first forty-eight hours of the operation, the identities of 11,600 Kikuyu were individually checked (screened) by the security forces; those suspected of allegiance to the Mau Mau were arrested. Eventually, by the end of the operation, on 26 May 1954, 50,000 Kikuyu had been screened, 24,100 of whom, including 2,150 women and 4,000 children, were detained.[5] The Mau Mau continued to fight for four more years, but, driven into the forests of the Highlands after Operation Anvil, their defeat was inevitable.

Colonel Grivas's Ethniki Organosis Kyprion Agoniston (EOKA, National Organization of Cypriot Greek Fighters) campaign in Cyprus in 1954–8 is another that involved a very significant urban element. Most of Grivas's armed bands fought in the rural areas of Cyprus, where British forces struggled to control them. However, throughout the emergency, EOKA terrorist cells operated very effectively in Nicosia. In addition to public demonstrations, Grivas had organized his eighty men in the city into fifteen groups. They specialized in street bombs and in the assassination of military personnel; notoriously, EOKA operatives shot off-duty soldiers and, on 3 October 1958, murdered the wife of a sergeant. As a result of these attacks, Ledra Street in Nicosia was renamed 'The Murder Mile'.[6] Cyprus was not self-evidently an urban conflict, but 'Grivas cleverly used his urban and rural groups in interaction'.[7]

Other colonial conflicts were similarly urbanized. Between 1964 and 1966, British troops were deployed to Yemen where they fought the National Liberation Front and the Front for the Liberation of South Yemen in Aden. The densest part of Aden, the Crater, had become a 'no-go' area, as insurgent groups, especially from the National Liberation Front, dominated the streets. Eventually, the British Army retook the city through the harsh actions of the Argyll and Sutherland Highlanders, commanded by Lieutenant Colonel Colin 'Mad Mitch' Mitchell, who crushed the rebellion.[8] In the cases of Malaya, Kenya, Cyprus and Aden, urban guerrillas were an important part of the insurgency. However, for the most part, they were driven out of urban areas by the sheer number of British troops.

The British post-war counterinsurgency experience was anything but unique. The Algerian War of Independence also involved very significant urban operations. It is true that, after 1958, most of the fighting in the Algerian civil war took place in the Atlas and Kabylie mountains and along the Moroccan border. Yet, the key battle of the war was fought in Algiers between Brigadier General Jacques Massu and his 10th Parachute Division and the Front de libération nationale (FLN). The battle began in January 1957, when, following a series of bomb attacks, 4,000 paratroopers were deployed onto the streets. They forcibly broke a general strike which the FLN had organized; they levered open the shutters of shops and physically dragged shopkeepers to their stores. This was followed by an intense ten-month operation, in which the paratroopers dominated the Casbah, arresting thousands of Algerian suspects, 3,000 of whom simply disappeared. On October 8, the French forces finally cornered and killed the last FLN terrorist leader, Ali la Pointe. The battle of Algiers was over, but the struggle continued until 1962, out in the field, where guerrilla bands fought French troops. As in Kenya and Malaya, French forces had driven the insurgents out of the city early in the conflict, although the methods they used would later lose them the war.

Vietnam was an overwhelming rural country in the 1960s. Consequently, it was all but inevitable that most of the war would be fought in the mountains, jungles and paddy fields, not least because the popular base of the insurgency lay in the peasantry of the south. Despite its political and military ineptitude, the US-backed South Vietnam regime dominated urban centres to the very end of the war. However, there was one notable, but telling, exception to this pattern: the Tet Offensive and, specifically, the battle of Hué in February–March 1968. The battle of Hué was, in fact, a conventional fight between the American and South Vietnamese against North Vietnamese forces. The Communist Party deployed the North Vietnamese Army's (NVA) 5th Regiment into the city. Assisted by local Vietcong, this regiment infiltrated successfully and seized control of the Citadel on 31 January. There followed a bitter two-week battle, in which a US Marine regiment and an army of the Republic of Vietnam battalion, eventually, and at great cost, retook the Citadel, eliminating the NVA force.[9] The battle of Hué was interesting, for, like Algiers, Malaya and Nairobi, it demonstrated that, in the twentieth century, it was extremely difficult for an insurgent force, even the size of the Vietcong, to infiltrate and control urban areas. The regime was strongest in towns and cities that were dominated by the security forces and a supportive population. It was hard for insurgents to gain a foothold there or to mount successful operations from them.

It is possible to identify a pattern across twentieth-century insurgencies. In most campaigns, there was a very significant urban dimension. These guerrilla movements frequently operated in cities and towns and some of their terrorist cells were highly successful in advancing the campaign and pressurizing the regime. Nevertheless, in each case, the rural insurgency predominated; the urban guerrilla was at most a supporting element of the uprising.

Insurgent Literature

Why did the rural guerrilla assume priority in the twentieth century? David Kilcullen and his colleagues have a clear answer to this: demographics. Cities were much smaller in the twentieth century, so it was more difficult to mount insurgencies in them; they provided nothing like the cover that the megacity of the twenty-first century potentially offers the rebel today. Yet, cities in the post-war period were large and complex municipalities. In 1957, Algiers, for instance, had a population of 900,000 with some 70,000 in the Casbah alone; Nairobi about 100,000 in 1954, Aden about 200,000 in 1966, Belfast more than 300,000 in 1970, and Saigon had 2 million in the 1960s. It might be thought that the demographics of these settlements were minimally adequate to sustain an urban insurgency of some kind. Yet, successful urban insurgencies were rare. It is something of a conundrum.

During the twentieth century, there was a rich literature on insurgency. Its primary aim was to educate potential revolutionaries. However, that literature also provides a very good answer as to why urban insurgencies were the minor form of action. Mao Zedong was the first major contributor to this genre; in 1937, he published *On Guerrilla Warfare*. Following the Second World War, a series of important insurgency manuals appeared; Che Guevara's *Guerrilla Warfare* (1961), Abraham Guillén's *The Strategy of the Urban Guerrilla* (1966), Régis Debray's *The Revolution in the Revolution?* (1967) and Carlos Marighella's *Minimanual of the Urban Guerrilla* (1969).

Most of this literature asserted that insurgency was a rural phenomenon. For instance, both Mao Zedong and Che Guevara were interested almost exclusively in the question of rural insurrection. Of course, in Mao's case, this reflected his own experience. In the 1930s and 1940s, China remained an agrarian civilization based on a vast peasant economy; its population was huge but cities were small and few in number. Mao led a rural insurgency against the nationalist Kuomintang regime. However, it was not only demographics that drove him into the field. When he did attempt to concentrate pre-emptively against superior state forces in 1934, he was defeated badly, and forced into the Long March. In the face of overwhelming state forces, the central principle of Mao's insurgency doctrine was dispersal; the effective guerrilla exploited space forcing opponents to spread out, thereby exposing their weakest points. The doctrine presumed a very large, remote theatre of operations that even superior regime forces could not hope to cover.

Guevara's approach to insurgency was similar. He, too, strongly advocated the exploitation of an inaccessible hinterland as a requirement for success:

> It ought to be noted by those who maintain dogmatically that the struggle of the masses is centred in city movements, entirely forgetting the immense participation of the country people in the life of all the underdeveloped parts of America. Of course, the struggles of the city masses of organized workers should not be underrated; but their real possibilities of engaging in armed struggle must be carefully analysed ... In these conditions, illegal workers' movements face enormous changes. They must function secretly without arms. The situation in the open country is not so difficult. There, in places beyond the reach of repressive forces, armed guerrillas can support the inhabitants.[10]

Guevara propounded a thesis of insurgency. In the twentieth century, rural insurgencies were effective because state forces simply could not dominate the countryside as they did the town; they lacked the personnel to penetrate every part of the countryside. Indeed, for this very reason, Fidel Castro himself had declared: 'The city is the cemetery of revolutionaries and resources.'[11] Castro noted bitterly that whenever guerrilla leaders had gone to the city to attend political meetings or engage in military action, they had been apprehended.

Mao and Guevara were certain that insurgencies had, of necessity, to be peasant movements. It was the only way to avoid state suppression. The other prominent insurgent theorists of the time adopted a different view. Brazilian revolutionary Carlos Marighella was, perhaps, the most important here, with his famous manual, written specifically for the urban guerrilla. His *Minimanual* advocated the critical role that the urban guerrilla might play in a revolutionary war. Precisely because urban guerrillas operated in cities, at the heart of government, the effects of their terrorism were amplified. They were able to 'threaten the triangle in which the Brazilian state system and North American domination are maintained in Brazil, a triangle whose points are Rio, São Paulo and Belo Horizonte'.[12] Clearly, the city was a more demanding environment than the countryside in terms of the human population, the physical terrain and the security forces. Consequently, urban guerrillas had to be more adaptable, flexible and cunning than the armed peasant if they were to stage their attacks, bank robberies and assassinations effectively. The urban guerrilla displayed unique characteristics. The terrorist had to be 'a good tactician and a good marksman' and 'a person of great astuteness', who embodied 'moral superiority',[13] but they must also be 'familiar with the avenues, streets, alleys, ins and outs, and corners of the urban centres, its paths and shortcuts, its empty lots, its underground passages, its pipes and sewer system, the urban guerrilla safely crosses through the irregular and difficult terrain unfamiliar to the police'.[14]

Nevertheless, while Marighella gave the urban guerrilla a distinctively prominent role – far more so than Guevara or Mao – even he did not believe that the urban guerrilla alone could bring down the government or liberate Latin America from US hegemony. This becomes clear only at the very end of the manual. There, he confirms that while the urban terrorist might bring militarists and dictatorships to 'the brink', the rural insurrection would, in the end, always prove decisive. Rural guerrilla warfare was the 'backbone of the revolution'; 'from this backbone will come the marrow of the revolutionary army of national liberation'.[15] Marighella does not contradict Mao or Guevara; he does not suggest that the urban terrorist replace the traditional guerrilla. Rather, especially in the specific metropolitan conditions of Brazil, he saw an opportunity for urban terrorists to catalyse the revolution. He does not discuss the reasons for this. Yet they are implied in his text: the urban guerrilla could not mount a revolution alone because state security forces were too massive and powerful in the city. Indeed, the urban guerrilla had to be cunning and covert precisely because of the potency of the security forces in urban areas. Ironically, Marighella's own career proved the point. He was shot dead in a police ambush in São Paulo on 4 November 1969, and his colleagues in the Action for National Liberation were arrested.

Abraham Guillén represents the other end of the spectrum from Mao and Guevara. If Marighella's work was a minimanual, 'Guillén's book is a maximanual for the urban guerrilla'.[16] He genuinely believed that an urban insurgency could work. Guillén was originally Spanish, but, having been imprisoned by Franco, he managed to escape and emigrated to Argentina in 1948. In 1960, he was a member of the Uturuscos, a radical group of Peronist revolutionaries. He took political asylum in Montevideo in 1962 and eventually became the leader of a radical terrorist group, the Tupamaros, in Uruguay. On the basis of his experiences in Uruguay, Guillén believed that the urban guerrilla could be the prime revolutionary force. While a rural insurgency was tactically and politically compromised, Guillén saw huge advantages to an urban uprising: 'It is absurd to engage in mountain guerrilla warfare when revolution can be decided in a few hours or days in the cities.'[17] He repeated the point: 'If 70 per cent of the country's population is urban, the demography and economics must dictate the specific rules of strategy of revolutionary combat. The centre of operations should never be mountains or villages, but in the largest cities where the population suffices to form an army of revolution.'[18] Guillén certainly believed that cities were large and discontented enough in the 1960s for an insurgency to be mounted in them.

Yet, Guillén's argument must be read cautiously. He certainly saw the advantages of the city, but he also recognized the difficulties of operating in metropolises of Latin America in the 1950s and 1960s. Consequently, he did not advocate mass urban uprising: it would be easily crushed. On the contrary, he developed a rather sophisticated understanding of urban topography. The urban guerrilla could not be concerned with territory. Indeed, to create obvious base areas, embedded in a specific neighbourhood, was to invite disaster: 'If revolution war does not spread to more than one district, then it involves linear battle that lends itself to defeat before the massive use of tanks, light artillery, cavalry and infantry.'[19]

Urban guerrillas should therefore form themselves into very small, highly professional and independent cells capable of moving about the city at will, never compromising themselves by staying in one location or with one population for too long; ' "the strategy of the artichoke" is the most prudent and safe one for the urban or rural guerrilla: to eat the enemy bit by bit'.[20] Skilled urban terrorists, therefore, mounted attacks across the city, demonstrating the weakness and corruption of the government, so that the people might 'arise *en masse* like an enraged lion'.[21] 'Today the same masses are being stirred by a handful of urban guerrillas.'[22] For Guillén, the city offered a unique political advantage. As long as they did not tether themselves to a location, guerrillas could remain completely anonymous, thereby evading detection and arrest. Yet, they could also generate spontaneous revolutionary fervour among the mass urban population through spectacular attacks. In this situation, urban guerrillas overcame the weakness of the traditional insurgency. They were able to mobilize the citizenry, without exposing themselves or the people to government repression.

It is an ingenious idea. Yet, it has never succeeded. Even urban guerrillas required a home base from which to mount operations. Ultimately, therefore, Guillén only affirms the position of Mao, Guevara and Marighella. He too recognized the great vulnerability of the urban guerrilla. Since state forces were strongest in towns and cities, it was impossible to mount a normal insurgency there from base areas. Guillén fully accepted that a territorial strategy must fail because the security forces would always have enough troops to counter such an offensive. As he himself notes, they would simply deploy tanks against the guerrilla strongholds. The crushing of the great urban insurrections in history illustrates the point very well. In 1830, 1848 and 1871, the Parisian insurrectionists were easily suppressed by mass state forces. For all his advocacy of the urban as not just the primary theatre of insurrection but the only necessary one, Guillén ultimately admitted how difficult it was to mount and sustain a revolutionary campaign in the urban domain. State security forces were so numerous that it was quite simply impossible for insurgents to operate effectively in this environment so close to the seat of government, its police stations, barracks, courts and prisons.

Kilcullen has claimed that the twenty-first-century insurgent has left the mountains. Yet, in fact, twentieth-century insurgencies often involved an urban dimension. However, as the history of those insurgents and the insurgent literature itself shows, insurgencies could operate effectively in urban areas only if they were highly adept or if their security forces were distracted and divided. These conditions pertained in Palestine and in Cyprus. Elsewhere, it was impossible for an insurgency to create a home base and to conduct significant operations from inside towns and cities. The security forces were too strong and, indeed, were repeatedly able to drive insurgents out of towns and cities; Nairobi, Algiers, Aden and Hué all demonstrate this process very clearly. In the twentieth century, the major insurgencies were usually expelled from the city quickly. It is not so much that twenty-first-century guerrillas have come out of the mountains into the cities, for they never really left the cities; they simply no longer needed the mountains any more, not only because cities have expanded, but also because state security forces have become so small.

The Battle of Belfast

The insurgent literature of the post-war era provides good evidence about the importance of force ratios to urban insurrection. A specific historic example will affirm the relevance of numbers. The 'Troubles' in Northern Ireland and, in particular, the violence in Belfast in the early years of this war offer a very good case study on urban guerrilla operations in the post-war period. Although not specifically recognized in the historiography of the Troubles, the struggle over Belfast between the Provisional Irish Republican Army (IRA) and the British Army between 1969 and 1972 is usefully understood as a discrete battle in a much longer war. Between 14 August 1969, when the army was initially deployed, and 31 July 1972, when, with Operation Motorman, the British finally overwhelmed the urban insurgency mounted by the Provisional IRA, there was an intense and bloody struggle for control of Belfast.

The history of the Troubles is well known.[23] From 1922 until the mid-1960s, there had been an uneasy peace between the Catholics and the dominant Protestant Unionist community in Northern Ireland. However, in the face of systematic discrimination in jobs, housing and the law, the Catholic community began to engage in marches and protests for civil rights. These marches escalated into open confrontations between the two sectarian communities. In July 1969, the Protestant marching season precipitated a new level of violence in both Londonderry and Belfast. By August, there were major riots along the Falls Road in Belfast, in which Protestants and Catholics mutually sought to drive each other out of their neighbourhoods (see Map 3.1). Numerous houses, especially Catholic ones, were burnt out in the process.[24] The Royal Ulster Constabulary (RUC) subsequently lost control of these riots and, exhausted, called for military support. On 14 August 1969, the British government ordered the British Army onto the streets. The battle of Belfast had begun.

Initially, the British Army succeeded in bringing order to Belfast. The troops successfully protected the Catholic areas from the Protestants and limited the predations of the RUC. Although the IRA was always opposed to their deployment, most Catholics were originally supportive of the British intervention. However, by the summer of 1970 the situation had changed entirely, as the army began to conduct aggressive searches of Catholic (but not Protestant) houses, to suppress riots violently and to harass, assault and arrest individuals.[25] The British Army was no longer seen as a neutral party – still less an ally – but part of the oppressive security forces of the Protestant-dominated regime in Ulster. On 3 to 5 July 1970, the British Army conducted a violent and destructive operation in Balkan Street, in search of IRA weaponry. The Balkan Street Search was the turning point. The result was a six-day riot, in which the British Army fired 1,454 rounds and imposed a curfew that, it transpired, was illegal.[26] The British Army had become the enemy.

The IRA had originally emerged during the War of Independence of 1921–2. It remained in existence, with a base in Dublin, throughout the twentieth century. However, as the Troubles began in 1969, the organization completely failed to protect the Catholic community. In light of the crisis in the North, the Provisional IRA split from the 'Official' IRA in 1969 and emerged as the prime terrorist movement in the ghettos of Londonderry and Belfast.[27] Although its leaders were mainly from traditional IRA families, the key figures, such as Martin McGuinness and Gerry Adams, were poor, working-class Catholics who had been born and raised in the Bogside and Falls Road. Rejecting the irrelevant Marxist doctrine of the 'Official' IRA, they developed a military strategy which they believed would force the British government to abandon the Province. Northern Ireland would gain its independence through unification with the Republic. To achieve this end, the Provisionals developed a twin-pronged strategy: they sought to create Catholic enclaves in Londonderry and Belfast, from which the security forces were excluded, so that they could begin to assert their political leadership over Catholics there and to create a home base from which

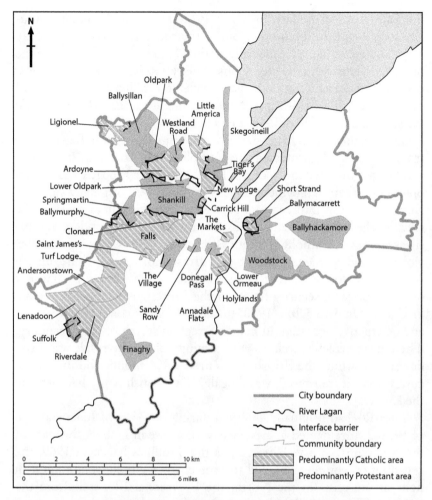

Map 3.1: Belfast, Catholic and Protestant areas
Source: Reproduced with permission from Peter Kumer and Marko Krevs, 'Understanding the implications of spatial segregation in Belfast, Northern Ireland', *Geografski vestnik*, 87(2) 2015: https://doi.org/10.3986/GV87204.

they could mount their attacks. From those enclaves, they planned to prosecute a deep battle against the city centres, mainly with car bombs.

In this way, the Provisional IRA sought to create no-go areas, through the use of barricades, riots, petrol bombs and small arms attacks against the RUC and British Army patrols.[28] In Belfast, the Falls Road never become a complete no-go area in the way Bogside did; although the British Army approved of the 'peace lines' along the Falls Road between the two communities, barricades around the

Catholic streets were forbidden. However, the RUC could not patrol the Falls Road alone. During the day, the British Army was consistently met with hostility (random abuse and local women following patrols banging dustbin lids, for example), organized rioting and shootings; it was even more difficult for the army to operate in these areas at night. Having studied the Cyprus and Aden campaigns, the Provisional IRA came to the conclusion that if they killed thirty-six British soldiers, the British government would concede.[29] However, although the aim was to assassinate soldiers, sniping was primarily used as a defensive tactic, intended to keep soldiers out of Catholic areas – or at least make access to them as dangerous as possible.

By 1972, the northern end of the Falls Road, around the Divis Flats, was a notable Catholic ghetto. The Divis Flats complex comprised modern apartment blocks, in the brutalist architectural style, located at the lower end of the Falls Road, nearest to the town centre beside St Peter's Cathedral.[30] Their construction had begun in 1966 and they were finally completed in 1972. They consisted of a ten seven-storey blocks, interconnected by concrete walkways, and a thirty-storey tower. Like many other new developments that appeared in British cities at the time, the concept behind the Divis Flats was positive, even noble. The planners and architects intended to remove 3,000 Catholics out of terrible Victorian housing and relocate them in new accommodation. In the event, the building quality was low, and poor Catholic families could not afford heating, so the apartments became damp and mouldy; the lifts did not work and the entire development quickly disintegrated. In the end, the Divis Flats became a sink estate: 'Divis Flats was a nightmare from an Escher drawing, a concrete warren of stairways, passages and overcrowded flats.'[31] It became known as 'the slum in the sky' (see Figure 3.1).[32]

The Divis Flats became notorious during the Troubles; in August 1969, the RUC killed a nine-year-old child who was sleeping when they fired a 0.5 Browning machine gun indiscriminately into the Flats.[33] Later, in 1972, Jean McConville, a mother of ten, was abducted from the Flats and shot by the Provisional IRA as a putative informer. The Divis Flats served two important purposes during the battle of Belfast. They were inhabited by a large Republican population, which supported the IRA strongly, and they therefore 'became a stronghold for armed resistance'.[34] They also occupied an important tactical position at the end of the Falls Road – a critical access point to the Catholic area. Their military importance was accentuated by their design. The roofs provided an ideal spot from which to bombard British Army

Figure 3.1: The Divis Flats
Source: Courtesy of *Castle, The Journal of the Royal Anglian Regiment* 17(1)
1973, 79.

patrols with stones and petrol bombs. With many floors and a complex network of walkways, they also afforded snipers multiple positions, hides and almost infinite escape routes. The walkways, in particular, were favourite sniping positions. During the battle of Belfast, the Divis Flats became a modern, concrete castle for the IRA; indeed, they became known as 'Fortress Divis'. A major operation in the Flats required two and half British Army battalions.

In 1972, the British Army's 3rd Battalion, the Royal Anglian Regiment, became well aware of the territorial significance of the Divis Flats. This battalion of about 600 soldiers was deployed to the lower Falls Road area in April 1972 for a four-month tour. Their headquarters was located in Divis Street, while the Divis Flats were in A Company's area of responsibility, stationed in the nearby Albert Road Mill. Immediately on their arrival, the Royal Anglians were subjected to a systematic assault by the inhabitants of the Divis Flats and by the Official IRA, which operated in the area. Indeed, the Royal Anglians named the first two weeks of their deployment 'The Battle of the Divis Flats'.[35] Trouble started in the afternoons with stone throwing and rioting, often in response to Anglian patrols. Gradually, during the afternoon and evening, confrontations increased, until the Anglians were subjected to significant gunfire, mainly from the Divis Flats themselves.

It would start at about 3:00pm in the afternoon and then go on until one or two in the morning, day after day. The point was they were using the Divis Flats as a base from which to shoot at us, usually from the links – the joins between the blocks of flats. We were very vulnerable coming out of Albert Street Mill base as it was completely overlooked from the flats.[36]

These gun battles were not small, isolated engagements. On the contrary, on 19 April, 177 shots were fired at the battalion, and on 26 April, 559 shots were fired, though the most violent day was 16 April, when the battalion was subjected to sustained fire from the Divis Flats mainly by adolescents armed by the IRA.[37] As one eye-witness observed:

I beheld a vision from hell: fifteen-year-old boys with sub-machine guns and semi-automatic rifles. They were gathered beside one of the now disused lift shafts, and they were receiving orders from some infant Rommel. Bullets were ricocheting everywhere, as these demented children emptied magazine after magazine into anything and everything.[38]

In fact, on this day, they did find a target. One of their rounds went through the observation slit in a Pig armoured vehicle; it struck and killed 2nd Lieutenant Nicholas Hull. Eventually, the offensive against the Anglians subsided, although they were attacked constantly throughout their tour; if not no-go areas, the Divis Flats and Lower Falls were enemy territory (or 'Indian country' as the Anglians called it) in which they could never patrol freely. The battalion suffered three fatalities during the tour, all shot by snipers.

As the 3rd Royal Anglians' tour shows, the Republican ghettos were militarily important for the Provisionals. When the security forces contested them, as they had to, Republican terrorists had the perfect opportunity to attack troops, or to provoke British soldiers into retaliating in ways that would alienate Catholics. These areas also allowed the Provisionals to mount a systematic attack on Belfast's commercial and business district. From March 1971, the Provisionals began to bomb the city centre with a view to inflicting economic damage on Ulster and showing that the province was ungovernable. While the defence of enclaves might be described as the close battle against the security forces, the bombing campaign was a deep battle against Ulster, the Northern Ireland government based at Stormont and the British state itself. After the Abercorn Bombing on 4 March 1972, when the Provisionals had been roundly condemned for killing and wounding innocent civilians, a

72-hour ceasefire was declared. As part of an attempt to reach a political settlement, the British government ordered the army to maintain a low profile; patrolling was reduced. As a result, the Provisionals were able to consolidate control over their enclaves and prepare themselves for a new offensive, which began on 22 June. On 9 July, 'Bloody Friday', the Provisionals detonated twenty devices in Belfast city centre between 14:10 and 15:13, killing nine and wounding 130. It was described as 'the worst day of death and destruction since the 1941 Blitz'.[39] It was seen as a direct result of the decision to withdraw security forces.

As a result of Bloody Friday, the British government decided on a new strategy. It refused to negotiate with the Provisionals any longer and ordered the British Army to bring Londonderry and Belfast under control. The no-go areas in the Bogside and the Falls Road were to be eliminated. Operation Motorman was the result. At 0400 hours, on the night of 31 July, the operation began. Troops flooded the two cities.[40] Royal Engineer armoured vehicles removed illegal barricades, while 22,000 troops were deployed into the Province. In Belfast, fourteen additional battalions reinforced beleaguered garrisons like the 3rd Royal Anglians; eleven units moved into West Belfast alone.[41] The force cleared the Falls Road and built a network of patrol bases throughout Republican areas. At a stroke, the military situation in Belfast had been transformed. Although they remained dangerous, even the Divis Flats were pacified. The nascent enclaves in the Catholic and Protestant areas were eliminated and the security forces took back control of the streets permanently. In place of informally erected barricades, a new network of patrol bases and observation points was the sole security architecture within the Catholic areas after Operation Motorman. Only the authorized 'peace walls' between the two communities remained intact.[42] The Provisionals could no longer protect their enclaves.

The battle of Belfast affirms the insurgency literature. The Provisionals sought to mount an urban offensive, believing it might be sufficient in and of itself to defeat the British in 1972. Yet, the results were predictable. The British government could not even begin to countenance political concessions of this magnitude, and was able to deploy more than 22,000 troops in order to suppress this outcome. In response to Operation Motorman, the IRA had no choice but to change its approach. In the short term, operators went to ground; leaders hid or went over the border to the Republic. Of course, violence remained high in Belfast throughout the 1970s. Riots, shootings and bombings were common. However, the Provisionals never again challenged the British for control of the city. Moreover, by the mid-1970s, the Provisionals had to revise their strategy completely. They transformed themselves into a professional urban terrorist organization, committed to a long war. Later, they formally adopted a dual strategy involving violence and politics: 'the Armalite and the ballot box'. They continued to plan bombs in Belfast and Londonderry, but, more significantly, mounted a campaign on the UK mainland, as the bombings in Guildford, Birmingham and, later, the City of London, Canary Wharf and Manchester showed. Meanwhile, the Provisionals' insurgency moved south to the border, to the bandit country of South Armagh. There, with full local support and a porous boundary, Provisional IRA cells could fight a war of attrition against the security forces. In effect, the Troubles imitated the geography of Algeria, Kenya and Malaya. Having lost a battle in the city, the Provisionals continued to challenge the British in the countryside – just as Guevara, Mao and, indeed, Marighella had recommended. The Troubles show that, in the twentieth century, the urban guerrilla often played an important role. However, they were always extremely vulnerable to the counteraction by massive state forces, which were normally able to drive them out of cities.

Force Ratios

The insurgents of the post-war period emphasized the difficulty of mounting an urban insurgency; there were simply too many security forces. Counterinsurgents of the same era also fully acknowledged that force ratios played an important role in counterinsurgencies. In order to interdict insurgents, it was vital to have enough troops to dominate the terrain physically, maintaining constant contact with the civilian population. For instance, Robert Thompson and David Galula, the pre-eminent British and French counterinsurgent theorists of the 1950s and 1960s, were very conscious of combat ratios. Thompson and Galula had served in Malaya and Algeria respectively; Thompson went on to join the British Advisory Mission in Vietnam. They had both written classic texts on counterinsurgency on the basis of their experiences. Thompson thought it impossible to put a precise figure on the ratio of counterinsurgents to insurgents, but Malaya and Vietnam suggested that approximately twenty counterinsurgents for every one insurgent were required.[43] Galula claimed that a 'ratio of force of ten and twenty to one between counterinsurgent and insurgent was not uncommon'.[44] Counterinsurgents in this period often worked off a rough force ratio of one soldier to every fifty civilians. In the intense period of a conflict, one soldier for every fifty civilians has often proved the minimum requirement for success. In 1957, the French deployed an extra 4,000 paratroopers into the Casbah of 70,000 civilians to reinforce the already sizeable security presence. During Operation Motorman in Belfast, the British state deployed more than 6,000 combat troops alongside the RUC, to control a Catholic population of 100,000. In both Algeria and Belfast, the security forces reached a force ratio of about one soldier to seventeen civilians. With these numbers, both the French and the British states were able to drive a nascent urban insurgency out into the countryside.

Force ratios have been inverted in the twenty-first century. In recent campaigns, security forces no longer always outnumber insurgents. Moreover, the population has often vastly outnumbered security forces. For instance, in the cities of Iraq after the invasion, the British never remotely approached the kind of force ratios they had enjoyed in the twentieth century. In Basra in 2004–8, the British experience contrasted drastically with Belfast between 1969 and 1972. At the height of the insurgency in Basra in 2006–7, the British commanders of Multinational Division South-East had only a single British Army battalion, along with the Iraqi Army and, often unreliable, Iraqi Police, at their disposal to secure a city of 1.3 million. General Richard Shirreff, who commanded Basra at that time and who had also been a soldier on the streets of Belfast in the 1970s, offered an illuminating comparison between the two campaigns:

> The single battalion commander responsible for a city of 1.3 million people told me that he could put no more than 13 half platoons or multiples on the ground, less than 200 soldiers on the ground, in a city of 1.3 million. You compare that, for example, with what I recall, as a young platoon commander in West Belfast in the late 1970s when there was a brigade on the ground.[45]

In radical contrast to Motorman, the British were operating with a force ratio of one to 370.[46]

Until the surge in 2007, the Americans also struggled with force densities. They fell well below the accepted ratio and, as a result, they struggled to control the streets. However, in Baghdad, Ramadi and Fallujah, especially after the surge, US forces thickened up their force densities and dramatically increased the size of the Iraqi Security Forces. By the mid-point of the surge in Iraq in 2007–8, security forces of all types (coalition, Iraqi, Sons of Iraq and private security contractors) outnumbered insurgents by ten to one or more, and enjoyed a

troop/population ratio of one to sixty; roughly 600,000 security forces
of all types operated amidst an Iraqi population of 30 million. However,
it was noticeable that the Americans were only able to reach these
figures through partnership with regular and irregular local forces.
The US surge itself consisted of an increase of about 35,000 troops,
from 130,000 to 165,000. This was a very large force, but it contrasts
starkly with the massive security presence in cities deployed by France
and Britain in Algeria, Kenya, Malaya, Cyprus and Northern Ireland.
It represented a force ratio of one US service person for every 181
Iraqi citizens. In the culminating battle of Sadr City, the ratio was even
higher, although the coalition never made any attempt to clear and hold
the neighbourhood. An urban area of about 1.2 million people was pacified by 3,000 US soldiers – aided, of course, by extensive Iraqi allies: a
ratio of about one US soldier to every 400 Shia citizens in that district.[47]
Because counterinsurgent forces have shrunk, it has now become much
harder for them to drive insurgents out of cities completely. Of course,
the enlargement of urban areas in the last few decades has only compounded the problem of force densities. In Iraq, insurgents were able
to hold terrain because, for much of the campaign, the US, the UK and
the Iraqi government simply did not have the troops to remove them.

Western states have not been alone in experiencing unfavourable
force ratios in urban areas. On the contrary, if anything, the wars in
Syria, Yemen and Libya have highlighted the problem of force ratios
even more clearly. Each of these wars is politically complex; their origins
and dynamics cannot be explained solely by numbers and force ratios.
However, force ratios in these insurgencies are striking. The Syrian civil
war offers a very significant and, perhaps, the most pertinent example
of the issue. The origins of this war affirm the demographic arguments
that most of the literature affirms. The conflict arose because of rapid
urbanization and the grievances it generated. For instance, the battle of
Homs exemplifies the model almost perfectly. Between 2000 and 2010,
the population of Homs expanded from 500,000 to 700,000 inhabitants,[48] mainly as poor peasants immigrated into its deprived districts.
At the same time, the city had become increasingly polarized, with a
privileged, globalized metropolis surrounded by impoverished shanties.
Eventually, disenfranchised residents, from areas like Baba Amr, occupied the Clock Tower Square in February 2012 to protest against the
regime. When they were attacked by President Bashir Assad's forces,
they formed themselves into antiregime militias.[49] Once the battle had
begun, insurgents exploited the asymmetric advantages offered by the
city.

Demographics may explain why the Syrian civil war started in its towns and cities. Yet, demographics alone do not explain its subsequent development. The urban uprisings began in 2011, but, in 2020, after nine years of war, the conflict was still urbanized. All the major battles have occurred in the towns and cities of Syria. The war started as an urban struggle and remained as one, with belligerents fighting for control of particular city sectors. It is necessary to explain this state of affairs.

Here, force ratios are instructive. Despite defeats by the Israelis in 1967, 1973 and 1982, the Syrian Army remained a large and well-equipped force. In 2013, in the early years of the civil war, it consisted of 178,000 soldiers.[50] However, the majority of this force was made up of conscripts drawn from the Sunni population, most of whom were rebelling. Consequently, the regime could trust no more than 65–80,000 of its soldiers, and only its elite troops, the Republican Guard, the 4th Armoured Division and its special forces were totally reliable.[51] In addition, the Syrian regime was supported by the National Defence Forces, numbering some 50–60,000, and the sectarian militia, Shabbihah. Eventually, Hezbollah and Iran provided significant additional forces. Consequently, the Assad regime fielded about 150,000 combatants during the war. It was not a small force.

However, the uprising eventually involved every major Syrian city and most towns, mobilizing a large part of the Sunni population. Regime forces attempted to suppress armed resistance in Aleppo, Damascus, Homs, Raqqa, Idlib, Latakia, Hama and Dera'a, as well as some other smaller towns. Between 2011 and 2018, a force of 150,000 was divided between eight major cities and many smaller ones. There, the regime employed considerable and indiscriminate force, but it rarely enjoyed the combat supremacy to defeat insurgents outright. Indeed, before the Russian intervention, in 2015, the regime decided to give up much of the country and focus on the 'rump' of Syria in the east, from Suwaida in the south to the coast in the north. The Syrian regime has been able to take back urban areas from the rebels only with the support of Russian airpower, Iran's Quds force (under the command of Qassem Soleimani) and Hezbollah. Even then, the fight has been bitter and protracted. Like the Americans and British in Iraq, the Syrian armed forces were confronted with a severe shortage of troops. Consequently, they were unable to drive their opponents out of the cities. The result was the notoriously long-running sieges which have characterized this dreadful war.

Brazil

In the 1960s and 1970s, the concept of the urban guerrilla was primarily a Latin American construct, advocated by Guillén, Marighella and Debray. Yet, in each case, the urban guerrilla, unable to secure terrain, had to operate as a highly adaptable terrorist and was normally defeated by overwhelming state force. States dominated cities at this time. The situation is now quite different. Insurgencies have urbanized substantially because of declining force ratios. Marighella provides a particularly useful counterpoint here. In the late 1960s, he orchestrated a revolutionary, leftist campaign against the military regime in Brazil. He failed completely; his urban gang based in São Paulo was defeated with ease. His urban successors are extremely interesting. They are no longer radicals, inspired by Marxist ideology. On the contrary, they are barely political at all. Marighella's urban guerrillas have been replaced by urban super-gangs, which now dominate large areas of ungoverned space in Rio, São Paulo and the other major cities of Brazil. Representing a genuine challenge to the state, the Comando Vermelho (Red Command) and Primeiro Comando da Capital (First Capital Command) are Marighella's true heirs. They provide a pertinent example of what twenty-first-century insurgency looks like – and how the reduction of state forces has facilitated their rise.

Favelas first emerged in Brazil in last decade of the nineteenth century. Returning from the Canudos War in 1898, demobilized soldiers, who had been falsely promised land, settled on Mount Moro outside Rio. The settlement became known as a *favela*, purportedly named after a rhododendron-like plant that grew in the area.[52] From 1900 until the mid-1970s, *favelas* proliferated on the margins of Brazilian cities. They were the site of poverty, poor health and endemic low-level criminality. *Favelas* began to change in the 1970s. Two processes played a critical role here: Brazilian penal policy and drugs. From the late 1960s, the Brazilian military regime incarcerated increasing numbers of criminals from the *favelas* in the infamous Candido Mendes Penal Institute on Ilha Grande. They were imprisoned alongside leftist political prisoners, some of whom were associates of Marighella.[53] While the leftists themselves had failed as urban guerrillas, they were highly effective in indoctrinating the young criminals from the *favelas*. These criminals were not interested in the finer details of Marxist theory, but the importance of organization and administration and the support of the people impressed them. The emergent *favela* leaders sought to apply these lessons to their own enterprises on release.

Coinciding with the *favela* leaders' growing political conscious-ness, cocaine became a major international drug from the late 1970s. Low-level criminal bands in the *favelas* quickly became major play-ers in the cocaine trade, acting as partners to the Fuerzas Armadas Revolucionarias de Colombia (FARC, Revolutionary Armed Forces of Colombia) and the Colombian cartels, trafficking the drug locally and internationally.[54] Inspired by a new ambition and funded by hith-erto inconceivable levels of wealth, the self-styled Comando Vermelho and Primeiro Comando da Capital emerged in Rio and São Paulo to monopolize the drugs trade. Later, other super-gangs emerged as rival factions split away from the two original gangs: Amigos dos Amigos and Terceiro.[55]

These super-gangs are utterly ruthless in protecting their interests. The leader of Comando Vermelho, William Lima da Silva, spent most of his life in prison and was personally responsible for the deaths of hundreds. Gang leaders are necessarily drawn into a cycle of violence and counterviolence to protect themselves and to deter rivals.[56] The most striking characteristic of the twenty-first century super-gang is that, quite unlike the urban guerrilla of the twentieth century, they dominate terrain. Brazil's super-gangs are all intimately attached to specific *favelas*, in which their leadership and organization are based. The *favelas* are crucial to the super-gangs because they allow the gang members to operate away from government interference. Because of the geography of the *favelas*, a major police operation is required to enter these areas. Consequently, *favelas* have become the perfect home base for the gangs, whose members can hide in plain sight, just a short distance from the centres of political power.[57] Drugs, contraband and weapons can be safely stored in the *favelas*, which makes it possible for the gangs to traffick drugs locally or to export cocaine internationally from these bases. In addition, the *favelas* provide the gangs with labour; young men and women are recruited as scouts, foot-soldiers, mules, traffickers and prostitutes.

The rule of the gangs is not benign. Individuals who are deemed to have transgressed by stealing or informing are killed; their bodies are rarely found. However, these gangs do publicly espouse the social democratic doctrines they were taught by political prisoners in the 1970s. They display a moral code of sorts and do attempt to provide employment, security, social services and justice to the inhabitants of their *favelas*. The Primeiro Comando's official sign is a yin yang symbol, with the motto, 'A way to balance good and evil with wisdom', while Comando Vermelho's motto is 'Liberty, justice and peace'.[58] Clearly, these emblems are more rhetorical than real. Yet, in the *favelas*, these super-gangs are able to out-govern the absent state, even though some of their methods might be deplorable.[59] Indeed, during the 2020 coronavirus pandemic, even as Jair Bolsonaro's government downplayed the virus and eschewed any attempt to introduce lockdown restrictions in Brazil, the gangs in Rio's *favelas* imposed their own quarantine regulations. They seemed to be more concerned than the state about public health. Brazilian gangs have achieved what the urban guerrilla failed to do in the 1960s and 1970s: they have created safe home bases from which to operate across the city and to supplant state sovereignty.

Since the 2010s, the Brazilian government has sought to challenge the super-gangs' control of the *favelas*. The state created a specialist paramilitary police unit in the 1980s, Batalhão de Operações Policiais Especiais (BOPE, Police Special Operations Battalion), to raid the *favelas*. BOPE has continued to play an important role to the present time, though its aggressive operations are controversial. Its raids to capture criminals have typically involved high levels of violence and often major gun battles. In readiness for hosting the FIFA World Cup in 2014 and the Olympic Games in 2016, Brazil developed a second type of specialist police unit, Unidade de Policia Pacificadora (UPP, Police Pacification Units), which does not mount raids; it is a stabilization force permanently based in *favelas* in order to wrest control of them from the gangs. By 2018, thirty-nine UPP bases had been established to patrol 763 *favelas*. However, despite the attempts of the Brazilian government to bring the *favelas* under control, they have lacked the security personnel to displace the gangs. Indeed, by 2019, the situation in the *favelas* had deteriorated. The pacification strategy was substantially abandoned and several UPP bases were decommissioned.[60] Jair Bolsonaro initially announced that he might seek an accommodation with the gangs.

Of course, it might be claimed that Comando Vermelho and their equivalents are simply criminal cartels. They are not political, as the classic urban guerrillas were. It is true that these gangs have no radical political agenda. They are not remotely interesting in bringing down the Brazilian government, still less the state; indeed, their leaders are not concerned with politics or political power in a formal sense at all. They are not at war with the state. Their violence is mostly used in a petty way to assert their local authority, imposing internal discipline or against rival gangs. They represent a political degeneration of Marighella's idealism.

Yet, periodically, when their interests are challenged, the super-gangs engage in orchestrated campaigns of violence against the state.

For instance, in May 2006, 765 Primeiro leaders were moved to high-security prisons.[61] Not only was this transfer insulting; it also threatened the gangs' operations, since the prisons, in which the leaders were held, acted as secure headquarters. The leaders were in constant contact with subordinates in the *favelas*, by means of mobile telephones. As a result of the transfer, Comando Primeiro staged major riots in São Paulo; there were nearly 300 attacks on police stations throughout the city. Similarly, when Comando Vermelho was threatened with a similar transfer later in the year, a leader declared: 'In the *favelas* I have one hundred thousand suicide bombers.'[62] It was a gross exaggeration. Yet, it usefully illustrates an important point. Brazilian super-gangs have accommodated the government as long as their operations have not been unduly affected. However, when the government has actively challenged their interests, these gangs become highly political. Then, they have used violence systematically against the state and its security forces in order to protect themselves and advance their interests. At this point, the gangs become political actors in a true sense, and their criminal violence, consequently, becomes indistinguishable from a genuine urban insurgency and, therefore, war.

Back to the City

The urban guerrilla is not new. Insurgents have not come out of the mountains in recent decades: they were always already in the city. However, cities have become a major – even the prime – theatre for insurgency in the twenty-first century. Insurgents now typically situate their enclaves inside cities; they dominate neighbourhoods, which they transform into no-go areas. The rise of the urban insurgent – instead of the placeless terrorist – can certainly be partly explained because cities have become so huge; their vastness quite overwhelms the security forces. As the Brazilian *favela* shows, slums are ideal havens for urban gangs; they are almost impenetrable for the security forces.

Yet, there is also an additional, often ignored, factor that helps explain why the urban guerrilla has become such an important actor in contemporary conflict: force ratios. Compared to their size in the twentieth century, state forces are now tiny. States today simply do not have the personnel to deploy one member of the security forces for every fifty citizens. So, while states could drive insurgents from cities in the 1950s, 1960s and 1970s, as Nairobi, Algiers, Aden and Belfast showed, they are no longer always able to dominate urban areas. They cannot patrol all the streets and alleys and, in this gap in the security apparatus, urban insurgents have proliferated in recent decades. Urban sanctuaries have emerged inside cities that are very difficult for the security forces to penetrate or clear. The chronic inner-urban stand-off, which has been such a feature of twenty-first-century urban conflict, has consequently appeared. Insurgents and state forces have been locked in an interminable struggle for supremacy inside the city itself.

4

Metropolis

The Global City

Up to now, the discussion has examined the armed forces, focusing specifically on the question of combat densities and urban warfare. However, plainly, it is impossible to comprehend urban warfare without some knowledge of the cities in which it takes place. In fact, in recent years, urban warfare has occurred in very particular human settlements: in globalized cities. Ironically, even small and apparently provincial towns have been globalized. But what does it mean to describe a city or an urban area as globalized? It is a commonly used concept, but it is a complex one, whose specific meaning is not always explained. Before we can begin to analyse urban warfare in any detail, it is imperative to define precisely what a globalized city might be. Against the proliferation of complexity in the academic literature, it is actually best to keep things very simple here. It is generally agreed that there are four essential elements that define the global city: size, height, polarization and globalization.

Size is the most obvious feature of the twenty-first-century city; urban populations have multiplied in the last few decades. There are now more cities with more than 100,000 inhabitants than ever before in human history; there are thirty-seven megacities worldwide. The major area of growth is in Asia and Southeast Asia, India, China and Indonesia. By 2050, seven out of ten people in the world will live in urban areas in this region. Yet, the trend is quite general. As a result of this population explosion, municipal areas are now bigger than ever.

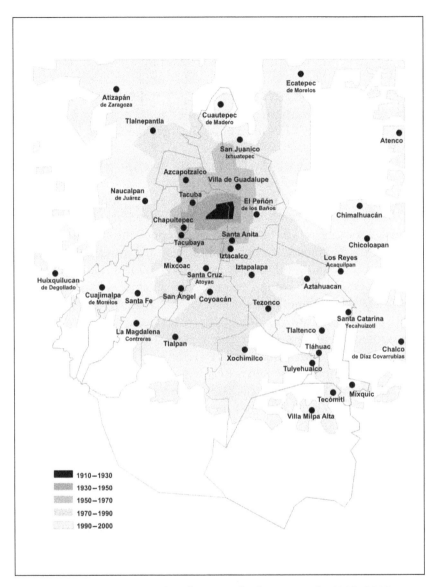

Figure 4.1: Mexico City horizonal urban growth, 1910–2000
Source: Yavidaxiu / Wikimedia Commons / Public domain.

Across the world, modern cities of the twentieth century have exploded into huge sprawling megalopolises. As cities have grown, they have merged with surrounding towns and suburbs to create vast leviathans. In the past, Los Angeles exemplified horizontal expansion at its worst, but this extrapolation is now widespread. In Europe, the Ruhr might be defined as one large urban area extending all the way to Amsterdam, as might the whole of south-eastern England. In China, new megacities are appearing with bewildering speed. As a result of massive increase in their populations, cities have expanded horizontally since the late 1990s. Mexico City displays the trajectory very clearly (see Figure 4.1). In 1960, Mexico City occupied an area of approximately 200 square miles; today, it covers 573 square miles. A large modern city has become a global megacity.

Cities have extended, then. Global cities have also grown vertically. Height has always been a feature of the city. Palaces, temples and churches have always been dominant, deliberately designed to inspire awe. In the late nineteenth and early twentieth centuries, the first skyscrapers appeared in US cities, and often under the influence of the International Congress of Architecture, very tall towers began to be built from the 1930s. When they opened in 1973, the ill-fated Twin Towers of the World Trade Center in Manhattan, at 540 metres high, were the tallest buildings in the world. However, as a result of changing architectural styles, new building materials, international capital and status competition between cities and states, it has been possible to build even taller skyscrapers. Commercial and business districts around the world have now converged on a common global style, consisting of truly vast vertical structures. In 2013, there were seventy-three supertall skyscrapers higher than 400 metres and two mega-tall structures of more than 600 metres: the Shanghai Tower and the Burj Khalifa in Dubai.[1] Ironically, many of the floors in these buildings are empty; it has been calculated that about 27 per cent of their height is superfluous. Yet, even in cities that cannot boast true mega-structures, soaring towers and vertiginous urban canyons have appeared. The proliferation of glass steles has mainly been driven by financial interests: 'It is clear that new super-tall towers act as key anchors within the wider construction of what Mike Davis and Dan Monk called "Dreamworlds of neoliberalism".'[2]

Moreover, as cities have ascended skywards, they have simultaneously descended sub-surface: 'Key urban geographical texts, meanwhile, rarely mention the extraordinary extension of cities above and below ground.'[3] Cities have always had a subterranean dimension; Roman cities normally featured underground water and sewage systems. Underground railways were an important part of the modern city. The world's first underground railway was opened between Paddington and Farringdon in London in 1863. As cities have extended horizontally, these underground networks have become more extensive and there is now a vast labyrinth of service tunnels and passages beneath the streets of almost every city. The topography of the global city is remarkable therefore; it has extended both horizontally and vertically. From a military perspective, the extension of the globalizing city is a major challenge. These huge buildings and subterranean passages complicate the battlespace, multiplying its acreage, impeding airpower and providing opponents with almost infinite cover.

As cities have grown spatially, they have also often diversified demographically and their social geographies have become highly complex. Of course, all cities throughout history have been demographically diverse; it is a defining feature of a city. Modern cities of the twentieth century were starkly divided into rich and poor areas, as classic texts like Friedrich Engels's *The Condition of the English Working Class* or Jacob Riis's *How the Other Half Lives* demonstrated. Indeed, a whole genre of Western literature and art was dedicated to exploring the urban experience and its depravations: Dickens, Dostoyevsky, Daumier, Baudelaire and the Impressionists all sought to represent the new urban lifeworld. Modern cities typically contained poor areas and ethnic minorities, often segregated into ghettos. However, especially in comparison with the post-war city of the mid- to late twentieth century, metropolises are no longer simply divided, but are actively polarized. There are two principal axes of polarization: economic and ethnic. The differential between the rich and poor in the global city has increased dramatically since the end of the twentieth century. This differentiation was first noted by geographers in the 1990s when they described the emergence of the 'dual city', characterized by extreme wealth juxtaposed against poverty. New forms of private security apparatus – walls, gated communities, CCTV, guards – signified this economic polarization, since it was specifically designed to keep the poor and the criminal out of affluent areas. Perhaps the simplest and most emblematic feature of the global city was the 'bum-proof' bench introduced into Los Angeles in the 1980s.[4] In order to overcome the problem of homeless people sleeping on park benches, Los Angeles introduced convex benches into parks and streets. Legitimate inhabitants could temporarily perch on these seats, but it was impossible to sleep on them. They signified the exclusivity of the global city.

At the same time, cities have become ethnically heterogeneous. In the twentieth century, cities typically contained an indigenous majority population and some minority communities. Today, many cities are not only more ethnically diverse, but these ethnic communities are also significantly bigger. The result is that a patchwork of increasingly exclusive ethnic enclaves is appearing in cities. There is nothing new about urban ethnic conflict, as Beirut and Belfast show. However, cities have become increasingly segregated spaces that are much harder to manage. Urban polarization has played a major role in recent urban battles and will influence military operations in cities in the future.

Finally, cities have globalized. Globalization has involved a dual process of localization and transnationalization. In the twentieth century, cities were broadly unified entities. They consisted of a concentrated population in a circumscribed area, with an obvious external boundary, under a single municipal authority. Cities were ordered in a national hierarchy, regulated by the state. In today's bloating conurbations, there is no necessary convergence between the urban authority and the population. Typically, the urban population extends well beyond the formal territory of what was once defined as the city. Sometimes, substantial terrain within the city is not governed or administered by the metropolitan authorities at all. Slums within the city often lie outside the domain of the municipal authorities. This process has led some commentators to claim that 'the basic nature of urban realities – long understood under the singular, encompassing rubric of "cityness" – has become differentiated, polymorphic'.[5]

Cities have always traded with each other, but cities today are immersed in global flows of finances, services and people. Of course, the truly major cities are more deeply interconnected than provincial towns. However, every single urban settlement has been drawn into an intensifying, transnational nexus of informational connectivity and socioeconomic interconnections. Cities have merged into a planetary urban entity: 'Urbanization has become planetary.'[6]

As a result, cities become more diffuse and less unified. Some districts are now deeply integrated into global economic and population flows. Global corporations clustered together into commercial and business districts might be more closely connected with other financial centres than they are with the neighbourhoods that surround them. Similarly, ethnic enclaves in one city may be as closely connected with related diasporic groups in another as they are with their fellow citizens: 'So extensive have the city's connections become as a result of the growth of fast communications, global flows, and linkage into national and international institutional life that the city needs theorization as a site of local-global connectivity.'[7] Globalized cities are no longer single, unitary spaces, organized around a centrifugal geographical and political point. They have become centripetalized settlements, consisting of heterogeneous elements, each integrated into the urban locale and global flows in quite different ways. Cities have been reconfigured. They have imploded inwards, with the creation of localized, exclusive enclaves, while also exploding outwards, as these enclaves are increasingly integrated into external global flows; urbanization has involved both concentration and extension.[8]

It would be possible to take almost any urban area to exemplify the reterritorialization of global cities. London's East End, formed by the trapezium between Wapping, Whitechapel, Stratford and the Isle of Dogs, is an obvious and familiar example: 'London Docklands [the Isle of Dogs] was indeed a symbol, the most spectacular example of a process that was occurring right across the capitalist urban world of the 1980s.'[9] From the industrial revolution to the 1970s, the East End was a poor but thriving commercial zone, as a result of its proximity to the Port of London and the Docklands. The area was the entrepôt of the British Empire, as the novels of Charles Dickens, Arthur Conan Doyle and Joseph Conrad so brilliantly described. Parts of the East End – especially around Whitechapel – were also always heavily populated by migrant refugees: Huguenots in the eighteenth century, Jews in the nineteenth. Yet, until the 1970s – migration to affluent estates in Essex and some Pakistani immigration notwithstanding – it was an overwhelmingly white area, populated by the working class, which was employed in the docks or associated industries.

In the 1970s, dramatic changes took place. In light of increased international competition and changing transport systems, the docks closed and the main source of employment for the indigenous working class disappeared. The Docklands became a post-industrial wasteland. In the 1980s, Wapping and the Isle of Docks were derelict; the warehouses and basins were empty. However, as a result of an initiative from the Thatcher government, the Isle of Dogs was designated for major renovation as the Canary Wharf enterprise zone. The execution of this project has been taken as an object lesson in how not to do urban development: 'Hardly anyone would now defend the Canary Wharf saga, whereby one of the largest urban developments in the world was started without the necessary transport system to move commuters in and out of it.'[10] Nevertheless, by the early twenty-first century, Canary Wharf had become a thriving centre of global finance, with many major companies located in its high-rises. New transport systems, one overground and one underground, connect it to the rest of London, and to Europe via City Airport. At the same time, the derelict warehouses of Wapping have been gentrified into expensive condominiums to house a growing professional population. Rather symbolically, in 1993, Millwall Football Club, originally located in the forbidding 'Den' on Cold Blow Lane on the Isle of Dogs and notorious for the aggressive localism of its mainly white, working-class fans, was relocated to a new stadium south of the river. Twenty years later, a global sporting mega-event moved into the area. Following the successful Olympic Games bid, the Stratford district of East London was designated as the location for the London 2012 Summer Games, involving renovation of the area and improvement of the transport infrastructure. Since the 1970s, Whitechapel and the surrounding area had become poorer and more ethnicized, with an increased Muslim population, mainly from Bangladesh, congregating in the area. Suggesting the importance of diasporic links to the global Muslim *ummah*, Stratford is also the site of a controversial Tablighi Jamaat mosque, propounding a conservative, if not fundamentalist, doctrine of Islam.

The East End has been reconfigured from postindustrial dereliction in the 1970s, when it lost its role as an imperial entrepôt, into a radically globalized space, with dense connections to the transnational flows of capital and people. The result is extreme contrast between wealth and poverty, white and Asian, Christian or post-Christian and Islamic, public and private. The East End has become a radically differentiated and highly complex district. London Docklands demonstrates the four features of the global city very well; the towers of Canary Wharf dwarf all preceding structures, it has a more extensive subterranean infra-structure, it is more heterogeneous and enclavized, and it is vastly more globalized. In short, Docklands today is taller, deeper, more diverse and more transnational than it was in the twentieth century. The East End has been globalized. It is a novel cityscape.

The City as a System

Cities have always been very difficult to understand. In the twentieth century, military forces often struggled to comprehend urban areas and how their opponents operated in them. For instance, following its intervention into Lebanon in 1982, the Israeli Army was ill-adapted to appreciate the political complexities of Beirut. State authority had collapsed in Beirut leaving competing ethnic groups struggling for dominance in the city. Consequently, 'the amorphous political, military and organizational apparatus in Lebanon did not "match" the combat methods and norms of a modern regular military'.[11] However, glo-balized metropolises are an even more profound challenge for the armed forces today. Because they are much larger and more heterogeneous than the twentieth-century city, it is much more difficult comprehend the dynamics of conflict within them. The problem experienced by the Israeli Defence Force early in the 1980s has now become acute. Cities are larger and more complex.

In order to operate effectively in these vast conurbations, refined intelligence and understanding are required. This is very difficult:

> There are two overarching challenges when conducting a military operation in an urban area. One is simply being able to understand the environment. The other is being able to understand how to operate in the environment. Both these challenges are harder to do in an urban environment than any other.[12]

Indeed, in his analysis of urban operations, Michael Evans, the British urban military expert, has gone so far to suggest that, in order to conduct successful urban operations today, it is necessary for the armed forces to understand the city not merely in a military sense; it is inadequate to identify key terrain, vital ground, dead ground, etc. The armed forces must also become urban sociologists if they are to operate effectively, as Michael Evans points out:

> In urban military operations all civil assets from water purification and electricity through garbage removal to securing medical infrastructure and public transport are invested with military significance. In this respect, the strategic policy-maker and military professional face many of the same problems as the urban planner or emergency services manager. In holistic terms, the concept of MOUT [military operations in urban terrain] is probably too narrow for the intellectual requirements of strategic studies. Developing a comprehensive urban lens will require that strategic studies consider embracing the broader concept of 'military operations as urban planning' or 'MOUP'.[13]

Whether the armed forces should aspire to becoming genuine urban planners is an open question. Yet, Evans's point is well made. In the twenty-first century, the military can no longer simply blunder into urban areas. Cities are complex heterogeneous ecologies, integrated into a global system, so the possibility of an error escalating from local events has been multiplied. The armed forces are too small to inundate a whole municipality, as the French did in Algiers or the British did in Nairobi and Belfast. Globalized cities defy their capacity to dominate them. Consequently, in order to have any military effect, the armed forces have had to interpret the city. They have to calculate where their intervention might have most impact. Yet, the city is a bewildering, all but infinite, environment.

John Spencer, a US Army officer who served as a company commander during the battle of Sadr City and went on to hold the Chair in Urban Warfare Studies at West Point, has, with his colleague John Amble, highlighted the interpretative challenge of urban operations today. Cities have become such a demanding environment for the armed forces that 'we need to figure out a better way to *think about* cities'. However, although the US Army is a highly professional organization, Spencer and Amble are concerned that it has no specialist skill in urban analysis. The results have been catastrophic:

> The chief problem is that because we don't understand cities nearly as well as we could and have demonstrated that we know even less about how to optimize military actions in them, we are like medieval doctors, lobotomizing patients and letting their blood without improving their health and too often causing death or such life-long damage that the patient survives as only a dysfunctional shadow of itself. We cause incredible disruption and even destruction, but without any research-based evidence that these efforts will save the city.[14]

Accordingly, in order to increase their effectiveness, Spencer has suggested that the armed forces must develop a better understanding of cities. Instead of mounting a blind attack, forces should learn to apprehend the workings of a city so that they can eliminate the opposition with minimal collateral damage and disruption. Spencer and Amble conclude: 'Need to excise a cancer like ISIS without disrupting the governance and service provision that the group has been conducting for three years? Turn to a military professional who has been trained and equipped to know how to do so.'[15]

Clearly, the development of a new urban military science is ambitious, to say the least. However, the armed forces have been trying to develop their analysis of cities. One of the most striking methods that they have adopted has been to try to analyse the city as an organism. They have developed a systems theory approach to the metropolitan problem. In 1965, Abel Wolman published a seminal article, 'The Metabolism of Cities', which suggested that cities might usefully be analysed by reference to the flow of inputs (water, food, fuel) and outputs (sewage, refuse and air pollution). On this account, a city displayed certain organic features. In fact, Wolman was concerned only whether American cities would have enough water and not be choked by air pollution.[16] However, his concept of the city as a metabolism has been interpreted very liberally and, in this wider guise, has been influential.

For instance, in *Wounded Cities*, Jane Schneider and Ida Susser follow Wolman to recommend that the armed forces see the city as a 'body politic': 'The city is a collective organisation to support human life and activities . . . Cities are constituted out of flows of energy, water, people, and all the other necessities that sustain life.'[17] Closely following Schneider and Susser, David Kilcullen has become one of the most prominent advocates of this systemic approach. He suggests:

> If we apply this notion [of metabolism] to the urban environment, noting that the primary threat in this environment comes from non-state armed groups, we can start to see what an urban conflict ecosystem looks like, and to develop an understanding of what we might call the microecology of urban violence.[18]

Conflict constitutes a pathology within the urban body. Kilcullen attempts to illustrate his metabolic approach by analysing gang violence in San Pedro Sula, Honduras, which at one point was 'the most dangerous city on the planet'. He concluded that gang violence could be best understood not in terms of the individual motivations of gang members or their leaders, but rather as the manifestation of deeper flows across the city:

> What seemed on the surface to be chaotic patterns of violence among a multiplicity of local gangs, narco-traffickers, and other groups turned out to be the result of a small number of macro-level flows that have accelerated over the past decade. These flows, along with the city's spatial layout, its geographic location as the country's main economic and transportation hub, and local conditions in a series of urban micro-habitats, account for virtually all of the observable violence in San Pedro Sula.[19]

As guns, money and drugs flowed into the city, gangs competed for terrain and markets.[20]

Kilcullen has not been alone in arguing that systems theory might help the armed forces to understand the complexities of conflict and violence in global cities. The armed forces have themselves sought to understand the city as a system consisting of flows and currents, which can be disturbed and interdicted at will: 'As a tool for guiding strategic appreciation, the use of a systems-theory based typology helps focus commanders and planners on the city as a whole.'[21] This methodology recognizes the importance of context, scale, density, connectedness and threats. However, a central concept is the idea of flow:

> Flow is the movement of people, resources or things into or out of a megacity. Just as a living organism relies on flows in (food, air and water), and flows out (waste) to stay alive, a city also requires flows. Vast amounts of energy and other vital goods must flow into the megacity, these goods must circulate throughout the urban space, and waste must flow out if the megacity is to remain healthy. Doctrinal approaches in the future must prioritize the preservation of key flows in order to maintain the health of the population. In so doing the Army will reduce the requirement for reconstruction efforts that inevitably follow major urban conflicts.[22]

By interpreting cities as systems, the armed forces hope to conduct surgical military operations in them, eliminating opponents while preserving the metropolitan infrastructure and its flows (see Figure 4.2). Systems theory is a way of executing military operations as urban planning.

Urban Sociology

It is obvious why the metabolic metaphor has attracted military analysts in the last two decades. Globalized cities have presented the armed forces with a highly complex problem. Sprawling urban areas, swarming with tens of thousands of inhabitants, are bewildering. They overpower human cognition and imagination. They defy the armed forces' attempts to map, analyse and define them, even though such documentation is essential. The armed forces need to understand cities; but global cities exceed comprehension. They are simply too large, multitudinous and mutable. The metabolic metaphor reduces the metropolis to mappable flows and currents.

As a general heuristic device, the concept of the urban metabolism is initially quite useful. Plainly, there are flows of material into and out of the city; water, sewage, electricity, gas, food and commuters, without which the municipality could not survive, flow into and out of the city on a daily basis. These flows exist and are relatively stable over time. Consequently, the urban metabolism model orientates the observer to the scale of the realities, focusing attention on the central elements

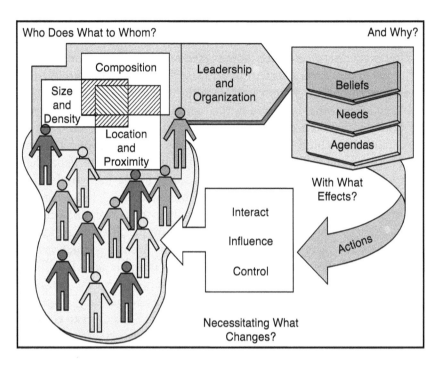

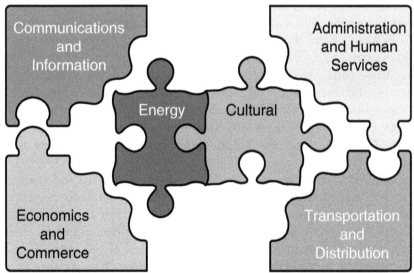

Figure 4.2a and 4.2b: The city as organism
Source: Headquarters, Department of the Army Field Manual 3-06, *Urban Operations* (Washington, DC: Department of the Army, 2006), 2.15, 2.19.

of the city. It also prevents fallaciously individualized accounts of this complex social reality.

However, there are also some extremely serious shortcomings with the urban metabolism model. Descriptions of the model presume that the urban system is in equilibrium, that flows are regular, stable and recurrent. In addition, the model presumes that urban areas are bounded entities, that there is a specific limit to the city, out of which and into which definite currents flow. On a metabolic account, the urban system is a unified, integrated, functionally interdependent entity. It is possible that, in the past, especially in pre-industrial settlements, cities were relatively closed and bounded. Yet, the globalized city of the twenty-first century flatly contradicts the concept of a closed, stable system. Expanding and changing very rapidly, cities are no longer stable; they are rarely, if ever, in equilibrium. A city in which armed forces might deploy will be, by definition, an unstable one. It will not be a self-supporting, self-equilibrating organism, but, on the contrary, a settlement whose inhabitants are fighting one another.

There are further problems. Despite Kilcullen's attempts to connect macro-flows with the 'microecology' of urban violence, systems theory operates at too general a level to interpret specific conflicts. Urban conflict is situated in the micro-geography of a city; it is constituted by warring parties who struggle for possession of concrete urban terrain. At best, the wider flows provide a context for any violence, but these flows cannot explain the actual dynamics of the violence itself, still less an urban battle. In San Pedro Sula, gangs periodically struggled for decisive locations, like road junctions, from which they were able to monopolize drug-trafficking. At the same time, the concept of urban metabolism depoliticizes a city. It reduces it to a series of physical, quasi-biological functions. Yet, in fact, cities are inherently and unavoidably political.

Cities are not organisms whose functions have evolved and adapted on the basis of what is objectively most efficient for their preservation or for the population as a whole; they are not organic bodies. On the contrary, cities are created, changed and maintained by their inhabitants. These inhabitants do not plan their city as rational and disinterested individuals. Instead, each and every city consists of a complex hierarchy of social groups. Cities consist of the government, state administration, political parties, churches, military and security forces, schools, universities, hospitals, professional groups, manufacturers, workers, criminals, families, neighbourhoods, clans, tribes and sports clubs. In a large modern city, the interrelations of these social groups are so intricate that it is empirically all but impossible to map them and their hierarchies comprehensively. There are numerous, overlapping groups. Some groups, such as occupations and religious or ethnic associations, are longstanding. Others, such as political or cultural movements, might be transitory; crowds form and disperse quickly. Moreover, urbanites belong to more than one group; they are employed professionally by a company or the state, but live in a specific neighbourhood, are bound by their own ethnic and kinship ties, go to different churches and support different football clubs. At any point, one of these affiliations might become more relevant for them. Groups overlap, merge and diverge. So, the social geography of the city is almost infinitely complex and always changing.

Nevertheless, although it may indeed be impossible ever to plot a truly comprehensive social geography of a city, it is crucial that cities are understood in terms of their human populations and, above all, their constituent social groups. Cities consist of groups, not flows. Indeed, the flows of water, electricity, goods and services that circulate around the city are never the product of neutral environmental adaptation. Always and everywhere, the physical topography of the city – its buildings, streets, parks and transport systems – are political achievements, arising out of the competition, cooperation and hierarchy of urban social groups. Take any built feature of the urban landscape. Somewhere and at some time, a specific social group, pursuing its interests, in collaboration with or opposition to others, built that edifice as it now presents itself; that group or its successors have maintained or changed their constructions. Human social groups build and sustain cities, not flows.

Urban sociology has often depicted the social constitution of the city very effectively. A prominent member of the Chicago school of urban sociology in the mid-twentieth century, Louis Wirth produced one of the most famous early studies of the city in his 1928 book on the ghetto. The ghetto is a long-established urban enclave whose origins can be traced back to the Middle Ages; the original ghetto was located in Venice, where the Jewish population was concentrated around the cannon foundry (it is probable that the word ghetto comes from this location). Wirth was not interested in the ghetto because of its fraught political history (which would take on a terrible significance after his book was published), but rather because it demonstrated urban existence generally: 'The ghetto may therefore be regarded as typical of a number of other forms of communal life that sociologists are attempting to explore.'[23] The city is never a vast anonymous mass. On the contrary,

it is made up of many small communities, located in specific neighbourhoods or united around particular functions; the city is actually just
a congregation of villages – or ghettos. Wirth argues that, although
isolated in some ways, the ghetto was also a rich and dynamic community, its members intensely bonded. It provided precarious migrants
with social security and economic opportunities as they arrived in the
city or continued to be excluded from better forms of employment. At
the same time, ghetto members exerted control over one another; they
were disciplined in a way that meant they contributed to the common
good. They adopted a common lifestyle, appearance and manners
in order to distinguish themselves from outsiders. Nevertheless, the
ghetto was never a totally separate entity from the city and other social
groups. Rather, the ghetto typically thrived only because it provided
crucial specialist, sometimes taboo services to the rest of the urban
population. Like every other association in the city, the ghetto is both
isolated and exclusive, but also integrated into the urban life. Finally,
the ghetto is never stable; populations necessarily cycle through ghettos,
with succeeding generations moving away physically and culturally as
they find new employment opportunities. Wirth noted how succeeding
generations of Jews in early twentieth-century Chicago moved to the
North Lawndale neighbourhood of the city as they gained professional
employment. Wirth's point is not that these individuals had departed
into an anonymous suburban population but, rather, they had moved
into a new, more expansive, advantaged kind of ghetto.

Wirth examined the interior dynamics of the ghetto. However,
his point was that cities were characterized largely by the interaction
of their ghettos. In his classic 1973 study, *Social Justice and the City*,
Marxist geographer David Harvey highlights the inherently political
character of the city. As a Marxist, Harvey prioritizes class as the master
explanation of urban geography. His preference for class explanations
does not need to be accepted. However, he usefully dismisses economic
theories of the city that explain the distribution of services by reference
to the neutral workings of the market – i.e., financial flows. For him, at
every point, cities are determined by the interests of the capitalist class.
The bourgeoisie have defined the city, imposing their profitmaking
interests on its very structure. This process becomes very obvious when
we look at the provision of public services across a city. They are never
spread fairly: 'The inability of market mechanisms to allocate resources
efficiently when externalities are present has posed a major problem for
economic theory.'[24] Harvey continues: 'Very little attention has been
paid to distributional effects, mainly because any theory of the distribu-

tion of external costs and benefits involves those ethical and political judgements about the "best" distribution of income which most of us prefer to avoid.'[25] He concludes:

> The very fact of the location of a public facility such as a fire station (or for that matter any public service) means that the population does not enjoy exactly homogenous quality and quantity of fire protection as far as consumption is concerned, even though they have the same quantity and quality of fire protection available to them in terms of production.[26]

Every building is at risk of fire. Yet, the provision of fire service stations is explained not by objective public need, but by capitalist interest; they cluster in the richer areas. It is not just fire stations. Transport, infrastructure, schools, hospitals and services reflect the distribution of social and political power in the city. Typically, poor areas are badly served because city councils are more influenced by important professional associations, political parties, businesses, dominant ethnic and social groups or specific neighbourhoods than by others. The geography of a city is an immediate manifestation of social hierarchy and group interest.

Sociology is of great relevance to understanding cities at war in the twenty-first century. Cities are not, and never have been, biological systems operating autonomously on the basis of functions and flows. They are congregations of human social groups. Consequently, they should be understood as concrete communities, each of which endeavours to protect or promote their interests with or against other groups. Cities are irremediably social and political entities, then. Their functions and flows are generated and channelled by the actions, interactions and interests of social groups located inside – and outside – the city. Urban conflict is not a product of autonomous flows, spontaneously generating tensions and fissures independently of group interest and conscious social action. It often arises accidentally, as social groups within the city compete with increasing ferocity for specific resources in the urban environment. Once the dispute develops, the belligerent groups form alliances with, and enmities against, other groups. As the conflict becomes more violent, and especially if it escalates into an urban battle, many of the complexities of the city evaporate or become irrelevant. At this point, the intricate social configuration of the city is distilled into the violent interaction between the belligerent parties, fighting over specific neighbourhoods, blocks and buildings.

The globalized city of the twenty-first century is complex. It has

become extended, heterogeneous, polycentric, localized and external-
ized. In their attempts to comprehend this bewildering new landscape,
commentators and military professionals have been attracted by the
idea of an urban metabolism. Yet, in fact, when we look beyond the
surface of a city, past the teeming flows of people, traffic, goods, matter
and waste, what we find at every street corner and in every institution
are people, acting as members of one or another social group. The city
is a thoroughly human environment. Like every other human ecology,
it consists ultimately of many social groups, interacting constantly with
each other. Even the globalized city should be understood as a hierarchy of more or less exclusive groups, gangs, ghettos, each defending,
extending and exploiting its own location in the urban terrain against
– or with – others.

5

Walls

Concrete

From antiquity, cities have always been synonymous with walls. Jericho and Çatalhöyük were walled, as were the city states of Sumer. Indeed, according to the anthropologist James Scott, 'the iconic founding act of establishing a Sumerian polity was the building of a city wall'.[1] Indeed, a city was often originally defined as a settlement with a wall around it; '"wall" and "city" were so tightly linked that one term could stand for the other'.[2] In Chinese, for instance, the character, 'cheng', was used for both city and wall. Consequently, since cities were originally almost by definition fortified habitations, walls have been a necessary, even constitutive, feature of urban warfare. From the earliest civilizations, urban warfare has involved building, scaling, breaching and undermining city walls. Consequently, since walls and urban warfare are all but coterminous, it is sensible to begin this analysis of urban warfare with fortifications. Walls provide a particularly privileged viewpoint into the anatomy of urban warfare today. Indeed, it is extremely noticeable that fortifications have played an increasingly important role in recent urban battles. They have proliferated within cities, delineating new battle-lines and circumscribing the locales of conflict.

After his experiences during the battle of Sadr City with 1st Battalion 68th Armor Regiment, John Spencer made a surprising observation about the Iraq campaign:

Ask any Iraq War veteran about Jersey, Alaska, Texas, and Colorado
and you will be surprised to get stories not about states, but about
concrete barriers. Many soldiers deployed to Iraq became experts in
concrete during their combat tours. Concrete is as symbolic to their
deployments as the weapons they carried. No other weapon or technology has done more to contribute to achieving strategic goals of
providing security, protecting populations, establishing stability, and
eliminating terrorist threats. This was most evident in the complex
urban terrain of Baghdad, Iraq.[3]

In the twenty-first century, US forces have been equipped with weaponry of unparalleled lethality, accuracy and range. Their operations
have been assisted by high-resolution surveillance systems and digital
communications capable of processing vast quantities of information
instantaneously. They are the most technologically capable force the
world has ever seen. Yet, in the cities of Iraq, concrete, discovered by
the ancients and perfected by the Romans, was one of the most important materials at their disposal. It is a remarkable survival. Despite all
the recent technological innovations, walls have become one of the
most useful military devices for urban warfare in modern times. Why
have walls become so important? How have they been employed in
contemporary urban warfare?

Throughout the ancient and medieval periods, the classic curtain
wall, enclosing the city, was, of course, the favoured method of fortification. The curtain wall became an important image in human culture.
The Bible discusses walls of this type frequently, often employing mural
imagery for theological purposes, while curtain walls appear frequently
in artworks from antiquity onwards. The defining feature of the curtain wall was height and thickness. The higher and thicker the curtain
wall, the greater its defensive value. Later, curtain walls were further
strengthened by the construction of towers and bastions. While their
advantages seem obvious, walls have, in fact, served five separate military functions: protection, fire, observation, movement and separation.
The first function is self-evident. Walls were always primarily used to
protect; they sheltered the inhabitants from external enemies.

The other functions are perhaps less obvious but no less important.
Walls also increased the effectiveness of weaponry. In particular, the
range and velocity of spears, arrows and slings were all enhanced by the
height of the walls, while diminishing the effects of attackers' arms. In
antiquity and the Middle Ages, walls were normally topped with merlons and castellations, from which archers could shoot without fear of

being struck by enemy projectiles. Arrow-slits, loopholes, embrasures, machicolations, towers, barbicans and hoardings were all designed to improve the performance of the defenders' weapons. Walls afforded advantageous positions from which to throw, drop or shoot weapons.

Precisely because they were high, walls have also consistently proved to be excellent observation points. Defenders were able to see further and more clearly than their attackers and therefore to identify enemy movements. Castles have often actively exploited hills, crags and high features to increase the defenders' view. Cities have not always been constructed on sites of purely tactical advantage. Most are located on rivers or around harbours. However, even when cities have not been in a prime location for observation, urban fortifications have tried to maximize defenders' fields of vision. Citadels, towers and donjons have been constructed on high points in the city so that, although observation at street level is often constricted, it is possible for the rulers and their forces to see out well beyond the polis.

Walls are useful for protection, observation and shooting. There is a fourth military usage that is a little more obscure, though no less important. Precisely because they protect defenders from external threats and, often, physically conceal them, walls also increase the mobility of defenders. Walls can allow defenders to move quickly and freely between positions, away from ground-level obstructions and protected from enemy attacks. City walls embody this feature. At Óbidos in Portugal or Dubrovnik in Croatia, it is still very easy to walk around the walls of the entire city, completely unmolested. Although they were not built around settlements, Hadrian's Wall and the Great Wall of China both exemplify the mobility function of walls very clearly. The precise function of some aspects of these remarkable fortifications is still under investigation. However, it is apparent that one of their prime functions was not defensive in a traditional sense. They were not intended to block Pictish or Mongolian incursions physically; they were not defensive lines. Rather, they both acted as protected, raised walkways along which imperial troops could march quickly to supply or reinforce frontier forts or to mount counterattacks. Although much smaller, the platforms and walkways of ancient cities and medieval castles served the same purpose; defenders could move swiftly to the points of attack. It seems rather contradictory, but, although dedicated to preventing movement, walls actually facilitated defensive mobility.

Finally, while walls have historically protected inhabitants from outsiders, they have also been employed with increasing frequency to separate urban populations from each other; here, their role is division.

Obviously, the oldest and most famous example of this internal separation were the Jewish ghettos of medieval Europe. This function has become ever more important today. It was very obvious in Belfast in the 1970s, where 'peace lines' were erected to separate Catholic Republican from Protestant Unionist populations. Similar constructions were evident in Berlin and Nicosia. Of course, ultimately, walls of separation of this type protected populations from each other. As such, they are plainly compatible with the classic external, curtain wall. Yet, their function is not primarily to repel, in the manner of a curtain wall, but to separate, thereby imposing peace and civic order.

Throughout history, walls have served five distinct but indivisible functions, then. However, as urban warfare has changed, walls have evolved to fulfil new military requirements. In terms of pure function, there is nothing new about the concrete walls and improvised barriers that have appeared in Fallujah, Sadr City, Aleppo, Donetsk and Marawi. Yet, their prime defensive function has changed. In the twenty-first century, for instance, walls have rarely been used to shoot from or as viewing points; airpower has superseded that role. They have almost never been used to move along; rather, they have been primarily employed to separate populations or to protect military forces from each other. The best way to appreciate the changing functions of walls in twenty-first-century urban warfare is to situate current developments in a longer historical sequence. It is useful to plot the evolution of the city wall through history. Although a knowledge of ancient fortifications is useful here, it is unnecessary to go all the way back to antiquity. Rather, in order to understand the distinctive function of walls today, a survey of urban fortification from the sixteenth century to the recent battles in Iraq, Syria and the Donbas is perfectly adequate. Indeed, an analysis of this period is highly illuminating. It is a striking fact that between the sixteenth and twenty-first centuries, defensive walls actually moved. They were physically relocated from around the city in the early modern period, to outside the city in the modern period, to inside the city itself in the twenty-first century. This relocation from around, outside, to inside cities denotes a reconstitution of the topography of urban warfare. Consequently, while urban warfare is as brutal today as ever, walls now bisect cities or circumvallate particular districts or defensive positions. A profound revision of the urban battlescape is under way, evidenced simply by the repositioning of walls in the last five hundred years.

Early Modern Defences

Gunpowder was first discovered and used in China at the end of the Tang dynasty in the eleventh century. However, its potential was not exploited for military purposes in ancient China. Gunpower and firearms were first used on the battlefield in the high Middle Ages in Europe. Edward III used cannon at the battle of Crécy in 1346, although, in fact, the battle was famously won by longbowmen. However, by the fifteenth century, gunpowder was being exploited by many medieval monarchs. The principal function of cannon was siege warfare. At the siege of Harfleur in 1415, Henry V employed cannon to breach the walls.[4] The direct battery of walls by cannon became a regular feature of Renaissance warfare between the 1420s and 1440s.[5] Firepower played a crucial role in the French defeat of the English in the Hundred Years War (1453), the reconquest of Spain (1492) and the Ottoman capture of Constantinople (1453). Castles had become vulnerable. In 1494, Charles VIII of France invaded Italy with a mobile artillery siege train that allowed him to take cities almost at will.[6]

The appearance of cannon in fifteenth-century Europe demanded a thorough reformation of urban fortifications. The curtain wall, so long the central element of all city defences, had become obsolete: 'The thin, tall medieval walls of Europe's towns and castles were quite inadequate when put to the test by the new artillery of the late fifteenth century.'[7] In particular, in response to the interminable rivalry between city-states and their vulnerability to attack, Italian cities redesigned their fortifications; the so-called *trace italienne* (bastion fort) appeared in the early sixteenth century. The key developments occurred between the sieges of Pisa in 1500 and Padua in 1509; walls were lowered and rein-forced against cannon fire, while a wide, dry moat impeded escalade.[8] From that time on, military opinion accepted the *trace italienne* as the best system of urban fortification. For instance, in his 1531 *Discourses*, Machiavelli declared that fortresses were superfluous and that an effec-tive prince should depend on his field army. Seven years later, in his *Art of War*, he extolled the 'double Pisan rampart'.[9] An efflorescence of literature on siege warfare and fortification in the early sixteenth century affirmed the revolution.[10] Albrecht Dürer, Michelangelo and Leonard da Vinci all made important contributions to urban fortifica-tion in this era.

The *trace italienne* consisted of four transformative features (see Figure 5.1). High curtain walls were everywhere replaced with low, thick ramparts with large gun platforms (terrepleins) for artillery pieces. At the same time, square fortresses were replaced by pentagons. As a geometric shape, the pentagon was invested with symbolic, even mystical, meaning:

> Fortification obeyed the same laws of organic symmetry as governed all branches of architecture . . . The organic ideal was expressed in geometrical terms, reflecting contemporary advances in surveying and cartography, and perhaps also a survival of medieval obsessions with mystical symbols and numbers. The pentagon was invested with magical significance.[11]

Be that as it may, the pentagon was adopted primarily because of its great military utility:

> This essential feature of fortifications evolved from its medieval form as a square then as a rounded tower to that of a five-sided polygon defined by its technical function – a gun platform with its head pointing aggressively outward but its neck tapering inward to provide flanking fire along curtain walls.[12]

A low pentagon could be struck only with glancing fire and increased the defenders' fields of fire. Third, a new system of triangular bastions, ravelins and hornworks defended the main walls, extending and widening the range of the defender's guns. Finally, wider, often dry, moats with a counterscarp were installed with a covered step for infantry and a glacis to act as a killing zone. In its most elaborate manifestations, the *trace italienne* was very expensive to build, but it was also easy to improvise a fortress of this type. During the Eighty Years War (1568–1648), for instance, the Netherlands successfully rebelled against the Spanish Habsburg Empire by fortifying the Low Countries with a series of earthen forts and modifying the medieval fortifications of towns or cities.

The *trace italienne* was originally designed and implemented by individual cities. However, it was normally built as part of a much wider defensive system. Newly fortified towns or cities were not just independent strongpoints, but part of a defensive network. Here, the fortresses interlocked into a mutually supporting system. The creation of such arrangements became widespread across Europe in the sixteenth and seventeenth centuries, as absolutist monarchies became richer and more powerful. The most famous example was, of course, constructed by Louis XIV and his chief engineer Sébastien Le Prestre de Vauban. Although he did not invent any new architectural features, Vauban

Figure 5.1: The *trace italienne*, Fort Bourtange
Source: © OpenStreetMap contributors
(https://www.openstreetmap.org/copyright).

was a genuine innovator in siege warfare; he invented the zig-zag sap and the counter-trench. Most significantly, he was responsible for the construction of the double *pré carré* (square field) line of defence in north-eastern France against the threat of the Habsburg Low Countries and their allies. These lines were eventually augmented by the Lines of *Ne Plus Ultra* (no further). Vauban built a number of new military forts in this defensive zone, but he also rebuilt the defences of the cities and towns of this area. Medieval walls were replaced with ramparts and bastions, and citadels based on the *trace italienne* model were introduced. Lille was one of the most famous examples of this process, where Vauban constructed a new citadel – the 'Queen of Citadels' – on the periphery of the city. The citadel and the city were taken by the Duke of Marlborough in 1708 as part of his Oudenarde campaign.

Early modern states invested immense resources in the construction of *trace italienne* or Vauban fortifications. As a result, siege warfare became a primary form of warfare from 1500 to the late eighteenth century. For instance, Dutch statesman Johan de Witt advised his young cousin to study siege warfare in 1659,[13] while Louis XIV claimed that 'great sieges please me more than any other action'.[14] The *trace italienne* revolutionized urban fortification; the early modern pentagon reconfigured the urban battlespace as walls ran *around* the city and the major siege action took place in this contested zone on the edges of the city.

Modern Defences

The *trace italienne* played an important role in Europe warfare until the mid-eighteenth century; indeed, it proliferated across the world as European empires expanded. However, from the 1750s, these fortresses became less important – if not redundant. This was not primarily due to advances in weaponry or to increases in the size of cities; it was almost exclusively the result of military expansion. As armies increased in size, Vauban-style forts and towns became irrelevant. After his conquests in the Netherlands in the 1740s, Maurice de Saxe, the famous French general, declared: 'I am not much of a student, but I have never been overawed by the reputation of Vauban and Coehoorn. They fortified towns at immense expense without making them any stronger.'[15] Saxe preferred improvised field fortification in vital strategic locations. The French revolutionary wars only proved his point. Although Napoleon did engage in sieges and, indeed, made his reputation at the siege of Toulon, the sheer mass of the Grande Armée reduced the operational and strategic significance of fortified cities. Chevalier du Theil noted that the 'fate of fortresses depends almost entirely on the outcomes of battle'.[16]

The *trace italienne*, or Vauban citadel, was becoming operationally irrelevant by the end of the eighteenth century. Nevertheless, it took several decades before it began to be replaced by a new system of urban fortifications. It is not easy to be absolutely precise here, as the appearance of 'modern' urban defences was a process rather than a single event. However, the year 1850, or the decade – the 1850s – might be taken as a useful switch-point when a new paradigm of defensive architecture emerged. By this point, as a result of industrialization, European cities had simply become too big to be contained within the outline of a *trace italienne*. Mass urban populations now sprawled well beyond the old city walls into new suburbs and slums. Cities had quite simply outgrown their walls. In addition, by the mid-nineteenth century, mass conscription had been adopted by all major European forces, so armies were truly huge. Furthermore, there had been dramatic advances in artillery in the early part of the century. Long-range artillery had been developed that far exceeded the capacity of the Napoleonic cannon. These new guns consigned early modern bastions and hornworks to irrelevance, since a city or fort could be bombarded from miles away, far beyond the line of sight. Improvements in artillery compelled urban refortification. The change was apparent in some of the major cities in Europe at this time.

During this period, Paris is of course always remembered for Baron Haussmann's renovation under the Emperor Napoleon III, partly in response to the 1848 Revolution. It is difficult not to be impressed by his radiant design. However, less noticeable to the modern tourist, some equally important military developments occurred outside the old walls of the city. Contemporaneous with Haussmann's internal reconstruction of the city, a new system of fortresses was built in a ring around Paris. Thirteen individually named forts were located beyond the city at strategic points (see Map 5.1). Some, like Mont-Valérien to the west of the city centre, are still in existence today and serve a military purpose. They were defended by large artillery pieces and garrisons in order to keep enemy field armies and their heavy artillery at a sufficient distance from the city so that it could not be bombarded.

After its victories at Sedan and Metz at the beginning of the Franco-Prussian War in 1870, the Prussian Army besieged Paris from outside this ring of forts. The new French regime capitulated without the Prussian Army having to fight for the city. However, during the subsequent Paris Commune, when the Communards held the city against the French Army, the line of forts was absolutely critical for its survival. On 30 April 1871, before the beginning of major hostilities, the Communards voluntarily evacuated Fort d'Issy in the south-west. The event was described as 'the worse military blow to befall the Commune' up to that point. Indeed, so vital was this fort to the defence of Paris, that Gustave Paul Cluseret, the Commune's Delegate of War, marched out with fewer than 200 men and retook the fort.[17]

Paris's new defences became famous in the Franco-Prussian War and the subsequent Paris Commune. However, other European cities also renovated their defences. Vienna was a particularly apposite example here. In 1683, Vienna, with the help of John Sobieski, king of Poland, had repulsed the last Ottoman invasion of Western Europe; the Vauban fortifications of the city had played an important role in protecting the city during the siege. However, by the middle of

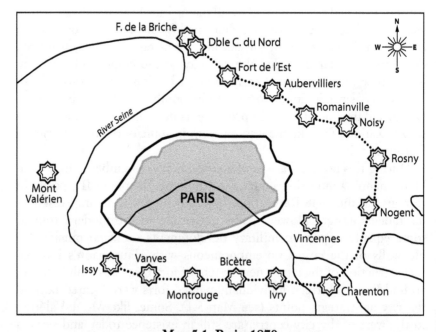

Map 5.1: Paris, 1870
Source: Based on map from Olivier Le Tinnier 'La Place Forte de Paris'
Mémoire & Fortifications, https://www.memoire-et-fortifications.fr/
fortifications/place-forte-de-paris/.

the nineteenth century, Vienna's old city walls had become obsolete.
Consequently, in 1857, Emperor Franz Joseph replaced the existing walls with the now famous Ringstrasse (see Map 5.2). The areas
opened up by the demolition were available for development, from
which modern Vienna emerged.[18]

Although Britain was protected by the sea and the most powerful
navy in the world, governments periodically contemplated the requirement for urban fortification. For instance, under the direction of the
Prime Minister Lord Palmerston, a series of forts were built outside
major naval bases, such as Plymouth and Portsmouth, in the early 1860s
in response to concerns about French naval strength. They protected
these cities from landward attack, in the somewhat unfeasible event on
a French invasion. They became known as Palmerston Follies – but
they useful showed the changing topography of urban fortification in
the nineteenth century. Later in 1869, Lieutenant General Sir John
Burgoyne, the Inspector General of Fortifications, proposed a defensive ring around London. It was never constructed. In the early modern

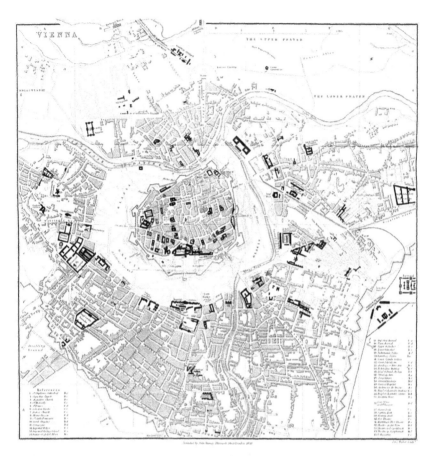

Map 5.2: Vienna, the Ringstrasse
Source: J & C Walker Sailp / Wikimedia Commons / Public domain.

period, walls were located around cities. In the nineteenth century, urban fortifications were repositioned *outside* cities.

This system of defence persisted into the twentieth century. Cities continued to grow, armies to expand and artillery to improve. Consequently, all the conditions that had recommended the installation of an external ring of fortifications persisted. The First World War is mainly remembered for the crucial role played by field fortifications on the Western Front. However, there were also some important urban battles. In 1871, the Austro-Hungarian town of Przemyśl in Galicia was converted into a strategically important fort; it dominated the last high ground before Russia. Seventeen main and eighteen subsidiary forts were constructed in a forty-eight-kilometre ellipse around the city. When the First World War broke out, many of these fortresses were antiquated, with insufficient artillery and inadequate protection.[19] Nevertheless, they played a decisive role in the siege of that city between November 1914 and March 1915. The Russian siege lines developed around the forts, the focus of much of the fighting. In October, for instance, there were bitter struggles over Fort I, Salis-Soglio, to the south-east of the city, which the Russians initially failed to take.[20] The siege eventually reached its climax on 19 March 1915, when Fort XI exploded.[21]

In the Second World War, cities had become so large and artillery and airpower so powerful that even these external defensive rings became less effective. Armies sought to defend their capital cities on fronts and defensive lines a long way from them, and sometimes on the very borders of national territory. Field fortifications had replaced urban ones. Nevertheless, an interesting feature of these field fortification systems was that, while their purpose was purely military, they were heavily influenced by urban architectural styles. For instance, in the face of the Allied invasion threat from 1943, Hitler ordered the construction of defences from the Netherlands around the entire northern coast of France to Brittany. The so-called Atlantic Wall consisted of a series of concrete forts, bunkers and strongpoints along the coastline. They were – and remain – remarkable constructions, which have impressed a number of scholars. The fortifications were fabricated from steel-reinforced concrete. These edifices actively implemented the modernism of the Bauhaus and Le Corbusier and anticipated the brutalist architecture of the post-war period (see Figure 5.2).[22] Albert Speer's Organization Todt, which was responsible for their construction, was simultaneously in charge of the development of the German road system and many urban buildings, such as factories. There was an architectural connection between the cities of the Reich and its bunkers on the coast of northern France. In stark contrast to the aestheticism of the pentagonal Vauban fort, with its often very fine detailing, these structures were utterly devoid of all extraneous features; they were completely functional. Yet, in their stark simplicity, they could often assume a surprising, if awful, beauty. The Atlantic Wall was not a form of urban fortification in any immediate sense; these were field defences. Yet, they represented the ultimate externalization of modern urban fortification. Unlike the forts of Paris, Vienna and Przemyśl, these defences were not only outside the city; they were as far from the city as it was possible to get. They were located on the very furthest edge of the Reich, on the boundaries of its territory: 'The ramparts that, in

Figure 5.2: The Atlantic Wall
Source: Supercarwaar / Wikimedia Commons / CC BY-SA (https://
creativecommons.org/licenses/by-sa/4.0).

preceding centuries, moved from the limits of the city to the limits of
the nation-state moved once again to the limits of emergent land.'[23]

The Atlantic Wall is an extreme example but it illustrates the topography of urban fortifications in the nineteenth and twentieth centuries.
Walls had migrated from their position around cities, to a new location
outside and even beyond them.

Twenty-First-Century Defences

Right up to the end of the twentieth century, cities were defended from
forts in the field outside them. This topography began to change in the
early twenty-first century and a new pattern of urban fortification is
currently emerging. Walls, as always, remain a central feature of urban
warfare, but their position and function have evolved. By 2020, the relocation of defensive walls had become obvious. However, the process of
refortification can be traced back to the 1970s. At this time, below the
level of interstate warfare, some important changes were taking place
in the way cities started to be protected and defended. In the 1960s,
the city became a site of increasingly intense contestation with the civil
rights movements, strikes, student protests (Paris in 1968), urban riots

(Watts, Los Angeles, in 1965) and, especially at the end of the decade, the emergence of international terrorism. Consequently, the question of protecting and defending the city, not primarily from an external enemy but from an internal threat, became an increasingly pressing problem.

A large literature emerged that either addressed this question or, on the radical side, rejected state repression and promoted civic rebellion. Indeed, a whole subfield of urban sociology in the 1970s emerged in response to the phenomenon of urban disorder, led by, among others, Henri Lefebvre, David Harvey and Manuel Castells. Oscar Newman's *Defensible Space* was one of the most interesting and important works of this period. Newman argued that, just as crime and violence were easier to commit in certain kinds of spaces, the possibilities for public disorder and aggression could be limited through design: 'Our conclusion is that the new physical form of the urban environment is possibly the most cogent ally the criminal has in his victimization of society.'[24] Architecture could be employed to dissuade potential miscreants: 'Design can make it possible for both the inhabitant and stranger to perceive that an area is under the undisputed influence of a particular group.'[25] Newman did not think that architecture could determine human practice. However, by changing the space in which humans interacted, he believed that design could influence social behaviour.

Newman's ideas about defensible space were not always directly incorporated into urban planning from the 1970s. Certainly, he did not advocate fortification and the construction of walls, which began to proliferate at this time. On the contrary, he was explicitly and wholly interested in reintegrating the urban poor – not excluding them. Nevertheless, the concept that cities should be rebuilt against an internal, civic threat was taken up very widely. Walls were increasing erected, not to protect the city from outside, but to ensure social order within it. The Berlin Wall of 1961 was a very early example of this internal fortification, although this wall was unusual in that it was a reflection of superpower politics. One of the first cities to be securitized against an internal threat was, of course, Belfast with its 'peace lines'. However, in addition to the peace lines, the British state simultaneously fortified other parts of the city. In response to the IRA's bombing campaign, a 'ring of steel' was erected around the city centre. Cars were banned from this commercial and business district, and civilian checkpoints were created at every access point to this area. Until the end of the Troubles in 1996, the centre of Belfast was defended by the construction of walls and barriers. Internal walls played a fundamental role in this conflict.

What took place in Belfast anticipated future urban fortification in the twenty-first century. 'Citadelization' has become a common phenomenon since that time. Internal walls, barriers and barricades have been erected around specific districts or buildings to protect them against criminality and terrorist attack: 'In lieu of going ostentatiously high-rise, the direction of development is towards protected, secured citadels, to internalize and shield the activities critical to the top tiers of global and national businesses.'[26] Since the early 2000s, terrorism has impelled urban refortification. In Britain, there was a precedent for this. In the 1990s, in response to the IRA's bombing campaign against commercial targets in mainland UK, another ring of steel was created around the City of London: 'As a result of terrorist attacks, and the risk of further bombings a series of defensive modifications to the landscape were constructed in the City, primarily between April 1992 and February 1997.'[27] These defences included police checkpoints, barricades (some permanent, some temporary) and an elaborate network of closed circuit television surveillance. The City was effectively separated from the rest of London.[28] The Islamist terrorist attacks of 11 September 2001 on New York and Washington, followed by continuing jihadist attacks, have only accelerated this refortification trend. In response to those attacks, urban defences have been reinforced. New walls, barriers and checkpoints have been erected in many European cities around the major commercial and political centres, with the aim of blocking attacks by suicide vehicles, in particular. In many cases, the barriers against vehicular assault have been obvious and ugly; large metal or concrete barricades and bollards now block pavements, entrances and avenues. Sometimes, these obstructions are deliberately obvious as a deterrent, but they are also often camouflaged as benches, sculptures or plant pots. An interesting example of this fortification is the new US Embassy in London, which, in stark contrast to the original, modernist building in Grosvenor Square, is actually a citadel (see Figure 5.3). Interestingly, this Embassy recalls many of the features of a medieval castle, with moat, barbican and drawbridge. The building is specifically designed to defend against suicide attacks.

Urban fortification has proliferated throughout the West. However, Jerusalem is probably the city that demonstrates twenty-first-century fortification at its most extreme. Certainly, it has attracted a great deal of academic and political attention since the 1990s. Its walls were initially intended to protect Israeli citizens and neighbourhoods in Jerusalem

Figure 5.3: US Embassy in London
Source: © Kieran Timberlake.

from the terrorist attacks that followed the Al-Aqsa Intifada in 2002. The walls have subsequently become part of a much more aggressive state policy on the West Bank and Occupied Territories. Israeli scholar Eyal Weizman has been a prominent critic of Israel's militarization of the West Bank. He is disturbed by the way in which architecture has been employed to oppress the already disadvantaged Palestinians: 'Architecture was thus conscripted to establish the state's control of its territories and help make uniform communities.'[29] Weizman identifies Ariel Sharon, the Israeli prime minister between 2001 and 2006, as the main culprit. He was responsible for the fortification of the West Bank. Interestingly, Weizman claims that Sharon had applied his early military experiences of fighting in Sinai during the Yom Kippur War to the pacification of the Palestinian community. Sharon had commanded a parachute brigade in that war and had eventually carried out assaults across the Suez Canal into Egypt. That war had taught him the importance of strongpoints in depth rather than lineal frontal defence. For Weizman, Sharon's strategy in the West Bank displays a similar character. It exploits fixed strongpoints and walls to create a comprehensive defensive system. Even nonmilitary structures have been recruited in this process. For instance, Sharon sponsored the construction of Israeli settlements that acted as anchors and observation points for the Israeli occupation: 'This geometric order seeks to produce what can in effect be understood as optical devices on a suburban scale.'[30] Together, these walls and strongpoints have not only secured East Jerusalem for Israel, but also impeded the formation of a Palestinian state. The walls divide Palestinian towns and villages so radically that unified sovereignty has become almost impossible.

Israel's use of walls in the West Bank is a notorious contemporary example of urbanized fortification. As states struggle to control their cities from internal threats, walls have become an increasingly common feature of the cityscape. Jerusalem may be unique, but it illustrates much wider trends. Barriers, barricades and checkpoints have been established to exclude not only terrorists, but also criminal gangs. Walls have, for instance, proliferated in Latin American cities, in general, and Brazilian cities in particular. Walls were constructed in São Paolo as the city became more fragmented and diversified.[31] As *favelas* spread, privileged districts or political or economic centres were fortified against attack. Internal fortification has become a major feature of Rio de Janeiro. In order to protect the Olympic Games of 2016, the government constructed a series of walls in Rio to separate the *favelas* and their criminal gangs, like the Comando Vermelha, from Olympic venues, the athletes' village or the main sites in which spectators were staying. For instance, a long corridor of walling was erected from the airport to the city centre, deliberately blocking the worst *favelas* from view and reducing crime. Rather than an inclusive global celebration, to many poor Brazilians the Olympic Games exemplified only their marginalization.

Barricades have long been a feature of cities in conflict. Throughout the nineteenth century, the barricade was the preferred instrument of the insurgent. Barricades were a central feature of the French Revolution and the subsequent Parisian uprisings of 1830, 1848 and 1871. In each case, insurgents erected barricades across the streets to defend themselves. Yet, there is an important difference between these and the walls that have been erected more recently against terrorists and criminal gangs. While insurgents once barricaded streets against the government, states and security forces now use permanent walls inside cities to control the population and defeat their enemies. Moreover, the function of these new walls is different from the Berlin Wall or the peace lines in Belfast. In each of those cases, the aim of the state was to increase their control of the population on both sides of the wall. Walls were part of an apparatus by which states supervised and protected their entire citizenry. Today, walls are not primarily built to extend state sovereignty but to mark its limits; they are internal cordons. In Jerusalem, Rio and São Paolo, the populations on the other side of the wall are segregated from the city and the state. These internal walls signify the recession of state authority over the city as a unified polity.

So, as we have seen, walls have reappeared within cities over the past few decades, constructed primarily to secure key locations within the city, and to exclude criminal, insurgent and terrorist threats. As such, they are state weapons in low-intensity urban conflict. However, as urban conflict becomes more intense and descends into a genuine urban battle, walls play an increasingly prominent role. Just as walls played a decisive role in siege warfare in the past, the new interior defensive lines within cities have become a critical part of the contemporary urban battle.

In the twentieth century, state forces were so powerful and numerous that they rarely used extensive fortifications to secure urban areas from their opponents. As we saw in Chapter 3, the armed forces could patrol the streets constantly. The situation has now changed radically. As troops numbers have declined and cities have expanded, it has proved impossible for military forces to secure cities as they once did; they simply cannot inundate neighbourhoods. Consequently, walls have played an increasing role, even in high-intensity urban operations. The US occupation of Iraq between 2003 and 2008 offers one of the best contemporary examples of how these interior, urban walls have become so militarily important today. The Americans found it impossible to secure Iraqi cities with their personnel alone; there were simply too many cities and they were too big – Baghdad alone had a total population of about 6 million. A classic strategy of military inundation was quite impossible, then. Even after the surge in 2007, US forces lacked the personnel to control all the urban neighbourhoods in Baghdad, Ramadi and Fallujah. Fortification – walls – compensated for numbers. They became a means of replacing human personnel. Consequently, concrete T-walls and gabions became the indispensable enabler of all operations. It is precisely in this context that John Spencer, cited at the start of this chapter, extolled the qualities of concrete. Concrete substituted for flesh. Lacking people, US forces built walls, barricades and barriers to save lives and restrict the movement of insurgent forces.

Concrete was a ubiquitous feature of the Iraq War: US forces employed it in all the major cities of Iraq to construct checkpoints or to isolate the warring sects and ethnicities. However, there are some particularly apposite examples, when walls played a critical tactical role. The most famous of these is the battle of Sadr City between 23 March and 13 May 2008 (see Map 5.3). During this period, the Shia Jaysh al-Mahdi, led by Muqtada al-Sadr, staged a major uprising against the Iraqi government of President Nouri al-Maliki. This involved heavy rocket and mortar bombardments of the Green Zone from Shia enclaves in Sadr City. The obvious response would have been to mount a clearance operation through the municipality. Yet, President Maliki forbade it, as he relied on Shia political support to sustain his position, even though he also wanted to crush the militants.

As a result, the Americans developed a novel course of action. US commanders decided to build a large wall along the major road, Quds Street (or Route Gold), which traversed the south-western end of

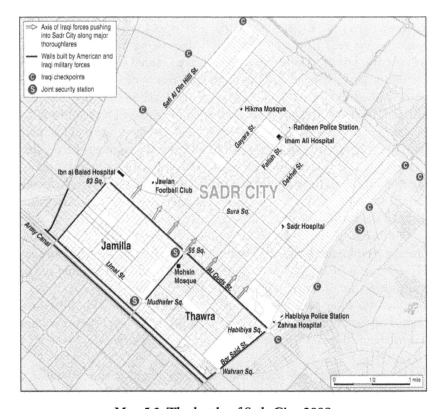

Map 5.3: The battle of Sadr City, 2008
Source: Map courtesy of the Institute for the Study of War:
http://www.understandingwar.org/operation/operation-peace.

Sadr City. The wall served two purposes. First, it pushed the Jaysh al-Mahdi rockets and mortars out of range of the Green Zone. Second, it separated the Jaysh al-Mahdi from its principal popular support bases in the two poor districts of Ishbiliyah and Habbibiyah. The wall on Route Gold was a classic form of siege warfare. Although walls are typically defensive, this wall had an offensive purpose. It was a deliberate and provocative act of contravallation against the Shia stronghold in Sadr City. The Americans knew that the Jaysh al-Mahdi would have to contest the wall, giving them an ideal opportunity to defeat their enemy without having to invade Sadr City itself. From the end of March, US forces began the laborious tasks of moving and lowering slabs of twelve-foot concrete T-walls into place along Route Gold. The reaction was predictable. The Jaysh al-Mahdi fought furiously against the construction of the wall. At first, it was impossible to build the wall during the day, since the risks were too great. Even at night, the fighting was intense. Battles raged around each section of the wall as it was erected. Especially in the first weeks of the construction, progress was very slow with only eight slabs being put in place on the worst days, but gradually the wall advanced, aided by reinforcements including tanks, mechanized infantry and layers of airpower, each to be described in the following chapters. As Jaysh al-Mahdi resistance faltered, the progress accelerated until finally the wall was in place. By that stage, the Jaysh al-Mahdi had admitted defeat. They had lost perhaps 700 fighters in the battle, while only six US soldiers were killed in action. Once the Jaysh al-Mahdi had been pacified, the function of the wall changed. It became a means of controlling and monitoring the Shia population, which had to pass through checkpoints to reach other parts of Baghdad.[32]

The battle of Route Gold has become a celebrated example of the military employment of walls within cities in the twenty-first century. However, it is by no means the only example. Walls proliferated across Iraqi cities; for a time, Baghdad became the world's greatest gated community. They have also been employed in subsequent battles since then. For instance, walls and barriers played a very important role in the battle of Mosul. ISIS used them to defend the city:

ISIS had set up an unbelievable obstacle network of concrete T-walls. They placed them at approach roads and set some other pieces of equipment. Then they would knock them down – into upturned Ts. To get them, we had to hook them up and pull them away. ISIS were skilled in defence.[33]

As they retook the city, the coalition erected many defensive walls against ISIS. It was essential to fortify their rear and flanks against counterattack, especially by suicide vehicles. Consequently, side roads were barricaded by tanks, armoured vehicles, craters, concrete walls or by rubble and detritus gathered from the local area.

During the battle of Raqqa, the Kurdish Syrian Democratic Forces adopted the same strategy of barricading their positions before mounting the next attack. In Marawi, the Filipino attackers fortified their advances:

> We used hard, solid and concrete walls to cover our front and sides and we extensively employed sand bagging (Hesco) to fortify our positions and get through open and killing zones. In an urban battle, whoever defends has all the advantages because of fortification and commanding positions in greater heights which they could readily select. Inside the structures, stairs, doors, windows and open areas are killing zones. In Marawi, everything inside the building was used by enemies as cover and protection.[34]

Micro-Siege

Concrete walls are certainly mundane – and unlovely, especially in comparison with the Vauban forts of the eighteenth century. It is easy to ignore them and be distracted by the allure of more sophisticated weaponry and equipment. However, the concrete wall has become a crucial part of the urban battle today. Walls are no longer built around cities, as they were in the sixteenth century, or outside them, as they were in the nineteenth and twentieth centuries. Rather, walls have migrated inside cities to create internal strongpoints, citadels and defensive lines. They have compensated for a lack of military personnel, replacing human beings with concrete or steel. In low-intensity operations, walls have segregated and divided; states have conceded control of significant parts of the city in order to assure their sovereignty over the rest of it. In intense urban battles, walls have proved no less important. They have been used aggressively to surround and isolate opponents, compromising their terrain; or to defend troops against counterattack. Circum- and contravallation has been rediscovered as vital military techniques. The proliferation of walls has transformed the topography of the urban battle, which has condensed into a localized, inner-urban siege; the fighting has coagulated around fortified points within the city itself.

Consequently, the concrete wall is likely to be as significant to warfare in the twenty-first century as the *trace italienne* was to early modern Europe.

6

Air

Volume

Throughout history, soldiers have operated in two dimensions. The earth on which people live and armies march is, after all, flat. Even in urban warfare, with its fortifications, armies have tended to orient themselves to terrain, not space, especially in the twentieth century when defences tended to be low and hidden. As we saw in the previous chapter, the micro-sieges that have developed inside cities in recent decades have been substantially fought out at the street level. However, at the same time, the sky above the streets has itself become an increasingly contested domain. Urban warfare has superseded a purely territorial framework and the airspace above cities has become an intrinsic part of the localized sieges taking place within them.

Indeed, from the 1990s, the two-dimensional view of the city came to be seen as increasingly inadequate to emerging military realities. Ironically, one of the first commentators to note this inadequacy was not an academic geographer; it was a US Army officer, Major Ralph Peters. His 1996 article 'Our soldiers, their cities', published in the US Army War College's journal, *Parameters*, was seminal. Peters presciently warned that, in the future, US troops would have to fight urban insurgencies in foreign cities. He also noted that with the rise of urban fighting, the battlefield would become three-dimensional:

At the broadest level, there is a profound spatial difference. 'Conventional' warfare has been horizontal, with an increasing vertical

dimension. In fully urbanized terrain, however, warfare becomes profoundly vertical, reaching up into towers of steel and cement, and
downward into sewers, subway lines, road tunnels, communications
tunnels, and the like.[1]

Peters's article has been cited by almost every subsequent academic
publication on urban warfare. A rich subdiscipline has developed that
explores the aerial, three-dimensional character of urban conflict.
Following Peters, Eyal Weizman played an important early role in
reorienting the study of urban warfare to the vertical domain:

> Geo-politics is a flat discourse. It largely ignores the vertical dimension
> and tends to look across rather than to cut through the landscape.
> This was the cartographic imagination inherited from the military
> and political spatialities of the modern state. Since both politics and
> law understand place only in terms of the map and the plan, territorial
> claims marked on maps assume that claims are applicable simultane-
> ously above them and below.[2]

According to Weizman, urban studies has been trapped in a two-
dimensional framework because it has been unwittingly influenced by
the way in which states and their security forces have traditionally
mapped – and controlled – the city. In order to subvert state power, it is
necessary for scholars to reimagine the urban battlescape.

Weizman's injunctions have been taken up very widely by scholars
across the social and political sciences. In *Cities under Siege*, British
scholar Stephen Graham, for instance, has become a prominent advocate of 'volumetric' thinking: 'The key concept driving current military
thinking and practice is "battlespace".'[3] Since the military itself has
colonized the airspace over the city, scholars must take to the skies
as well. In another of his books, *Vertical*, Graham has highlighted the
inadequacy of existing approaches. Urban scholars need to treat cities
as three-dimensional spaces, not just as terrain. To this end, Graham
professes his 'ambitious agenda': 'To inscribe the politics of our three-
dimensional world into critical debates about urban life, cities and
geography.'[4] Since states and their security forces operate in the vertical
axis, so must scholars.

The point has been taken up more widely. For instance, geographer Stuart Elden has recently called on fellow scholars to 'secure
the volume'. The pun is deliberate. Because states are committed to
securing not simply urban territory but space itself, it is essential that

scholars are similarly orientated to think volumetrically too: 'Thinking about power and circulation in terms of volume opens up new ways to think of the geographies of security. Just as the world does not just exist as a surface, nor should our theorizations of it; security goes up and down; space is volumetric.'[5] Many studies of urban conflict still focus on what happens at street level. This is not unreasonable, since, for all the extension of the cityscape and the proliferation of aircraft, most human violence still takes place on the ground; ultimately, military forces have sought to seize and hold urban terrain. Nevertheless, commentators from Ralph Peters onwards make a very valuable point. In comparison with conventional warfare, the contemporary urban battle is notably vertical; cities are tall and extend below the ground. This is particularly so in the globalized cities of the early twenty-first century that have become so uniquely perpendicular. Consequently, the urban battle has a different geometry from that of conventional ground combat, accentuated by the recent growth of very large structures and the increasing role that airpower has played in urban warfare.

Airpower in the Twentieth Century

Volumetric scholars are right to highlight the cubic character of urban operations today. The urban battlescape has become more vertical in the early twenty-first century. However, some care needs to be exercised here. Certainly, scholars recognize that airpower has been used over cities since the early twentieth century. However, in rightly professing the importance of volume in the twenty-first century, they risk the danger of overstating the case. For instance, from the earliest origins of cities in Mesopotamia, urban fortifications exploited height to gain an advantage over attackers. The walls and towers of Sumerian cities introduced a vertical dimension into urban warfare from the outset; castellation increased the range and lethality of their weapon systems, while reducing the effectiveness of their enemies' arms. In the assault, walls had to be physically climbed. Indeed, almost every feature of ancient and medieval fortifications used height in order to exploit the force of gravity: machicolations, merlons, arrow-slits, loopholes, hoardings, portcullises – all relied on altitude. These architectural developments altered the geometry of the ancient battlefield. Vertical walls were themselves undermined by subterranean tunnelling.

The vertical dimension was always already a feature of urban warfare from antiquity. Arcane avian methods have long been employed in siege warfare. For instance, a military compendium from the late

Ming dynasty recorded the use of birds to attack cities. The work recommended capturing hundreds of small birds from an enemy's city. Incendiary almonds could be attached to their feet so as to ignite roofs and provisions as they returned to their roosts.[6] These were noteworthy, if esoteric, developments. However, genuine aerial warfare is self-evidently a much more recent phenomenon. The first systematic use of airpower in urban warfare relied on the development of military aircraft. Balloons began to be used for military purposes in the late eighteenth century as airborne observation posts. The first offensive use of airpower occurred over Venice in 1849 when the Austrian Army experimented with dropping incendiary bombs from balloons onto the city. Fortunately, the experiment failed.

Aerial bombardment became a military reality only in the twentieth century, and in the First World War, in particular. The first ever recorded aerial bombardment from an aircraft occurred on 1 November 1911, when Lieutenant Giulio Gavotti bombed Ain Zahra in Libya. During the First World War, the potential of air raids began to be explored. One of the very first air raids took place in December 1914 on the great Austro-Hungarian fortress of Przemyśl. This fortified city on the frontier between the Austro-Hungarian and Russian empires was besieged by Russian forces from November 1914. Following a failed counterattack by the Austrian Field Marshal Conrad von Hötzendorf, the Russian renewed their siege of the city in late November. On 1 December, Russian aeroplanes appeared over the city. The defenders opened fire as the planes dropped their bombs. In the course of the siege, the Russians dropped 275 bombs, targeting the San bridges and military installations around Przemyśl, to little effect.[7]

Przemyśl is notable, but the most significant early uses of the air raid during the First World War took place in Britain and Germany. The German Zeppelin raids on British cities were particularly important both in themselves and in their subsequent influence on airpower thinking. From 31 May 1915 to 20 May 1918, the German Air Force conducted a series of raids on London involving, in total, 13 Zeppelins and 128 aeroplanes. The raids started 224 fires and destroyed 174 buildings.[8] Other cities, especially ports, were also targeted: 'Who that saw it will forget the nightly sight of the population of a great industrial and shipping town, Hull, streaming out into the fields on the first sound of the alarm signals?'[9] The British mounted several air raids on German towns and cities.

While the air attacks of the First World War caused considerable panic among the civilian population, they did little material damage.

Nevertheless, these air raids and the subsequent use of air attacks during pacification operations in East Africa, Sudan and the Northwest Frontier by the British Royal Air Force (RAF) and by the Italian Air Force in Abyssinia convinced some airpower proponents of the strategic potential of this weapon. The Italian Air Force general, Giulio Douhet, was the central figure here. In 1921, he published his highly influential, if not notorious, work, *Command of the Air*. He recommended strategic airpower as the means of overcoming the attritional warfare of the First World War. Douhet perceptively noted that the war on the Isonzo and the Western Front had been particularly invidious because the civilian population had, for the most part, been quite unaffected by it: 'Since war had to be fought on the surface of the earth, it could be waged only in movements and clashes of forces along lines drawn on its surface. Behind those lines . . . the civilian population did not directly feel the war.'[10] Airpower promised to revolutionize the lineal and planar geometry of warfare; warfare would take flight and become volumetric. In this way, the topography of warfare would be fundamentally revised. For the first time in human history, it would become genuinely three-dimensional.

As a result, the destructive potential of airpower was, Douhet believed, almost limitless. Flight rendered all natural and artificial defences obsolete. Planes could fly over mountains, rivers, forests, walls and fortifications; 'aerial warfare admits no defence'.[11] 'There is no practical way to prevent the enemy from attacking us with his air force except to destroy his airpower before he has a chance to strike at us.'[12] As armies became irrelevant, the central purpose of the air force was to destroy cities and terrify civilian populations, coercing them into surrender or deterring them from starting a war in the first place. Douhet's essay was, therefore, ultimately a manual on urbicide.[13] It specifically advocated the strategic use of air bombardment to destroy civilian targets in cities. Indeed, a genuinely strategic effect could be achieved only by bombing cities, where factories, infrastructure and people are clustered: 'Such bombing expeditions cannot be undertaken successfully unless they are directed against very large centres of the civilian population.'[14] This bombing had two effects; it destroyed critical infrastructure and spread terror: 'Tragic, too, to think that the decision in this kind of war must depend upon smashing the material and moral resources of a people caught up in a frightful cataclysm which haunts them everywhere without cease until the final collapse of all social organization.'[15] In order to achieve this moral collapse, Douhet recommended that bombing raids had to be large enough so that city centres could be destroyed in one shock attack. He noted that if ten planes could destroy an area of 500 metres in diameter from 3,000 metres, bigger raids with a mixture of explosives, incendiaries and poison gas could be truly devastating. In the twenty-first century, the original conception of airpower has often been forgotten or sanitized, but after the First World War, strategic airpower was designed for a single purpose alone: the destruction of cities.

Douhet's position might be regarded as extreme. Yet, in the inter-war period, his doctrine of airpower was extremely influential. In the literature and art of the period, the fear of air attack was palpable, as the writings of H. G. Wells or Picasso's painting *Guernica* demonstrated. Military historian Basil H. Liddell Hart affirmed its dreadful potential:

> There is no reason why within a few hours or at most days from the commencement of hostilities, the nerve system of a country inferior in air power should not be paralysed. Imagine for a moment London, Manchester, Birmingham, and half a dozen other great centres simul-taneously attacked, the business localities and Fleet Street wrecked, Whitehall in a heap of ruins, the slum district maddened into impulse to break loose and maraud.[16]

Substantially as a result of Douhet's writing, airpower thinkers, espe-cially in the US and Britain, aspired to a genuinely strategic – that is, city-destroying – air force. Billy Mitchell in the United States and Hugh Trenchard in Britain began to build strategic bomber forces, whose purpose was to prevent war through deterrence or end it quickly once it had started, by inflicting insupportable damage on cities and their civilian populations.

In fact, the early years of the Second World War belied the prophe-cies of airpower advocates and the jeremiads of pacifists: 'No force in 1939 was prepared to carry out an annihilating, war-winning "knock-out blow" of the kind Douhet had envisaged.'[17] Bombers were, in fact, disappointingly ineffective. Rather than being able to destroy cities with impunity, early air operations showed that it was actually often quite difficult to hit them at all. The German Air Force had caused considerable damage during its Blitz bombing campaign in 1940–1, notably in its raid on Coventry. Yet, the destructiveness of the air force, still more its ability to terrorize the civilian population and government into submission, was not high. The performance of the British RAF in the early years of the war was instructive here. Up to August 1941, RAF attacks on German cities were ineffective. The Butt Report of 1941 recorded that only 15 per cent of aircraft bombs landed within five miles of their target.[18] In many cases, German air defences could not determine which city was the RAF's intended target, so random was the bombing pattern.

This changed after 1942. Under the leadership of Air Marshal Arthur Harris, the RAF gained strategic direction, new equipment and a new discipline, which transformed the performance of the force, and, while falling well short of an aerial apocalypse until the very end of the war, it began to inflict serious and sustained damage on Germany. Harris dismissed the aspiration – attempted by the Americans – for precision bombing of industrial nodes in cities. Whenever RAF bombers attempted to hit precise targets like railways or synthetic oil plants, they missed them.[19] Instead, Harris perfected a system of attritional night-time bombing aimed at the general destruction of the industrial and civilian infrastructure of German cities. Even if factories could not be completely obliterated, the destruction of housing would reduce the effectiveness of the labour force: 'The targets chosen were congested industrial areas and were carefully picked so that the bombs which overshot or undershot the actual railway centres under attack should fall on these areas, thereby affecting morale.'[20] The US Army Air Forces (USAAF), equipped with its excellent Norden bombsight, attempted precision daytime bombing. Its attacks, especially later in the war when German defences were weak and bombers were escorted by fighters, were, relative to the RAF attempts, reasonably accurate. However, even then, they could not really be described as precise, and the victims of their attacks found it difficult to distinguish between the two techniques.[21]

In contemporary imagination, the major urban battles of the Second World War took place between armies: Stalingrad, Manila, Berlin. Yet, in fact, urban air battles were far more common and, overall, far more destructive. For instance, the joint RAF/USAAF campaign over Germany between 1942 and 1945 eventually resulted in the destruction of large parts of almost every major city in Germany. In the Pacific, the USAAF, untroubled by ethical issues, firebombed Japanese cities at will, until the final denouement at Hiroshima and Nagasaki. Urban warfare in the twentieth century very substantially involved air bombardment, not ground attack. In Europe, Harris was its master; in the Pacific, it was Curtis LeMay.

Many scholars and military professionals have suggested that urban warfare has become volumetric in the twenty-first century. However, since the air raid was the most common form of urban battle in the twentieth century, urban warfare has consistently involved an intrinsically cubic element for about a hundred years. From 1939, the airspace above the city has been as important a part of the urban battle as the streets. However, even though urban warfare has been volumetric since bombers started to fly over cities, assertions and presumptions about the aerial topography of the battlescape need to be avoided. In particular, we need to examine how the airspace above a city during an urban battle was organized in the twentieth century. Only once this is established will it be possible to develop a precise and accurate understanding of its three-dimensional character in the twenty-first century.

The Battle of Hamburg

From 1942 to 1945, the RAF and the USAAF mounted hundreds of raids against German cities. Any one of these might exemplify the twentieth-century urban air battle. The battle of Hamburg, fought between the nights of 24/25 July and 2/3 August 1943, was one of the most striking and significant engagements. The battle was given the appropriate code-name Operation Gomorrah and involved four large-scale attacks on Hamburg (24/25 July, 27/28 July, 29/30 July, 2/3 August) each employing more than 700 bombers (see Map 6.1). The USAAF mounted two smaller daylight raids on 26 and 28 July. Operation Gomorrah was the first RAF attack in which 'Window' (strips of aluminium dropped from aircraft) was used to block German radar signals. The result was that the first two raids were the most destructive mounted by the RAF until the very end of the war. On the first night of the battle, a defenceless city was attacked. Helped by the warm summer weather and wooden buildings in the medieval city centre, the RAF was able to achieve a hitherto impossible concentration of bombing, igniting the first 'firestorm' in the history of warfare on the night of the second attack.[22]

Gomorrah was a disaster for the city – known later as the 'Catastrophe' – but it exemplified the way the airspace was organized by both attackers and defenders. The RAF's night attacks were organized differently from the USAAF raids; the USAAF flew their B-17s in dense formations for self-protection. RAF bombers flew in large streams along attack corridors from their bases in Britain to their targets and back. To deceive the Germans about the ultimate target, the bomber streams flew a series of dog-legs out over the North Sea and Germany. At each switch-point, Pathfinders dropped coloured flares to assist navigation. Over Hamburg, each raid was oriented along different axes in order to maximize the bomb damage; the 24/25 July raid attacked from the north-west, bombing the western quadrant of the city; the 27/28 July

Map 6.1: Operation Gomorrah attack plans, 1943
Source: Based on maps from Martin Middlebrook, *The Battle of Hamburg*
(London: Cassell and Co., 1980).

raid attacked from the west, destroying the eastern districts; the 29/30
July raid attacked from the north; and the final 2/3 August raid attacked
from the south (although, due to a storm, it was ineffective).

In planning raids, the RAF organized airspace into a long corridor
to and from the city. Over Hamburg itself, Pathfinders and bombers
were assigned to a corridor of between 18,000 and 25,000 feet above
the city. The stream itself was further coordinated by time. The
Pathfinders arrived over Hamburg first to lay Target Indicators (TIs,
flares) over the aiming points. They were immediately followed over
the next hour by the rest of the stream flying in waves, squadron by
squadron. Although tight concentrations were achieved at Hamburg,
bombing was necessarily dispersed – 'creep back' was unavoidable. On
seeing the TIs and fires already burning from incendiaries, there was a

tendency among RAF crew to release their bombs early. Consequently, the bombing pattern never consisted of a dense circle of destruction around the aiming point, as might be expected, but rather an oblique ellipse or triangle stretching back from the aiming point along the direction of attack. RAF planners fully knew of this phenomenon and, therefore, adjusted for it. During Operation Gomorrah, the aiming point was positioned in the centre of Hamburg because, although there was no specific target at that location, large swathes of the city would be destroyed as the bombardment inevitably crept back from it.

The RAF delineated the airspace for their bomber crews in order to maximize damage. The German defenders also organized the space above and around Hamburg carefully. Hamburg had an evil reputation among RAF pilots. On the coast, the Germans had erected a radar screen called the Kammhuber Line, through which every single bomber had to pass. The Kammhuber Line consisted of a series of aerial boxes monitored by radar, which identified incoming bomber streams so that Luftwaffe night-fighters could intercept them. Hamburg's own defences, consisting of searchlights and anti-aircraft guns, formed a twenty-mile circle around the city, through which it took a bomber fifteen minutes to fly. In July 1943, the city had fifty-four batteries of heavy flak, armed with 166 88mm flak guns, ninety-six 105mm guns and sixteen 128mm guns, twenty-four batteries of searchlights and three smoke-generating units.[23] In addition, there were three flak towers in the centre of Hamburg, two in Heiligengeistfeld and one in Wilhelmsburg. These remarkable modernist structures consisted of tall concrete towers, above the elevation of the surrounding roof tops, topped with large platforms for guns and observers. The searchlights and flak guns normally covered the space above the city up to about 30,000 feet. Once one searchlight had found an RAF bomber, all the others 'coned' that aircraft and the city's guns were turned on it. A 'coned' aircraft rarely survived.

During the battle of Hamburg, the air defences did not work because 'Window' jammed German radar. Consequently, on 24/25 July the bomber stream flew straight through the Kammhuber boxes unmolested and, since the searchlights were also coordinated by the radar, many were not operating; Hamburg looked that night as 'if a black swath had been cut through a sea of light and flashes'.[24] There was little anti-aircraft fire. The airspace was uncontested. However, the German defenders reacted quickly. On the second firestorm raid of 27/28 July, the Germans dispensed entirely with their reliance on radar. Additional searchlights were brought in that operated up to a level of 18,000 feet, targeting all low-flying aircraft for the guns.[25] Above this altitude, in a second box of airspace, the Germans assigned their new 'Wild Boar' squadrons of night-fighters. These fighters were not coordinated by radar but simply attacked bombers as the opportunity arose, using running radio commentaries to facilitate their actions.[26]

The airspace above Hamburg assumed a distinctive shape during Operation Gomorrah, then. It consisted of a series of air corridors, zones and boxes, created and organized by the attackers and defenders, which overlapped and intersected. The RAF flew along a narrow, angled air corridor from Britain until they reached the bombing zone above the city. Meanwhile, the Germans had organized the airspace above the city into two large twenty-mile-diameter cylinders; one up to 18,000 feet, which was assigned to searchlights and guns, the second from 18,000 upwards, which was occupied by Wild Boar squadrons. Contemporary theorists are absolutely correct to emphasize the three-dimensional cubic character of urban warfare. However, this phenomenon is not new. Cubic battlespace appeared with strategic airpower. Consequently, as early as July 1943, urban warfare displayed a complex volumetric shape.

Airspace in the Twenty-First Century

The bombing campaign of the Second World War proves that urban warfare was already three-dimensional before the twenty-first century. Nevertheless, some important changes to the airspace above cities have occurred in recent decades. Although urban warfare has not only just become cubic, its aerial topography has become distinctive. It is necessary to be precise about the exact way in which the airspace above cities has evolved since the end of the Cold War.

During the Second World War, airpower had been informed by an attritional philosophy. Bombing was almost always inaccurate. Guided munitions were first used by the US Air Force in Vietnam at the end of the 1960s. Their development began to transform the theory of airpower. Instead of bombing cities as a whole, individual targets inside the city could now be destroyed. For instance, rather than crudely destroying factories and damaging morale, specific structures and installations could be reliably eliminated. By the end of the Cold War, precision had replaced attrition as the central principle of airpower. The Gulf War of 1991 was the first true demonstration of the potential of precision weaponry. During that conflict, US generals beguiled the media with video images of precision munitions destroying buildings and bridges. The terrible Al-Firdos incident on 13 February 1991 only proved the point. In that strike, the Americans destroyed the Al-Firdos military bunker in Baghdad, killing more than 400 Iraqi civilians. With a savage irony, although the effects were terrible, the strike itself was extraordinarily precise; one laser-guided bomb punctured the concrete roof, while a second penetrated the hole to detonate inside.

In Kosovo, accuracy became even more refined. In 1995, a US Air Force officer, John Warden, published a now celebrated article called 'The enemy as a system'.[27] It contrasts nicely with Douhet's *Command of the Air*. Warden's work advocated that a regime consisted of five rings: the fielded military, the population, the infrastructure, organic essentials and the leadership. He recommended that a precise air campaign could systematically target key elements of each ring to undermine a regime. Precision strikes alone could destroy the enemy system, where strategic airpower in the 1940s had sought only to obliterate its cities. Later in the decade, Warden's theories were tested. In 1999, during the Kosovo conflict, NATO subjected the Serbian regime to a precise campaign of air coercion, striking critical targets in Serbia and Belgrade itself until the government conceded defeat. Precision remains central to airpower today. Contemporary military doctrine identifies the central features of airpower as 'ubiquity, agility and concentration'. Airpower is able to operate everywhere, quickly and powerfully, primarily because it has become so precise: 'Precision technology means that significant airpower effects can be created without the need for large numbers of aircraft; imposing psychological shock that may be crucial to military success.'[28] Airpower remains a critical part of the urban battle, but air forces have evolved a long way since Douhet and the strategic bombing campaigns of the Second World War.

Precision has transformed the airspace above the city. In order to bomb precisely, air forces have had to reconfigure the space. Precision airpower played a major role in the Gulf War, and in the Bosnia and Kosovo campaigns. However, the true urban potential of airpower became apparent only during the Iraq War and specifically during the occupation, as the insurgency began to accelerate after 2004. Most commentators identify a critical historical moment for the transformation of airpower at this time: the second battle of Fallujah (Operation New Dawn/Al-Fajr) from 7 November to 8 December 2004. The second battle of Fallujah was a major land battle fought by two regimental combat teams from 1st Marine Division, with heavy US Army support and in partnership with the Iraqi Army, against Al Qaeda insurgents who had taken over the city and were using it as a base to mount attacks on Baghdad and surrounding areas. It was the single biggest urban battle of the Iraq War. Fighting in the city was brutal and provides many insights into the character of modern urban warfare, to be discussed later. In the air, the situation was instructive: 'Fallujah marked the unveiling of an urban warfare model based on persistent air surveillance, precision airstrikes, and swift airlift support.'[29] Indeed, following the conclusion of the battle, the concept of a 'Fallujah model' became a common part of the military lexicon; it referred to the complex way in which the airspace had been organized above the city in order to support ground operations.

Fallujah was unusual in the variety of aircraft employed by US forces during the battle. In Hamburg, the RAF had used four types of bombers (Lancasters, Wellingtons, Halifaxes and Stirlings); each had different capabilities but they were closely compatible and dropped the same ordnance. In Fallujah, by contrast, 1st Marine Division employed a diversity of airframes: attack helicopters (Apaches and Cobra), drones (Predators and Hawks), jets (F-16s and Harriers), AC-10 Spectre gunships and, finally, electronic surveillance aircraft. In all, the marines employed twenty different kinds of aircraft over the city: 'The skies over Fallujah are so crowded with US military aircraft that they are layered in stacks above the city, from low-flying helicopters, and swooping attack jets to a jet-powered unmanned spy drone that flies at 60,000 feet.'[30] The potential for confusion and collision was plainly extremely high in this situation, and the airspace about the city had to be coordinated very carefully. The US forces instituted a system, which has become known in the armed forces as 'high-density air control' (HIDAC).

In Fallujah, the airspace above the city was organized into a tall cylinder from ground level to 60,000 feet. This cylinder was itself divided into a series of layers to which particular types of aircraft were assigned. Each layer was separated by 1,000 feet to prevent collision. Artillery was assigned to the airspace below 8,500 feet; high trajectory artillery munitions can hit friendly aircraft. Aircraft, beginning with attack helicopters, were assigned to altitudes above 9,000 feet. There was a primary altitude of 13,000–15,000 feet where most of the aircraft flew, and a secondary altitude of 18,000–20,000 feet.[31] The result was a distinctive cubic topography: 'We call it the wedding cake. It's layered all the way up.'[32]

This 'wedding cake' was further subdivided to create a system called the 'keyhole concept', instituted by Lieutenant Colonel Gary Kling, an F-18 pilot and the lead air force officer in 1st Marine Division. The keyhole concept worked in the following way:

The keyhole concept was basically a template with two rings gradu-
ated in nautical miles. The centre of the template was placed on a
reference point, which then positioned the rings. This inner ring,
called the engagement ring, was five nautical miles from the centre
of the template. In the case of Fallujah, the template's centre was
located on a very distinct road intersection in the geographical centre
of the city, making it an easily identifiable feature. Between the two
rings, the circle was divided into four blocks based on the cardinal
points north, south, east and west. The blocks were further divided
by altitude to provide vertical spacing. For example, the north block
might have an altitude of 16,000 to 18,000 feet, south block 19,000
to 21,000, east block 13,000 to 15,000, and west block 17,000 to
19,000.[33]

It is worth clarifying this statement. The keyhole method consisted
of two rings around Fallujah; supporting aircraft were stationed in an
outer eight-mile circle. They were then called into the five-mile inner
circle to make a strike. When a target was identified, air controllers
determined which type of ordnance and, therefore, which airframe was
best designed to deliver the strike. At this point, a specific airframe –
an attack helicopter or F-16, for instance – was called into one of the
quadrants in the inner ring above the city. From here, the analogy of
the keyhole became apparent. Attacking aircraft flew into a quadrant
in the inner circle, dropped their munitions on the objective, and then
withdrew back to their position in the holding pattern outside the city.
The airspace to which attacking aircraft were assigned assumed the
shape of a keyhole, with a large lower entry point tapering to a target
point.

The keyhole method also meant that aircraft could be assigned to
simultaneous targets in the city without fear of fratricide, since their
attack runs took different courses and altitudes. As one of the US officers who employed it in Fallujah noted:

> The keyhole CAS (close air support) concept was simply a template
> for airspace coordination. A template you can place anywhere, and
> automatically all the players know who's where. It further facilitates
> the integration of surface based fires and multiple sections of aircraft to
> keep them from bumping into each other – [typically] twelve aircraft,
> four to six ISR (intelligence, surveillance and a reconnaissance) plat-
> forms: Predator, Pioneer, Scan Eagle and Dragon Eye, three artillery
> batteries, and associated mortars; 81s, 60s and 120s.[34]

The Fallujah model was a major development at the time, but it is not unique. On the contrary, the layered system of close air support, which was first introduced during the battle of Fallujah, has now been institutionalized. US armed forces employed a similar model throughout their operations in Iraq and it was used to support Iraqi Army units during the battle of Mosul in 2016–17. The battle of Sadr City, fought between US–Iraqi coalition forces and Shia insurgents in March–May 2008, was one of the most well-documented examples of layered airpower. Unlike Fallujah, the population remained in Sadr City and, consequently, artillery was severely restricted. The operation was even more dependent on airstrikes than Fallujah. Instead, Sadr City relied on persistent intelligence and surveillance from U-2s and joint surveillance acquisition and reconnaissance aircraft, such as Global Hawks, at the highest altitude under the operational-level command of the Multi-National Corps–Iraq (MNC–I). The result was twenty-four-hour surveillance of the city. Small drones (Falcons and Shadows), attack helicopters and aircraft were assigned to the lowest altitudes and put under the command of the tactical forces, the 3rd Brigade Combat Team and the 1st Infantry Division (see Figure 6.1). Initially, the headquarters of the 3rd Brigade Combat Team under Colonel John Hort struggled to cope with the amount of aerial reconnaissance information they received.[35] However, although the Brigade and even its subunits were employing strategic air assets that were normally assigned to the MNC–I, it quickly became capable of coordinating reconnaissance and strikes. In the end, the operation involved strikes with 120 Hellfire missiles, 6 guided multiple launch rockets and 8 air force guided bombs.[36] As in Fallujah, the battlespace above Sadr City was complicated. A cylindrical 'wedding cake' was created, facilitating permanent surveillance and rapid, precise strikes.

The Fallujah model has continued to be developed and refined. For instance, by the time of the battle of Mosul the airspace had become even more complex. Indeed, one report observed:

The Battle of Mosul turned joint terminal attack controllers into what at times seemed like air traffic controllers managing up to 40 aerial platforms. In the past, fire support personnel would arrange platforms by time, space, and desired effects, call them to the target area, and quickly take them out of the 'stack'. A Special Operations Task Force-North senior joint terminal attack controller described this by saying that he had never seen anything like the dense old Mosul; it was like a micro-airspace with extraordinary challenges when talking on close air support.[37]

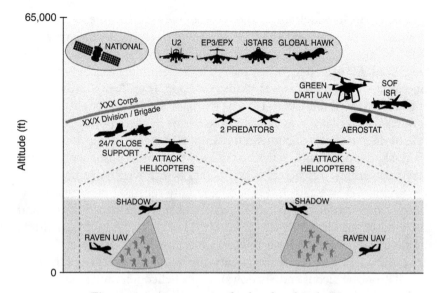

Figure 6.1: Airpower in the battle of Sadr City
Source: Based on graphic from David H. Petraeus, 'CENTCOM Update,
Center for a New American Security', briefing, 2009.

There is no question that the United States, with its allies, has developed the most sophisticated system of urban airspace management ever seen. However, these are not the only state forces to have employed airpower extensively in recent urban battles. In some cases, other states have not been nearly so concerned about precision. On the contrary, during the Syrian civil war, neither President Bashir al-Assad nor his ally, Russia, was much troubled by precision or collateral damage. Indeed, in many cases, they deliberately sought to create as much local destruction as possible. Russia entered the Syrian war in 2015 to shore up the collapsing regime. Its airpower proved crucial both in pushing the antiregime elements back and also in Assad's eventual victory. The Russian Air Force rarely had the aircraft, the pilots or the ordnance to mount a precision campaign of an American type; only its SU-34s were armed with precision munitions. It could not have implemented the US keyhole method. However, during the battle of Aleppo, the Russian Air Force eventually deployed drones and a variety of aircraft, including Su-34s, Su-35s, Hind attack helicopters, with Su-33s and Mig-29s flying from the carrier *Admiral Kuznetsov* in the Mediterranean. In order to deliver close air support in Aleppo, they refined their management of the airspace. Although the precise details of that system are not yet in the public domain, the Russians presumably organized the airspace by altitude and zones so that aircraft could be called into specific targets without fear of fratricide. The US might, therefore, be the most advanced and precise military in the world but their peers have converged on a compatible system of airspace management above the urban battle. For all these forces, the airspace above the city now consists of an invisible, aerial architecture of zones, layers, quadrants and corridors.

Aerial Architecture

Urban warfare has always involved a vertical dimension. Defenders have sought to exploit height and, therefore, gravity against their assailants. With the advent of the military aircraft, the airspace above a city has become as integral a part of the urban battle as the fighting in the streets. We are indebted to today's volumetric theorists for highlighting the spatial dimensions of urban conflict, which is so often ignored. Weizman, Graham, Elden et al. are absolutely correct to insist that war in cities takes place not just on terrain but in a space. However, some refinement of their arguments is required. While urban warfare became truly volumetric with the air raid, airspace has evolved over the last century.

In the Second World War, as the battle of Hamburg showed, operating in the airspace above the city was not simple. Both British attackers and German defenders constructed corridors and boxes in which their planes, searchlights and guns functioned. Many of the techniques originally developed in the 1940s for airspace management remain in use today. By the first decade of the twenty-first century, however, urban airspace management had evolved so far as to be a quite distinct, if not actually a fundamentally different, practice. Urban airspace is now organized into a carefully segmented structure of cylinders, zones, layers and quadrants. Although, to the naked eye, the airspace above a city seems empty, it has, in fact, become a complex, variegated space. The development of this aerial architecture is intimately related to conditions on the ground. The airspace has been reorganized so that troops committed to localized sieges in the city are given constant support by attendant airpower. In Sadr City, for instance, the airspace was organized elaborately precisely so that US troops on the ground could build the wall along Route Gold. Although apparently quite separate, the airspace above cities has become as much a part of the urban battlescape as the walls within them. Walls and air are indivisibly connected. The micro-sieges that have appeared inside cities take place both in the streets and also in the air above them. Commentators are absolutely right, then. War in the twenty-first century is, indeed, three-dimensional. However, its topography can be truly appreciated only when the airspace above cities is itself submitted to close analysis.

7

Fire

Flames

Fire has always been a central element of urban warfare. An ancient siege typically culminated in the looting and burning of the city. Indeed, the archaeological evidence testifies to the ubiquity of fire in urban warfare. The city of Hamoukar, in north-eastern Syria, was destroyed by fire in 3500 BCE.[1] Nineveh's acropolis mound of Kuyunjik, all its great palaces and temples show clear evidence of incineration in 612 BCE, including vitrified cuneiform tablets.[2] Fire was not only used to burn cities once they had been taken; it was employed extensively throughout antiquity as an offensive weapon. In his treatise on siege warfare, Aineias the Tactitian was convinced that, in siege warfare, fire was a prime weapon.[3] Indeed, the Greeks developed an incendiary weapon that seemed to have been an early form of napalm. At the siege of Plataea, in 428 BCE at the start of the Peloponnesian War, the Spartans, under Archidamus II, piled brushwood, covered with sulphur, pitch and possibly arsenic, along the wall, while throwing as much brush over the wall in an effort to spread the fire – 'this fire, however, was indeed a very big one, and it very nearly finished the Plataeans off'.[4] At the siege of Parium (c. 362–359 BCE), Iphiades of Abydus ordered his troops to fill wagons with twigs and roll them up to the walls, where they were ignited. Once the flames had spread to the gates, Iphiades' soldiers took advantage of the distraction to scale the walls at another point and take the city.[5] Fire was central to Chinese warfare: 'From the Warring States onward it became a crucial part of Chinese theory and practice.'[6] Fire was equally effective in defence, destroying the weapons and equipment of besiegers. For instance, the Thebans used a flame-thrower against Athenian attackers at Delium:[7] 'By attaching a bellows to an iron-plated, hollowed-out wooden beam with a curved iron tube that reached from a cauldron of fire through the beam, the Boeotians were able to blow an intense flame through the beam against the wooden walls of the Athenian camp.'[8]

Fire itself has always been an important siege weapon, then. However, siege warfare presented attackers with a distinctive problem: they had to get into the city; they had to breach the walls or batter down the gates. Here, fire alone was less useful unless they could burn down the gate itself (as Iphiades tried to do at Parium) or the walls were made of wood. In order to destroy walls and fortifications, battering rams and catapults, employing kinetic energy, were vital. Although many of the weapons and techniques already existed, and Assyrian kings took great pride in their role as takers and destroyers of cities;[9] the Assyrians became adept at using battering rams and mines. When he took Lachish in 701 BCE, Sennacherib employed both methods to breach the walls and assault the city, as palace friezes in Nineveh show. The Assyrians employed relatively crude kinetic weapons. However, in Greek city-states major advancements in siege technology were made as catapults were developed; later, mangonels and trebuchets appeared. It is technically wrong to call these weapons 'firepower'; they depended on human or animal strength, gravity, tension and torsion, not flames. However, these kinetic weapons had the same effect on cities as cannon and artillery would much later. Projectile weaponry harnessing kinetic energy was an early form of 'firepower'.

Nevertheless, while projectiles have been an eternal part of siege warfare, genuine firepower has a shorter history: about 600 years. Firepower became important when European states started to exploit the military potential of gunpowder in the fifteenth century. From that time, siege cannons played a crucial role in urban warfare. Artillery remains essential to urban warfare. However, today, firepower takes two main forms: airpower and artillery. Both have been extensively employed to support ground operations in urban areas in recent decades. In addition, of course, machine guns, automatic rifles and grenades have played a crucial role in urban warfare, especially as the lethality of hand-held weapons has increased. 'Fires' are, then, a central feature of contemporary urban warfare.

Some commentators have claimed that the use of firepower in urban warfare has not changed significantly in over a century. Alice Hills,

for instance, argues that 'the most effective tactics for urban warfight-
ing appear remarkably consistent across decades'.[10] There is no real
difference between Stalingrad and Mosul in her opinion. In both battles, unadulterated firepower blasted through buildings and defensive
positions, and killed opponents. Firepower is certainly not new; there
are plainly major continuities with the twentieth century. The sheer
violence and destructiveness of contemporary urban combat endures.
In some cases, such as the need for close and direct supporting artillery fire to destroy specific bunkers in front of attacking infantry or
the use of small arms, little seems to have changed at all. However, it
is necessary to be cautious here. Continuity cannot be assumed just
because firepower remains important and is equally terrible in its
destructiveness. In fact, while firepower may persist as a central feature
of contemporary urban warfare, it is important to be sensitive as to how
it might have been employed in cities since the early 2000s. Above all,
it is difficult to ignore the increasing precision with which firepower has
been used in recent urban battles. This does not mean that firepower
has always been employed accurately. On the contrary, in some cases
there has been little attempt to be precise. Yet, even then, firepower
has congregated onto specific targets in the city itself. Fire has become
a critical part of the micro-sieges inside cities that have become such a
striking feature of urban warfare today.

Targeting

Firepower relies on mapping. Without accurate mapping, it is impossible for long-range artillery to fire accurately, especially in urban areas.
In the twentieth century, cities were a major challenge to military mapping because of their dense, complex topography. Nevertheless, no one
doubted the importance of detailed maps. For instance, the US Army's
doctrine during and after the Second World War recommended that
urban operations required 'careful and thorough planning';[11] an attack
'must be based on a detailed study of the city, as well as enemy dispositions'.[12] Standard travel publications or guidebooks were recommended
to generate the 'best intelligence'.

Sometimes, detailed mapping was available. During the battle of
Aachen, for instance, in October 1944, 1st Infantry Division, under
VII Corps, assigned two infantry battalions, 2nd and 3rd Battalions
26th Infantry Regiment, to clear the town. VII Corps was well supplied
with detailed maps at a scale of 1:25,000, 1:62,000 and 1:10,000, the
first two in colour and the last one detailed enough to show individual

buildings within the city. The 26th Infantry Regiment received 500 maps of Aachen in the week before the assault.[13] There were extensive aerial photographs of the town too. In addition, 'the assaulting force had at least one copy of a brochure for the spa complex at Farwick Park, including a floor plan for Hotel Quellenhof.[14] Consequently, the 26th Infantry Regiment was able to number every single building in the town and to clear the city systematically.

In this century, the armed forces have continued to employ large-scale maps and aerial photographs in urban areas in order to identify targets. Indeed, contemporary urban doctrine continues to emphasize the importance of detailed, accurate mapping: 'The mission specific military map can be a topographical map or an image map of a city that is usually at a large scale (1:5000, 1:10,000 and 1:25,000 are common).'[15] However, 'identifying or referring to a particular piece of urban terrain using a six or eight figure grid reference can prove imprecise and slow'.[16] Urban areas should, therefore, be divided into colour-coded zones with all the buildings numbered: 'High resolution mapping or aerial photography should be divided into alphabetical sectors, individual buildings identified by target reference points and main routes by numerical spots.'[17] The importance of identifying individual buildings is very important: 'Special mapping products can supplement or replace topographic maps as the basis of navigation and are often called "Spot Maps" due to having coloured routes and numbered spots providing those reference points.'[18] Indeed, the Land Component Commander during the battle of Mosul, General Joseph Martin, confirmed that, in urban areas, 'mapping is key'. He carried a 1:25,000 map in his pocket throughout the battle in order to be able to brief his subordinates.[19] The Iraqi Counter-Terrorist Service conducted operations in Mosul from a wall-sized map of the city in its field headquarters. The map located the Counter-Terrorist Service's current position on two small polygons, and other sectors were cross-hatched blue, green and red to denote whether they had been seized by the Counter-Terrorist Service, the 16th Iraqi Infantry or 9th Iraqi Armoured Divisions, or were still in ISIS hands.[20] Similarly, in Marawi, conventional mapping played an important role and spot maps were developed for the Filipino forces: 'I found the use of numeric targeting where each house/structure in a map is marked or designated with numeric code an effective and efficient way of determining targets. This avoids confusion and misinterpretation in identifying Targets. We learned this method during the Zamboanga siege and employed the same during the Marawi siege.'[21]

The importance of accurate, shared mapping to urban warfare is most forcefully demonstrated by incidents when it has not been available. Lack of accurate mapping contributed to Russia's disaster in the opening phase of the first battle of Grozny in December 1994 and January 1995. The Russians did their initial planning on 1:50,000 and 1:100,000 scale maps; they lacked larger scale maps or aerial photographs.[22] Poor mapping and battlespace management played a major role in the battle of An Nasiriyah on 22 and 23 March 2003 during the Iraq invasion. The entire operation was mounted by the US Marine Corps' Task Force Tarawa very quickly, without adequate preparation. As they entered the town, 1st Battalion, 2nd Regiment Marines were engaged heavily and the battalion quickly fragmented into isolated company groups each fighting its own desperate battle. C Company was isolated and surrounded at the northern bridge over the canal on the edge of the city. At this point, C Company radioed its headquarters for air support, stating that they were at 'the' bridge (over the canal in the north) and required support. The battalion called for air support but, because they had not mapped and coded the buildings and streets, there was complete confusion about C Company's location: 'Grabowski [the commanding officer] wasn't clear about the exact location of the different companies.'[23] Tragically, officers in the headquarters assumed that C Company had to be at the southern bridge over the Euphrates because they were sure that 'No one is north of 3-8 grid. There are no friendlies north of the canal.'[24] Airstrikes were subsequently called in on C Company, killing ten marines.

Urban targeting demands accurate mapping, then. However, military professionals have recognized the limitations of traditional two-dimensional mapping for the demands of contemporary urban operations. Two-dimensional military maps have become inadequate to the prosecution of precise, joint firepower. At the battle of Mosul, for instance, coalition forces sought to strike not simply a building, but a specific floor and even a room in a dynamic environment in which buildings were being destroyed or damaged and targets were moving. Mapping had to keep up with this destruction. At other times, firepower has even been used to strike moving targets. Consequently, it has been necessary to go beyond two-dimensional cartography. As General Martin noted:

> It was necessary to have simultaneous 3-D imagery for the purposes of the ground force, for Fire Support Coordination lines, and to optimize joint fires from mortars to airpower. We designed the air space and

changed it on the east side of the river and the west side. As the city got
smaller, it was more difficult for aerial platforms at 5,000 feet. It was
difficult to coordinate them at that altitude and it changed every day.[25]

During the battle of Mosul advanced mapping and modelling systems
were required, especially since it was so difficult to establish a common
picture of the city with Iraqi allies:

> In dense urban terrain, the environment changes quickly. Disputes
> over the common operating picture and the location of Iraqi forces
> within Mosul demonstrated the need for a consolidated, multi-system
> compatible, digital common operating picture ... During the Mosul
> fight, the target engagement authorities sometimes questioned the
> validity of a target observed by an in-contact ground element based on
> outdated imagery. On the ground, the difference between a building
> and a pile of rubble was measured in hours as opposed to the speed at
> which the imagery was updated (at best several days).[26]

The same lesson was learnt at Marawi:

> Initially we used a tactical map which gave us wider perspective on the
> physical elevations and contours of Marawi. When things got more
> complicated, we later resorted to aerial photos that provided us better
> perspective as it depicts the real picture on the ground. To reinforce
> this, we also employed drones which provided us excellent descriptions
> of the main battle area – the height of the buildings and structures,
> streets and alleys. The use of drones gave us better ground appreciation
> as well as enemy activities on a real time basis.[27]

In light of these experiences, contemporary NATO doctrine has
advocated a new approach:

> The urban environment requires multidimensional understanding. As
> with all terrain, it consists of airspace and surface area; but also the
> subterranean and supersurface (rooftop) areas must be considered and
> planned for. Equally important are considerations of the exterior and
> interior (intrasurface) space of buildings. Military maps do not provide
> sufficient detail for proper terrain analysis.[28]

Consequently, the armed forces have experimented with three-dimensional modelling and live imagery:

Data on the layout, structure and organization of the majority of urban areas in the world will often be readily available through open source as well as military means. In addition to imagery from satellite and air reconnaissance, commercial mapping and satellite imagery may be more immediately available. Google Earth and similar 3D visualization tools are used extensively for planning by commercial agencies and town plans, communication, power and transport networks can be accessed from government agencies, utility companies and often directly off the worldwide web.[29]

The Royal Engineers in the British Army, for instance, are currently conducting an initiative called Project Crocker, in which they are attempting to exploit the potential of three-dimensional imagery for military purposes. They are exploring the possibility of purchasing automated civilian software that represents the city with holographic imagery. The aim here is not simply to represent the city topographically, but also to generate visuals that assist a commander to make decisions in real time. Above all, these new systems of imaging are intended to facilitate precision strikes.

Airstrikes

Two types of firepower have been regularly used in recent urban battles: airstrikes and artillery fire. Of course, in reality, airstrikes and artillery fire have been closely coordinated and often simultaneous. The armed forces categorize them both as 'fires' and see them as interchangeable. However, while continuous in practice, in order to understand the development of urban firepower in recent decades, it is sensible to examine them separately.

Let us consider airstrikes first. Chapter 6 illustrated the evolution of aerial choreography in the twenty-first century through a comparison of the battle of Hamburg and the Fallujah model. The recent development of airstrikes can be best illustrated by a similar historical comparison. Some caution is required here, though. Since the early 2000s, airpower has been primarily employed in urban operations in a close support role, in immediate cooperation with troops on the ground. We need to find similar examples from the twentieth century. There is a problem here, though, in that there are only a few such examples. In the Second World War, the RAF and USAAF dedicated themselves to the strategic bombing of cities, so the sample is much smaller. However, there is one well-known example from this era; the second battle of Seoul in 1950.

Following the debacle in the summer of 1950, when Republic of Korea and US forces were pushed all the way back to Pusan, General MacArthur famously conceived of an amphibious counterstrike at Inchon, named Operation Chromite. Against all expectations, the landings were a complete success and, having landed, 1st Marine Division was quickly engaged in the second battle of Seoul. US mapping of Seoul was seriously underdeveloped.[30] More than 6,000 maps (1:12,500) were produced but they were not all on the same grid system and there was no complete photographic mosaic of Seoul until two days after the landing.[31] Targeting was therefore difficult during the battle. Nevertheless, especially as they advanced out of range of naval gunfire, 1st Marine Division drew on the close air support provided by the Marine Air Wing. Air support typically operated during the day, artillery at night. This air support consisted mainly of low-flying Corsairs, armed with napalm, which was most effective, along with 1,000 or 2,000-pound bombs or 20mm cannon. The Corsairs flew mainly from Kimpo airfield, five minutes' flight time from the city, in squadrons of six aircraft; 55 per cent of all their missions were in the city.[32] The Corsairs were controlled by forward observation officers on the ground or forward air controllers in light observation aircraft. These controllers identified visual targets for the pilots as they flew over the city. The strikes were surprisingly accurate, engaging targets within 150 yards and sometimes 100 yards: 'US Army units, which were not used to being supported by marine aircraft, lavished praise on the support they received.'[33] Although there is little doubt that air support in Seoul was sometimes very close, most attacks occurred at a greater distance. In particular, napalm and bombs could not be dropped so close to American troops. In Seoul, the Corsairs, therefore, attacked static defensive positions – buildings – some distance in front of the attacking troops.

The battle of Seoul is an important reminder that, while rarer, urban close air support was practised in the twentieth century. However, it quickly becomes apparent that US-led air operations over Fallujah, Sadr City and Mosul differed markedly from the example of Seoul. In particular, where close air support was intermittent and roughly accurate in Seoul, it has now routinely become ubiquitous, constant and, especially in the case of Western forces, extremely precise. Above all, video footage has become an intrinsic element of the precise airstrike today. For instance, during the battle of Sadr City, US forces had employed live feeds constantly. The coverage over Sadr City was so complete and the resolution of the imagery so good that the headquarters of Colonel John Hort's 3rd Brigade Combat Team, 4th Infantry Division, were able to plot the movement of Shia rocket and mortar teams back to their supply points or command locations. In their parlance, they 'watched the rail' in real time, so that in a single strike they were able to eliminate multiple insurgent teams as they congregated in apparently safe areas; five of seven 107mm rocket teams were destroyed in strikes like this.[34] In Mosul, the US-led coalition also exploited high-resolution real-time video footage to an even greater extent.[35] As a result, the coalition were able to hit small, mobile targets – individual vehicles, or small teams of ISIS fighters – as they operated against the Iraqi forces.[36] Indeed, the US became adept at interdicting suicide vehicles; in Raqqa, for instance, they destroyed 84 of the 125 suicide vehicles launched by ISIS.[37]

US urban airstrikes have become increasingly precise and have been commonly used against mobile targets. Yet, the development of airstrikes has involved a second, perhaps more interesting and profound process. In the twentieth century, air forces primarily engaged in strategic attacks on cities or, more rarely in urban areas, provided close air support. Since the early 2000s, the US has perfected what might be called deep urban strikes. These strikes have been very accurate, but they have sought both to kill enemy fighters and also to incapacitate their urban systems, using specialist or very heavy ordnance normally held at a high level of command. This technique was used against suicide vehicles in Mosul. Although the coalition was very successful against suicide columns as they attacked, air commanders responsible for the battle became dissatisfied with this approach. They regarded it is as purely tactical reactive activity, which did not exploit either their intelligence and surveillance assets or their airpower to their fullest potential. So instead, in the course of the battle, the air planners identified the factories in which suicide vehicles were being made, the locations where they were being armed and, indeed, particular individuals who were playing a critical role in constructing and launching the suicide missions. In short, the airstrikes began to target the network of production and command itself, executing deep strikes across the city to interdict suicide attacks before they were ever even mounted: 'We went after the network – to the production. We were doubling down on VBIEDs. If we saw it anywhere we would strike it.'[38] In all, the US coalition made 558 airstrikes and dropped 10,115 munitions, a significant proportion of which were launched at deep targets behind the immediate battlefront.[39]

In order to mount these deep strikes on urban targets, US forces refined their conception of battlespace. On current operations, American land forces divide the battlefield into deep, close and rear areas. Each area is assigned to a specific level of command. Normally, the close battle is assigned to a division, and the deep fight to a corps. At the battle of Mosul, for instance, the deep battle was the responsibility of the Joint Task Force (a corps-level command, Operation Inherent Resolve), while the close battle belonged to the Land Component Command (a US divisional headquarters in support of Iraqi forces). 'Deep' and 'close' referred to actual physical terrain on the ground, divided by a conceptual line called the Fire Support Coordination Line. The battlespace beyond the Fire Support Coordination Line is assigned to the corps level that prosecutes targets in the deep fight with its the long-range, heavy artillery and specialist airpower. On field operations, the distinction between the close and deep battles is very clear; the Fire Support Coordination Line is normally located about fifteen miles in front of friendly troops beyond the range of divisional artillery. During the battle of Mosul, by contrast, the distinction between the deep battle of the Joint Task Force and the close battle of Land Component Command became very fine indeed; 'In urban fights, deep may equate to only a few city blocks from the front lines'; this meant that US forces had to 'rethink the application of battlefield geometries, such as Fire Support Coordination Line, to optimize the integration and synchronization of air assets with manoeuvre'.[40] In Seoul, Corsairs sometimes strafed in the immediate vicinity of US troops. However, as a result of this precise delineation of deep and close battlespaces in Mosul, the US delivered operational and strategic level air munitions within a few hundred metres of Iraqi troops on the ground.

Western forces have sought to be very precise with the use of airpower in the twenty-first century, especially in comparison with the past. With radically reduced forces, it has been necessary to be far more efficient with the use of firepower; precision has, therefore, become important. However, US-led Western forces have also been concerned with accuracy in order to sustain their legitimacy. Predicated on a concept of legal, liberal interventionism, their operations have to be seen to be precise and proportional, avoiding excessive collateral damage. Of course, many other states have not been so constrained by the international legal context. The Saudi attacks on the Houthis in Sana'a Yemen were not characterized by restraint at all. Similarly, in the Syrian civil war, the Assad regime, fighting an existential war of survival, has been indifferent to civilian casualties and collateral damage. On the contrary, as his use of gas has shown, Bashir Assad has periodically sought to maximize civilian casualties in order to intimidate his opponents. From 2015, Russia has supported Assad closely, especially through airpower. Consequently, in alliance with Assad, it has applied firepower ruthlessly. Russians are much less sensitive than the West about the accusation of war crimes. Moreover, they lack the aircraft, the pilots and the weaponry to be very precise. They dropped a large number of dumb bombs in Syria.[41] Nevertheless, although they may not have been so concerned with collateral damage, the Russians eventually developed a relatively accurate system of airpower primarily because it was more militarily effective. They certainly wanted to avoid a repetition of their experience of airpower in Grozny. There, during the first battle, the Russian Air Force struck the presidential palace successfully on 17 January 1995, but, for the most part, its 'targeting was scandalously imprecise'.[42] Indeed, Russian troops stopped calling on close air support for fear of fratricide, preferring to rely on artillery.

The first Russian airstrike in Syria occurred on 30 September 2015. Although they could not imitate the precision of the Americans, the Russians eventually developed a targeting system which was at least compatible. By October 2015, they had developed a series of measures to improve the precision of their airstrikes.[43] They introduced the Forpost drone into the theatre, and this became central to their air operations in Syria.[44] For instance, during the battle of Aleppo, Forpost drones played a crucial role, monitoring the city twenty-four hours a day and producing detailed images of enemy positions.[45] Like the Predator or the Global Hawk, the Forpost loitered over areas, permanently feeding targets to the Russian Air Force, which was then able to strike them with reasonable accuracy.[46] In the case of SU-255M strikes, the method 'ensured accuracy of target destruction of several tens of metres'.[47] In this way, Russian aircraft provided constant close air support to the regime's Desert Hawk Brigade and Tiger Force, as they took back the city.

Urban airstrikes in the twenty-first century have not always been precise. Yet, they have at least become highly localized; strikes have concentrated on decisive points in the urban battle. The US and Russian close air campaigns over Iraqi and Syrian cities have often left these cities destroyed; after the battle, Aleppo, Mosul and Raqqa looked much like Berlin, Hamburg or Dresden. Yet, the eventual result of the battle should not obscure a quite different process of destruction. In the twentieth century, air attacks destroyed cities blindly. Close air support was rarely used, especially in an urban environment and, although it might be released close to troops, it was inaccurate. Today, the situation is quite different. Airstrikes are often objectively accurate. They are relatively very precise in comparison with the past. The result is that bombs and rockets have concentrated on specific targets inside cities themselves.

Artillery

It has become impossible to ignore airpower as a feature of twenty-first-century urban warfare. However, artillery, the original siege weapon, remains essential in urban combat to this day.[48] Artillery has been used for two missions in recent urban battles: to strike targets in the deep, or to fire directly at targets at close range in immediate support of troops. There has been some confusion about these roles in the literature. For instance, on the basis of the analysis of direct fire, it has sometimes been assumed that the use of firepower in the urban environment has not changed. It is a category error. In order to understand the evolution of artillery in the twenty-first century, it is important to distinguish between indirect and direct fire missions. They are quite different functions and have evolved separately. In particular, while indirect, deep strikes have become increasingly precise, direct fire remains perhaps the most unchanged element of contemporary urban firepower.

The development of deep artillery strikes can be highlighted most effectively by considering the use of artillery in the twentieth century. Artillery was used prodigiously, even profligately, in twentieth-century urban battles. For instance, during the battle of Berlin in April/May 1945, the Red Army employed vast quantities of firepower to support their attack: 12,700 guns and mortars, 21,000 Katyusha rocket systems and 1,500 tanks.[49] As Soviet commander Vasili Chuikov remarked: 'A battle within a city is a battle of firepower.'[50] The adage remained true throughout the twentieth century.

During the first battle of Grozny, the Russians employed artillery extensively and indiscriminately. They bombarded the city on 26 December 1994 before the main assault. As already discussed, that assault was a disaster and the Russians had to withdraw. The Russians, then, reconfigured the operation completely and cleared the city systematically. They employed extremely heavy, and often very inaccurate, artillery bombardments to destroy buildings, kill fighters and intimidate the local population. The bombardments were followed by a slow advance of heavy mechanized forces. The city fell to the Russians in late January: 'They suffered incredible losses in the first week of fighting and then drew on the experience of artillery forces and storm detachments to collect themselves and conduct block-by-block fighting.'[51] The Chechens were driven out of the city. Grozny was bombed indiscriminately again in early August 1995 when Chechen forces retook large parts of it.

Although the Russians had defeated President Dudayev in 1995, Chechnyan troops regained Grozny in 1996 and continued to assert their autonomy. Vladimir Putin sought to reimpose Russian authority on the region in 1999, and to snatch power from President Maskhadov, who had succeeded Dudayev after the latter's assassination. The Russians had learnt from their dreadful experiences of 1994–5. They recognized that the Chechen rebels inside Grozny would employ the city as a killing zone as they had done in December 1994. So instead of advancing into the city, from October 1999 the Russians began a mass artillery and air bombardment of it, even though the city was still in ruins as a result of the 1994–5 attack. By 23 December 1999, the Russians were fighting on the outskirts of Grozny and, having blockaded the rebels, began to advance on three axes in January 2000 under massive fire support. Assault teams seized key nodes, while artillery interdicted and killed Chechen fighters across the city. The Chechens eventually capitulated and President Maskhadov declared a unilateral ceasefire.[52]

Artillery has proved no less important for US and Western forces in the twenty-first century. Indeed, US artillery played a vital role during the Iraq occupation and subsequent war against ISIS. However, unlike Russian artillery in Grozny, the Americans have always sought to be precise with their use of urban artillery strikes. Consequently, the Guided Multiple Launch Rocket System (GMLRS) has begun to play a, perhaps the, leading role in artillery fire in urban operations. The precision of this rocket systems may be surprising, as these weapons have a 200-pound warhead and a range of over twenty miles. They are also very destructive. A marine in Ramadi in 2016 recalled their lethality: 'I would use the GMLRS throughout my time in Ramadi. I discovered that one rocket on target would suck the life right out of a building and paint the walls red; two in the same building would bring it to the ground, and there'd be no need for a search afterwards.'[53] Yet, despite the size of their warhead and the distance from which they were fired, they have been extremely accurate. For instance, in Ramadi on 7–8 December 2006, Al Qaeda mounted a major counterattack against US forces and their new Sunni tribal allies. There was a heavy assault on US Marine Emergency Check Point 8 in the centre of the city. Completely surrounded and in danger of being overrun, the marines called for fire support. Five rockets struck at 'danger-close' targets 165 meters from the marines' base: 'When the rockets hit, their warheads detonated with a sharp, but somewhat muffled explosion. We barely felt any shockwaves even though we were less than two football fields away.'[54]

During the battle of Sadr City, as US forces struggled to erect the wall on Route Gold, the GMLRS was used against individual mortar teams. Sometimes, rockets struck even more difficult targets. For instance, on 6 May 2008, a GMLRS strike targeted and destroyed a Jaysh al-Mahdi command post; several important insurgent leaders were killed in the attack. The Shia militants declared a ceasefire a few days later. In Mosul too, the GMLRS played a critical role. Indeed, so accurate were the rockets that 'multi-round missions' were often used; the first round breached the position, the second destroyed the enemy inside.[55]

The GMLRS has become very important as a long-range precision weapon for Western forces. However, more traditional field artillery has also continued to provide important fire support. For instance, in Mosul, 105mm and 155mm guns were extremely useful, especially when augmented with precision equipment: 'The Precision Guidance Kit on the 155mm served as low-cost alternatives, allowed greater flexibility with battlefield geometries (low-angle fires) and was in greater supply.' In particular, artillery pieces could be moved more easily than GMLRs to create different trajectories of fire. While an enemy position might be initially protected from fire by a covering building or structure, the US forces became adept at moving their artillery pieces in order to achieve an optimal angle of fire: 'Fighting the urban canyon fight, the gun target line had to be perfect in order to get the projectile in there to get effects. If it wasn't perfect, we had to resort to something else.'[56] In Grozny, the Russians had employed mass, attritional fires, still broadly consistent with Chuikov's doctrine at the battle of Berlin. In Mosul, by contrast, coalition artillery was employed for precise fire missions against individual targets, identified positively and cleared for collateral damage. The trajectory of the rounds was organized carefully in order not only to have maximum impact, but also to avoid unnecessary civilian casualties and destruction.

In Mosul, suicide vehicle-borne IEDs were the priority target for the coalition; airpower struck these vehicles as they attacked, and eventually the coalition sought to destroy the production system. However, the coalition also targeted another major element of ISIS infrastructure in the city: checkpoints. 'The way ISIS projected infantry was not what you or I would expect; their Command and Control was not typical.'[57] In order to defend Mosul, ISIS established a series of checkpoints throughout the city, manned by about three or four dedicated ISIS fighters, 'the party faithful'. These checkpoints initially controlled the population; they were a vital part of the security mechanism. As the battle for the city started, they provided a more explicitly military function. As ISIS reinforcements entered the city, the new troops were passed through the checkpoints. At each checkpoint, recruits' paperwork was confirmed, they were provided with bread and water and given instructions and orders. A US officer serving in Iraq at the time gave a hypothetical example of how a checkpoint might function to feed battalions into combat: 'The security mechanism was used to move uneducated forces to check points. If Battalion A was coming up the road, the checkpoint would be told to move it up the road and told not to talk to Battalions B and C.' Checkpoints were critical to ISIS's control of the battle, then, but they were also a weak point: 'ISIS enablers and vulnerabilities were the same' because ISIS 'could not project forces further than their security apparatus'. Consequently, once the coalition had understood the significance of these checkpoints, it began to strike them: 'If you destroy the checkpoints or the security system it takes longer for them to move troops. Then, we jammed communications. That further confused them. If forces were confused and isolated, we were able to kill them.' In the course of the battle, artillery became increasingly important for destroying ISIS's security infrastructure in the city: 'Initially, operations in Mosul involved air-based fires: drones. As we developed a more nuanced approach, we went more surface to surface.'[58] In addition to being unaffected by the weather, artillery could also suppress ISIS fighters in Mosul, stopping them from moving and firing, rather than simply destroying buildings themselves.

Indirect artillery fire has played a crucial role in recent urban battles, striking precise targets in the deep. However, direct fire cannot be ignored as a feature of recent urban battles. Direct fire has, of course, always been important in siege or urban warfare. In order to breach a city and its defences, it is necessary to destroy enemy walls and fortifications. Traditionally, this was always the function of artillery. Ultimately, no attack on a city could be mounted without massive quantities of artillery firing directly in support of the infantry. In Stalingrad, the German Sixth Army found armoured 'Sturmgeschütz' (a tank with a short-barrelled gun) to be indispensable when squads assaulted buildings. Similarly, at the battle of Hué in February 1968, marines employed M-48 tanks and

ONTOS tracked vehicles, armed with recoilless rifles, to knock down walls and suppress North Vietnamese Army soldiers in the Citadel.

Direct fire has continued to be critical to urban combat to this day. It is probably the type of firepower that has changed least over the past 100 years. Even now, tank and artillery crews fire over their open sights at targets at extremely close range, as they did in the Second World War. The battle of Marawi may be the best example of direct urban fire. During that battle there were many scenes reminiscent of twentieth-century warfare. The level of firepower used by Filipino forces was staggering. For instance, one company from 2nd Infantry Division employed 10,000 mortar rounds in three months. Eventually, the Filipino forces developed a systematic approach, gradually constricting and weakening the insurgents with firepower:

> In each sector it located and then isolated the militants by arranging forces or fire effects around their position, then constricted them by shifting soldiers or fire effects inwards, and finally eliminated them with explosive firepower followed by infantry assault. The evolved SLICE approach was slow and deliberate; attack on each building planned in detail.[59]

Direct firepower became very important in this fight. For instance, the Filipino forces used 105mm pack howitzer artillery pieces in the direct fire role. The guns were brought up to the front line, positioned in buildings or on their roofs, packed in place with sandbags, and then fired at targets at an extremely close range 'to penetrate the thick concrete walls' with 'infantry platoon leaders directly liaising with the gun crews'.[60] The effects were devastating; defensive walls were breached for attacking Filipino troops, while the insurgents inside were disabled or killed.

Of course, although artillery and tanks have often provided the most devastating direct fire in urban combat, infantry weapons constitute the most common, immediate and probably the most important firepower in the close urban battle. Machine guns, automatic rifles, grenades, grenade launchers and pistols have long been an integral part of street fighting. Indeed, the expenditure of small arms rounds in the urban environment is always very high, as combatants struggle for position at close range. However, although it is very difficult to prove, it seems likely that the amount of small arms fire now used in urban warfare has increased. Contemporary military doctrine suggests that consumption rates for small arms ammunition 'can be between 4–6 times greater' than in open terrain.[61] It is also noticeable that both insurgent and state forces are much better armed today than they were in the past. This is especially true for urban guerrillas, who, in the twentieth century, were often disadvantaged by poor weaponry. Marighella and his colleagues were lucky if they possessed a few rifles, submachine guns and grenades. By contrast, 'the Comando Vermelha is generally better organized, better funded, and better armed than the government. It uses its machine guns, grenades, and antiaircraft weapons to both combat and corrupt the forces of the state'.[62] In Fallujah, Mosul, Bint Jbeil and Aleppo, nonstate forces were exceptionally well provisioned with heavy and medium machine guns, sniper rifles, automatic rifles, rockets, sophisticated IEDs and, increasingly, drones. In some cases, they have all but matched their state opponents in terms of firepower at the small unit level. Indeed, during the Second Lebanon War, Israeli soldiers, used to low-intensity operations in the West Bank, were shocked by the firepower which Hezbollah fighters brought to bear against them.

Of course, state forces are also far better equipped than they once were. In many cases, precisely because force numbers have declined, it has been necessary to increase the combat power of the remaining personnel. For instance, in addition to its automatic rifles, a US Army platoon of three infantry squads and one weapons squad is now armed with six light machine guns, six grenade launchers, two medium machine guns and two Javelin rocket launchers.[63] A US infantry platoon can, therefore, generate an unprecedented weight of fire with much greater range and accuracy than its predecessors. Indeed, the British Army claimed that its platoons deployed in Helmand in 2008 had forty times the firepower of their equivalents in 1939.[64] It is difficult to ascertain how such a figure was calculated. Yet, it is not ridiculous. Indeed, despite the increase in small unit firepower, the US Army is currently seeking to enhance the combat power of its units and subunits by a factor of ten. This multiplication of capability does not just refer to firepower, still less to platoon weapons, but firepower is an important part of this enhancement. The improvements in weaponry at the small unit level have created problems for state forces in cities, which demonstrates just how significant firepower has become. Armed with automatic weapons, soldiers are likely to consume their ammunition too quickly in the urban fight. Consequently, doctrine recommends:

> Small arms engagements are often conducted at very short range and involve close quarter battle or reactive shooting. They are not just the preserve of the infantry, but may be applicable to anyone operating

in the urban terrain. Ammunition consumption can quickly outstrip supply with the risk that troops become non-effective. Therefore, aimed shots and rapid fire are preferred to automatic fire.[65]

The increase in firepower at the small unit level is materially relevant to urban warfare. Precisely because close combatants are more heavily armed, it means that urban operations have become more challenging. An assault requires increasing quantities of firepower. It is difficult to attack a well-entrenched, well-armed opponent who can generate a huge volume of defensive fire. In turn, attacking forces have relied on increasingly heavy firepower in order to suppress the improved weaponry of their opponents. A self-reinforcing cycle is evident. At every level, the urban battle of the twenty-first century has become more intense. More and more firepower is being used in ever contracting areas. The increase in firepower has contributed to the deceleration of urban operations; it has encouraged forces to slow their attacks and engage in positional warfare. Rapid and ambitious manoeuvre has become too risky.

The Fire Sermon

There is currently much talk of precision fires. Sometimes this has led to the suggestion that urban warfare has become less brutal and more surgical. There is little evidence of this. On the contrary, raw firepower remains an intrinsic element of the urban battle. Although no army could now amass the huge artillery concentrations of the twentieth century, urban combat still requires vast quantities of firepower.[66] Cities in which major battles have occurred have been ruined – as they always have throughout history.

Indeed, although the amount of ordnance may have declined in absolute terms after 1945, in relative terms, urban battles today involve intense concentrations of air and artillery fires. During the battle of Berlin in April 1945, the Red Army used 35,200 artillery pieces to support a force of 2.3 million soldiers against a German defending force of 766,000; there was one Soviet artillery piece for every twenty-two German soldiers. At Mosul, by contrast, the Iraq Security Forces were supported by a battalion of artillery from 2nd Brigade Combat Team, 82nd Airborne Division, which fired 6,500 rounds, most of them precision munitions. The French and Iraqi Armies provided additional artillery support, but most of this was normal ordnance which restricted its utility.[67] Objectively, the coalition had far fewer artillery pieces than the Red Army, then; the coalition deployed about fifty artillery pieces (rocket systems and guns).[68] Yet, the coalition was opposed by a fighting force of only about 6,000 ISIS fighters. Consequently, the combat ratios were much closer than might initially be thought; the coalition had one artillery piece for about every 120 ISIS fighters. Proportionately, the Soviet army employed about six times the artillery as the coalition in Mosul. Yet, of course, the Iraqi Security Forces in Mosul also enjoyed constant close air support, which dropped more than 10,000 munitions on the city. Moreover, coalition firepower in Mosul was far more accurate and, therefore, more effective. The coalition targeted and destroyed specific ISIS strongpoints in sequence, concentrating all their fires on an objective, before moving on. It is difficult to be mathematically precise here. Yet, relative to the size of the forces and in the light of the accuracy of the munitions, it is probable that as much firepower has been used in recent urban battle as ever – and probably even more.

Consequently, the urban battlescape of the twenty-first century is distinctive.[69] In the twentieth century, mass firepower was applied inaccurately to the urban area in general; cities were struck by destructive but blunt air bombardments or artillery barrages. Many buildings were damaged or destroyed which were not immediately involved in the defence of the city. The cities themselves were, then, the target.

Today, coordinated firepower from both air and artillery has condensed onto specific locations within urban areas. The targets are in the city. Sometimes, especially when Western forces are involved, these fire missions have been very precise indeed. Yet, even when other forces, such as the Russians, have prosecuted these attacks, strikes have congregated on specific targets. The Russians no longer use firepower as they did in Grozny; in Ukraine and Syria, they have sought to strike identified targets. In those targeted areas, the amount of fire is truly staggering. The result is that, from the perspective of fires, the urban battle has changed. It no longer consists of broad swathes of blind destruction, sweeping across entire cities; it is no longer a conflagration. Rather, infernos have erupted in particular neighbourhoods. Air and artillery have struck from a distance, while direct fire support and small unit weapons have engaged their enemies at extreme close range. Typically, these firestorms have exploded around the walls that mark the siege fronts inside cities today. For the soldiers and civilians operating in the streets, the wider topography of urban battle has been irrelevant. Just as in the twentieth century, they have been imprisoned within a terrifying blitz. Yet, although the personal experience of an urban battle may not have changed, the battlescape itself is quite different. Barrages, destroying everything in their path, have been replaced by localized furnaces, where fire from air and artillery has descended with a previously unachieved intensity. The bombardment has been replaced by the precision strike.

8

Swarms

Fractal Manoeuvre

Since the early 2000s, scholars have become very excited about a revolution in urban tactics that they see as reflecting the transition to a more fluid global era. Eyal Weizman, for instance, has been prominent in this respect. His work on walls around Jerusalem was discussed in Chapter 5. However, he has also observed the appearance of putatively new forms of urban manoeuvre in the twenty-first century. Previously, mass, citizen armies engaged in lineal frontal warfare. The battle-lines in Stalingrad, for instance, traversed the whole city. For Weizman, the Euclidean geometries of the twentieth century have been displaced. Military forces have now dispersed throughout the city and have begun to execute complex, nonlinear manoeuvres. Urban operations have become quantum.

Weizman examines the Israeli Defence Force, especially in the period 2002 to 2006 during the Second Intifada, when it carried out major operations against Nablus and Jenin in the West Bank, and when it was under the influence of Shimon Naveh's Operational Theory Research Institute (OTRI). Shimon Naveh is a prominent Israeli military scientist who has produced a number of important writings, including a highly influential book about network warfare, *In Pursuit of Excellence: The Evolution of Operational Art*, published in 1997. On the basis of his work, Naveh had set up the OTRI as a military think-tank, which informed Israeli military doctrine, training and education. Somewhat unfeasibly, Naveh began to interest – and some would say bewitch –

senior officers in the IDF in contemporary continental philosophy, including works by Jean Baudrillard, Gilles Deleuze, Félix Guattari, Georges Bataille and Guy Debord. Naveh sought to postmodernize Israeli military theory. Instead of thinking of combat ratios, firepower and front lines in traditional terms, Naveh encouraged officers to contemplate the virtual and cognitive dimensions of warfare, dislocating the perceptions of their enemies, rather than just blowing them up. He advocated a hyperreal approach to warfare for a postmodern age.

Naveh's work is of immediate relevance to urban warfare – and especially urban manoeuvre, because, as Weizman writes, for him, 'urban warfare is the ultimate postmodern form of warfare'.[1] Naveh asserted that 'belief in a logically structured and single-track battle plan is lost in the face of the complexity and ambiguity of the urban mayhem'.[2] The multidimensionality of the global city has defied traditional unidirectional military methods. In a lecture in 2004, Naveh replaced existing military concepts with new Deleuzian terms supposedly more adequate to this reality. His central point was that, against 'Formless Rival Entities' (i.e., Palestinian insurgents), 'fractal manoeuvre' was necessary. By this, he meant nonlineal, noncontinuous, noncontiguous tactical actions, conducted by dispersed military swarms; operations should be fracted.[3]

Weizman suggests that the battle of Nablus in 2002 demonstrated Naveh's postmodern theorizing in practice. At Nablus, Israeli paratroopers did not mount a conventional lineal assault of the city, clearing it block by block. Instead, they engaged in swarm tactics: 'Instead of linear, hierarchical chains of command and communications, swarms are polycentric networks, in which each "autarkic unit" (Naveh's term) can communicate with the others without necessarily going through central command.'[4] 'Walking through walls' was key here.[5] In order to penetrate the insurgent strongholds in Nablus, the paratroopers moved through buildings and houses themselves, smashing and blasting 'mouseholes' through interior walls (see Figure 8.1).

The IDF also employed 'fractal' manoeuvres in Palestinian refugee camps, including Balata. As one Israeli officer noted: 'We completely isolate the camp in daylight, creating the impression of a forthcoming systematic siege operation . . . [and then] apply fractal manoeuvre swarming simultaneously from every direction.'[6]

Weizman has been perhaps the most prominent proponent of the idea of fractal manoeuvre in the urban environment. However, he is not alone. Rejecting traditional forms of urban attrition, retired US Marine Lieutenant General Paul van Riper has advocated a concept of decisive

Figure 8.1: Mouseholing
Source: Lance Corporal Dalton Swanbeck, U.S. Department of Defense
gallery.

manoeuvre in the urban environment that 'penetrates gaps in enemy defences'.[7] Moreover, other Israeli scholars have been impressed by the evolution of urban tactics. In their work on urban operations in the Second Intifada, Eyal Ben-Ari and his co-authors describe a changing urban topography, which exceeds the lines and fronts of the twentieth century. 'Bubbles' of noncontiguous, evanescent military action have taken the place of static positions and battle-lines:

> In place of unit cohesion at the centre of the organizational structures, we would posit the importance of modular units and task cohesion . . . This conceptualization should be coupled with a move from imagining units as concerted formations that are usually concentrated territorially toward an idea of a much more dispersed set of 'bubbles' operating in separate (if adjacent) territorial cells. In other words, we suggest the shift of sociological analysis from linear warfare to one that is much more networked and dispersed.[8]

For Ben-Ari, military forces in the twenty-first century operate as interconnected swarms, moving freely and independently through the urban space in small flexible subunits.

Mouseholing

The vision of urban warfare proposed by Naveh, Weizman and Ben-Ari is seductive. According to them, manoeuvre has been liberated. It is exciting to think that military forces have transcended the temporal and spatial limitations of twentieth-century warfare and can now flow freely through cities. The brutal attrition of Stalingrad has been superseded by rapid, decisive, frictionless strikes. Flexible, flowing tactics seem appropriate for the complexity of globalized cities. At an intellectual level, the concept of fractal manoeuvre is also highly convenient. Many scholars have been deeply impressed by the concepts of postmodernism and postmodernity. Twentieth-century rationalism has been replaced by a relativistic society, in which traditional racial, ethnic, gender, class and sexual hierarchies have been subverted. According to the Polish sociologist Zygmunt Bauman, we are living in an era of liquid modernity.[9] Consequently, many scholars want to see postmodernism wherever they look. For military scholars, influenced by these currents of contemporary thought, Israeli actions in Nablus in 2002 conveniently proved their point; their cognitive biases were affirmed. Just as the metropolis has become postmodern, so has urban warfare.

Although it is difficult not to share these scholars' enthusiasm, it is, unfortunately, very doubtful that urban manoeuvre has become fractal over the last decade or two. Indeed, the claim is easily disproved. For instance, while the Israeli paratroopers' use of mouseholing in Nablus was certainly noteworthy, it cannot be claimed that it was remotely new. On the contrary, mouseholing is an old and, indeed, ancient military tactic. In fact, it was a technique used by Israeli fighters themselves more than fifty years before Nablus. When 600 guerrillas from the Irgun Gang assaulted Jaffa during the War of Independence in 1948, they used the technique extensively. The Irgun attacked Jaffa on 26 April 1948 and, after six days of fighting, dislodged the Arab defenders. In the course of the battle, the Jewish guerrillas mouseholed through buildings in order to advance on Arab defences: 'Using pick and sledgehammers, the men would create "mouseholes" through the houses, with the outer walls providing natural cover until they reached Arab lines.'[10] After two days of labour, the Irgun had carved 'two jagged parallel "aboveground tunnels" through blocks of houses' and were in a position to mine and, then, seize the Arab strongpoints.[11] Apparently, the Irgun were already engaging in Deleuzian postmodern manoeuvre in 1948.

The Irgun's use of mouseholing at Jaffa was striking, but the guerrillas were anything but original in their use of this method of urban

manoeuvre. In December 1943, during the Italian Campaign of the
Second World War, the 2nd Canadian Brigade was ordered to seize
Ortona, a large town on the Adriatic coast south of Venice. The town
was held fiercely by German paratroopers. The 1st Battalion Loyal
Edmonton Regiment, supported by the Brigade's Tank Regiment, led
the attack. Exploiting the firepower from their tanks and field guns,
the Canadian infantry advanced house by house. However, they were
eventually blocked by the main avenue, Corso Umberto:

> Failing in their attempt to outflank the enemy by striking up the Corso
> Umberto I, the Edmontons reverted to their former practice of work-
> ing forward house by house. Having to get from a captured house to
> the next one forward, without becoming exposed to enemy fire along
> the open street, produced an improved method of 'mouseholing' – the
> technique of breaching a dividing wall with pick or crowbar, and taught
> in battle-drill schools from 1942 onwards. Unit pioneers would set a
> 'Beehive' demolition charge in position against the intervening wall
> on the top floor, and explode it while the attacking sections sheltered
> at ground level. Before the smoke and dust had subsided the infantry
> would be up the stairs and through the gap to oust the enemy from the
> adjoining building.[12]

The 2nd Canadian Division used the same technique to clear Groningen
in the Netherlands in April 1945. Mouseholing was a widespread practice in urban combat in the mid-twentieth century. 'Walking through
walls' is by no means a twenty-first-century tactic.

In fact, mouseholing was already a common feature of urban warfare
well before the twentieth century. It was, for instance, used extensively by the French Army throughout the nineteenth century. Marshal
Thomas-Robert Bugeaud's celebrated essay, *La Guerre des rues et des
maisons* (*The War of Streets and Houses*), discussed the technique with
great clarity. Having personally commanded the suppression of urban
insurrections in Algiers in the 1840s, Marshal Bugeaud was a leading
French practitioner of urban warfare. *La Guerre des rues et des maisons*
was a distillation of all the methods he had learnt during those operations. Much of the work discusses how to pacify riots with minimum
force. Yet, at certain points, he claimed the army had to be prepared
to assault the insurgents' barricades. These fortifications posed a very
significant tactical problem, for it was impossible to approach them in
the traditional columns used in the field.[13] Consequently, Bugeaud recommended more complex tactics that involved firing on the barricades

from concealed positions while approaching them obliquely. It is at this moment when mouseholing became highly effective:

> Some barricades are too strong to be cleared by infantry. Then, one penetrates in the first building on two sides at the start of the street, and this is where the petard is very useful because it attains the objective quickly; one climbs to the top floor and pierces successively through the partition walls, in order to arrive at the barricades. Once this has been achieved, the infantry in the houses which overlook the barricade can kill defenders with gunfire.[14]

For Bugeaud, mouseholing enabled his troops to outflank insurgent barricades by covert, oblique, vertical manoeuvre. Even in 1848, troops were exploiting the three-dimensional urban space.

Indeed, mouseholing is even older. In 431 BCE, at the very beginning of the Peloponnesian War, when the Theban soldiers marched into Plataea in an attempt to take control of the city, the Plataeans devised a counterstrategy:

> They became aware that the Thebans were not there in great force and came to the conclusion that if they attacked them, they could easily overpower them ... They decided therefore that the attempt should be made, and, to avoid being seen going through the streets, they cut passages through the connecting walls of their houses and so gathered together in numbers.[15]

Moving through their mouseholes, they struck the Thebans at night and expelled them from the city.

The historical evidence is very clear. Although Israeli paratroopers were ingenious in Nablus in 2002, the practice of 'walking through walls' cannot be claimed as evidence of some new technique of urban manoeuvre. Soldiers have been 'swarming' through buildings for as long as they have been engaged in urban and siege warfare. It is the most effective way of advancing in an urban environment when the streets themselves are so obviously vulnerable to fire from all directions. If mouseholing is the only evidence for swarming, then we would have to conclude that fractal manoeuvre is not new.

Close-Quarters Battle

Mouseholing is not new. Nevertheless, there have been other innovations in urban infantry tactics in the early twenty-first century that might be taken as evidence of a new form of manoeuvre: namely, 'close-quarters battle' (CQB). In contrast to mouseholing, there is a strong case to be made that CQB tactics constitute a genuine advance in urban manoeuvre. These tactics might be seen to signify a move to fractal manoeuvre.

CQB tactics are relatively new. Throughout the twentieth century, conventional urban infantry tactics developed little. From the First World War onwards, when assaulting a building, soldiers were taught simply to throw grenades into rooms and then to spray them with automatic firepower. For instance, urban combat doctrine, even in the 1990s, prescribed a method of room clearance that was exactly the same as those in 1944:

> Get in fast; fire automatic. As soon as the hand grenade goes off, rush into the room as fast as possible. The first man into the room backs quickly against the near wall where he can observe the entire room. He should engage any targets with short bursts of automatic fire.[16]

There was no significant innovation of urban tactics among the regular infantry in the twentieth century; things began to change only in the early 2000s. At this point, conventional infantry started to become interested in CQB tactics in response to increasingly urbanized operations. In the West, this move was led by the United States, whose troops were struggling to manage in the cities of Iraq and villages of Afghanistan. The battle of Fallujah in 2004 was a key moment here, when the US Marines recognized that their infantry was ill-prepared for urban combat. A rapid series of innovations followed, as regular infantry began to adopt CQB techniques. The dissemination of CQB is now quite widespread. European countries have followed the US closely. As a result of their experiences in the West Bank and Gaza, the IDF has also adopted CQB tactics, as have India and the Philippines.

CQB is a specialist technique of moving through buildings. It was developed in the 1970s and was bound up with the emergence of the Special Operations Forces at that time.[17] Following the Munich Olympic crisis of 1972 (when Palestinian terrorists broke into the Olympic village, took hostage and killed eleven Israeli team members) and the rise of international terrorism, Western governments began to develop specialist counterterrorist units capable of conducting hostage rescue missions. Between 1972 and 1976, Western Special Operations Forces units developed new methods of assaulting buildings, planes and ships in order to eliminate terrorists while minimizing the risks to their hostages. These methods of rapid entry and precise marksmanship became known as close-quarters battle. They were most famously utilized in the SAS's assault on the Iranian Embassy in London in May 1980.

Precision is the central element of CQB. Soldiers must fire accurately in order to kill terrorists without hitting their hostages. The principal skill in CQB is therefore marksmanship. Since the 1970s, CQB training has always involved intense range-work to improve the accuracy of soldiers' shooting. However, while accurate shooting is imperative, assault squads have to get themselves into positions in buildings and structures, so that they are able to shoot accurately without themselves first being killed or wounded by their enemy. CQB, therefore, also involves a method of manoeuvre, which enables soldiers to move stealthily, smoothly and safely through a hostile urban environment. It is relatively simple to move through a building as an individual. However, this is far more complex for a squad. The urban environment poses a quite different challenge to the field: 'Urban areas present an extraordinary blend of horizontal, vertical, interior, exterior, and subterranean forms superimposed on the natural relief, drainage, and vegetation.'[18]

Urban manoeuvre has to overcome two central problems. First, buildings necessarily channel assault teams down corridors or stairwells, separating them as the squads clear rooms individually. Even more than in the field, the squads can quickly become separated and dispersed, unable to see or hear one another. The urban environment breaks up regular combat formations, therefore, and generates role-turbulence among the assaulting force; individual soldiers may find themselves at any position in the assault squad performing a suite of tasks. Furthermore, while open warfare demands dispersion of troops in order to mitigate the effects of firepower, troops involved in urban combat are necessarily forced to operate in confined spaces in close proximity to one another, increasing the chances of physically interfering with each other (bumping into or knocking each other over) or injuring each other. It is exceptionally easy for assault troops to point or fire weapons at each other as they move around the constricted urban space with patently serious implications.

Second, room clearance is a complex tactical problem; threats are multiplied at every point. In open warfare, an infantry platoon is typically tasked with eliminating a small enemy position usually consisting of a bunker or a trench. In conventional combat, there is, therefore, a single threat (a position) or a few closely contiguous ones (two or three positions), which are neutralized by the selection of one option by the platoon commander. Urban combat inside buildings is quite different. In any building, there are numerous rooms, each of which may contain enemies, booby-traps or civilians; corridors and rooms lead off in unseen directions from which it is possible to be enfiladed. Stairwells, cellars, attics and furniture can all conceal dangers. An assault team is presented with a taxing collective action problem, then. In each building and in each room, soldiers have to identify all the threats, prioritize them in terms of their relative danger and assign team members to their neutralization. CQB consequently demands high levels of coordination within the teams so that threats are neutralized quickly, without the need for excessive discussion.

CQB tactics have reduced the problem of urban manoeuvre through the development of a repertoire of drills that enable teams to move quickly through buildings together. For instance, one of the most common drills is the 'five-step entry'. This is the basic CQB drill and refers to entering a room. Once inside a building, infantry squads break up into smaller groups, called 'stacks'. A stack refers to the line made by a group of about four soldiers as they wait alongside walls to enter a room; the soldiers literally 'stack' up by the door. In the five-step entry drill, the stack lines up by the door and, on a signal, enters the room. The first soldier clears the near corner, the second the back of the room and the blind corner, followed by the others until they stand in the 'dominant position' in the room. The method has been proven as the best way to clear a room.

The five-step entry is the basic CQB method, but CQB tactics involve an extensive repertoire of established manoeuvres. There are established drills for rooms and buildings of every type, which soldiers or marines follow together and which can be adapted for a variety of contingencies. Consequently, the most professional CQB troops, and above all the Special Operations Forces, have refined their drills to such a point that, in the face of almost any structure, assault squads resort to a set drill that they have already conducted in training. Ultimately, expert assault teams will develop a comprehensive repertoire of collective drills for stairwells, corridors, T-junctions, left and right junctions, square, oblong and L-shaped rooms. At this point, drills become so ingrained that every member of the assault team can perform any of the functions of the stack: 'Baseline knowledge of the

Figure 8.2a, 8.2b and 8.2c: Close-quarters battle:
the five-step entry method

techniques and fundamentals is common to all.'[19] Since every soldier operates to the same pattern, individuals can initiate a drill on seeing a threat, knowing that their teammates will respond automatically.[20] This collective flexibility – based on ingrained procedures – is regarded as essential for success; when these highly trained teams encounter an unusual structure or threat, they are best positioned to respond to it – they simply apply or adapt the appropriate algorithm. One team member will initiate a drill, to which others react in predetermined ways. Ironically, the tactical flexibility of the assault team relies on collective drills inculcated through endlessly repetitious training. As a result, squads or stacks adopt a highly distinctive posture, advancing steadily forwards together while looking carefully through the sights of their raised weapons, as they scan the rooms and corridors for threats. Stacks flow through buildings, 'rolling' past each other, 'popping' doors and corners smoothly.

CQB tactics have involved a new method of manoeuvring through urban terrain. Its choreographies are very distinctive. They might not be quite what scholars have in mind by swarming or fractal manoeuvre, as they are very controlled and careful. Yet, CQB represents an important tactical innovation at squad level. Infantry soldiers now move through buildings differently from their twentieth-century predecessors; stacks flow into and through buildings. Certainly, these stacks seek to be faster, more precise and more mobile with these tactics.[21]

Swarming

Close-quarters battle tactics are new for infantry squads. They constitute a novel method of urban manoeuvre, even if this is not precisely the equivalent of swarming. However, in recent decades, there is some evidence that, on occasions, military forces have employed tactics in cities that might genuinely be described as 'swarming'. Here, swarming involves rapid, dispersed, simultaneous action by autonomous small units.[22] Military swarms are seeking to achieve the same objective, but manoeuvre quite independently against their enemies to achieve it. Swarming is perhaps most obvious among light infantry. In the first battle of Grozny, Chechen swarms inflicted heavy casualties on Russian attackers. The Chechens had approximately 6,000 fighters in Grozny in 1994, organized into hunter-killer squads of about 20–30 fighters, armed with AK-47s, rocket-propelled grenades, explosives and, sometimes, heavier weapons. These squads were assigned sectors of the city to defend that they knew intimately and in which they were free to move at will. The Chechens had no artillery or airpower and, consequently, the problems of fratricide were minimized. The squads were instructed to wait until the Russian columns had advanced into the city centre before mounting their attacks on a pre-designated signal. At this point, the squads engaged the Russians from rooftops and upper storeys, but they quickly manoeuvred around their sectors inside and between buildings, through conduits, tunnels and sewers. In short, the Chechens engaged in very effective defensive swarm tactics. A very similar strategy was adopted by Hezbollah during the Second Lebanon War, especially in the town of Bint Jbeil.[23] The Lashkar-e-Taiba's attack on Mumbai in November 2008 could also be described as swarming. The attackers (Pakistan-based Islamist terrorists) dispersed into small groups, normally of two fighters, and, over the following four days, attacked major tourist and commercial sites in the centre of Mumbai.

It is not only insurgent fighters who have employed swarming tactics, though. In Baghdad, between 2003 and 2008, the US Joint Special Operations Forces Command adopted a strategy that might be described as swarming, although it was certainly a highly specialist and unusual variety of it. Almost every night, Special Operations Forces teams descended on precise locations in the city to kill or capture Al Qaeda leaders, and to seize evidence on the terrorist network. Simultaneous raids often took place in different parts of the city on the same night, all coordinated from the headquarters in Baghdad. The teams inserted unpredictably, appearing suddenly out of the darkness, and then extracted rapidly, often by means of stealth helicopters. Of course, the Special Operations Forces conducting these raids employed CQB tactics, flowing through buildings and structures to their targets. Assisted by night vision goggles, digital locators, satellite radios and laptops, these raids seem to have embodied precisely what theorists like Naveh or Weizman meant by 'fractal manoeuvre'.

It is clearly far easier for insurgent forces, especially when they are defending their home cities, or for highly equipped Special Operations Forces to adopt swarm tactics. It is much harder for conventional heavy state forces, concerned with casualties and fratricide, to manoeuvre through an urban area. Nevertheless, since the early 2000s, state forces have occasionally conducted rapid, deep raids and penetrations into cities, even if these actions do not constitute genuine swarming tactics. The most famous raids of this type were the US Army's 3rd Infantry Division's 'thunder runs' into Baghdad in April 2003. The 3rd Infantry Division served as the leading attack formation during the invasion of Iraq, reaching the outskirts of Baghdad in early

April. The original plan was for the Division simply to besiege the city and wait for the regime to collapse. However, the commander of 2nd Brigade Combat Team, Colonel David Perkins, decided that the Iraqi Army and Fedayeen fighters were sufficiently close to capitulation that it was worth attempting an attack on them in the capital itself. On 5 April, the Abrams tanks of the 1st Battalion 64th Armored Regiment advanced in a column up Highway 8 to the airport, engaging Iraqi fighters ferociously for most of the route. On 7 April, the 2nd Brigade mounted a second thunder run, with the entire formation attacking with a view to reaching the Republican Palace itself in the heart of Baghdad. The aim was not merely to raid, but to stay in the city. The attack was a deep penetration of the city on a single axis. As with the first run, the velocity of the attack was startling; the column moved at about forty-five kilometres an hour.[24] In order to ensure that the attack force seizing the Republican Palace could be resupplied and reinforced, the 2nd Brigade secured three key motorway junctions on Highway 8, code-named Moe, Larry and Curley, where there was intense fighting, especially at Curley, where US troops were nearly overrun, even as the rest of the 2nd Brigade was engaged in heavy combat at the palace (see Map 8.1). On this second thunder run, four discrete 'bubbles' of combat developed across Baghdad. The actual battle assumed a fracted geography.

Today, Western forces remain actively interested in the potential of urban swarming. The British Army provides an interesting example here. Since withdrawing from Afghanistan, the British Army has been engaged in a series of reforms to ready itself for new, higher-intensity operations. The introduction of a Strike Brigade has been a signal development here. This Brigade is a medium-weight, mechanized force equipped with Boxer wheeled infantry fighting vehicles and Ajax tracked reconnaissance vehicles. Both Boxer and Ajax vehicles are able to travel and support themselves at significant range – 1,100 and 500 kilometres respectively. Strike Brigade has developed a concept of employment in which not only will it deploy at great range, but its subunits themselves will also disperse widely, congregating only at decisive points. Since 2017, Strike Brigade has been testing this concept of dispersed fighting. Although the concept of strike is most applicable to the field, this Brigade has also been exploring the possibilities of dispersal in the urban environment. For instance, in 2018, it conducted an urban planning exercise followed by a virtual, simulated urban exercise. The Strike Brigade has not used the term swarming. Yet, it is clear that the idea of dispersing in the urban environment and exploiting the speed

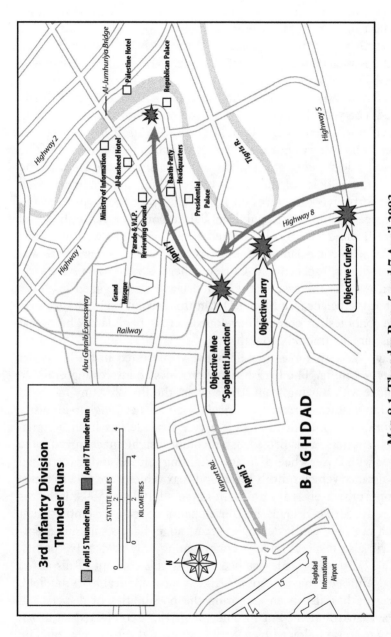

Map 8.1. Thunder Run, 5 and 7 April 2003

Source: Reproduced with permission from Michael R. Gordon and Bernard E. Trainor, *Cobra II: The Inside Story of the Invasion and Occupation of Iraq* (Pantheon, 2006), xxv.

and mobility of its vehicle is a form of swarming. The Strike Brigade may be engaging in fractal manoeuvre.

The Return of the Siege

In the early twenty-first century, it is possible to identify certain tactical innovations – close-quarters battle, thunder runs, Special Operations Forces, the Strike Brigade – which might be taken as examples of swarming. These cases are deeply interesting in themselves and are not to be dismissed. Nevertheless, although not completely artificial, these examples do not seem to be particularly representative of contemporary urban operations. On the contrary, these moments of mercurial manoeuvre seem to be the exception rather than the rule. The basic reality of urban warfare in this century has not been rapid manoeuvre, but, on the contrary, slow attrition. Rather than liquifying and accelerating, urban warfare has coagulated and slowed in the last two decades.

A consideration of the sheer length of today's battles illustrates the point; urban battles have become very long indeed. Although the Stalingrad campaign lasted from August 1942 to February 1943, when the German Sixth Army surrendered, the battle for the city itself burnt out in late November after the Soviet encirclement. The greatest urban battle in history, therefore, lasted less than three months, from September to November 1942. Other major twentieth-century urban battles were similarly short – and intense. The battle of Manila lasted a month (February to March 1943); the battle of Berlin, two weeks (April to May 1945); the second battle of Seoul, six days (September 1950); the battle of Hué, one month (30 January to 3 March 1968); the battle of Khorramshahr, two months (September to November 1980).

The contrast with more recent urban battles is marked. The battle of Mosul lasted nine months, from October 2016 to July 2017; the battle of Aleppo, four years (2012 to 2016); the battle of Marawi, five months (May to October 2017); the battle of Donetsk Airport, six months (July 2014 to January 2015). It might be thought that, because far fewer forces fought in these battles than they did in their twentieth-century equivalents, and state forces often fought against relatively weak irregular forces, they would have been concluded much more quickly. Yet, on the contrary, urban battles, which were completed in weeks in the twentieth century, now take months or years. This is significant. Urban warfare in the twenty-first century rarely involves rapid manoeuvre, but rather a grinding war of position.

The deceleration of the urban battle seems paradoxical. We have entered an age of unparalleled communication and travel. Data moves around the world instantaneously, people and goods very quickly. Some weapons are also able to traverse the world extremely fast. Paul Virilio, the French cultural theorist, has claimed, for instance, that long-range ballistic missiles have accelerated the pace of war; it is now possible to destroy cities in seconds.[25] For him, war has become instantaneous. Yet, while communications may indeed have accelerated in globalized postmodernity, the inconvenient truth is that urban warfare has gone in the other direction: it has actually decelerated. It is not conducted on digital time; it is neither immediate, nor rapid. On the contrary, it has resumed the form of ancient warfare; the siege – conducted at glacial pace, rather than lightning speed – has returned. Some observers have noted this development: 'When looking at the conduct of warfare since the end of the Soviet Union, one thing becomes very clear – the siege is a defining feature of modern warfare across the globe.'[26]

There are a number of reasons why the urban battle has actually decelerated in the early decades of this century. The topography of the city has become more complex; combatants are better armed with more lethal weaponry. Casualties have also played a key role here. In the twentieth century, it was assumed that casualties in urban fighting would be very high. In Stalingrad, for instance, between 21 August and 17 October 1942, the German Sixth Army suffered 40,068 casualties and probably more than 100,000 before the Soviet counteroffensive in November – over 25 per cent of its overall strength.[27] Its combat divisions engaged in urban fighting suffered even more grievously, however, probably losing more than half their personnel in Stalingrad. In the 1990s, the US army calculated that a rifle company of 100–120 soldiers could take a defended city block in about twelve hours, but only by suffering a 30–45 per cent casualty rate.[28] In other words, a city block consumed the equivalent of one infantry company as an effective fighting force per day. These figures are now much disputed and some scholars have claimed that, in fact, urban combat in the twentieth century was not necessarily much more costly than combat in the field.[29] During the battle of Manila, for instance, even though they enjoyed a numerical superiority of only 1.5:1, the 37th Infantry and 1st Cavalry Divisions incurred 780 killed and 4,700 wounded, a casualty rate of about 20 per cent, while they killed 16,665 Japanese defenders.[30] Nevertheless, no one would deny that urban combat typically involved very heavy casualty rates.

By contrast, it is very noticeable that casualty rates in the last two decades have not approached their twentieth-century levels. During the second battle of Fallujah, between 8 November and 7 December 2004, a US force of 13,000 suffered 63 killed in action and a further 535 wounded: a casualty rate of less than 4 per cent for the whole force.[31] Of course, casualties were concentrated in combat companies where the rates were higher. Yet, the 1st Marine Division, which commanded the battle and provided most of forces, was never close to losing a company. During the battle of Mosul, the Iraqi Army lost many more. As noted in Chapter 1, officially, 1,400 Iraqi soldiers were killed and 7,000 wounded, but the casualties were probably much higher; perhaps 15,000. Yet, 94,000 soldiers were involved in the operation, so the overall casualty rate was far lower: between about 10 and 15 per cent of the whole force. Casualties were certainly heavier in the leading combat units. For instance, the Counter-Terrorist Service reportedly incurred a 50 per cent casualty rate; fourteen of its battalion commanding officers were killed in the fighting.[32] Yet, even the Counter-Terrorist Service's heavy casualty rate was much lower than traditional averages. In the course of the entire battle of nine months, it approached a casualty rate which, in the twentieth century, would have been expected in one day of urban fighting. Similarly, in the battle of Marawi, the Filipinos incurred heavy losses in their Special Operations Forces companies at the front of the fight. Nevertheless, in comparison with the twentieth century, casualty figures in urban operations today were much lower.

The reduction in urban casualty rates is not because urban warfare is now less dangerous. Rather, it is primarily because, knowing that they have very limited numbers of troops, political leaders and commanders have been much more cautious in their approach to urban operations. They no longer have the mass armies of the twentieth century, and the small, often professionalized forces at their disposal are too valuable to waste. Even for an authoritarian regime, there would be serious political consequences to catastrophic casualties. Although Assad, for instance, was not concerned about civilian casualties, he was careful to protect his own quite limited forces. Consequently, commanders have tried to preserve their force, preferring slower, more deliberate but, therefore, safer operations, to the bolder, riskier attacks that often characterized twentieth-century urban battles. Mosul took nine months precisely because Iraqi generals did not want to expend their forces unnecessarily. The armed forces may, therefore, dream of fractal manoeuvre, and in exceptional circumstances it may be possible, but faced with the prospect of high casualties, they have almost always preferred measured, attritional attacks.

Significantly, although Weizman announced a radical transformation in urban manoeuvre when he discussed Nablus, he himself eventually acknowledges the attritional character of urban warfare today. He notes that while paratroopers in Nablus infiltrated cunningly, Israeli troops in Jenin were far less successful. They engaged in a costly, traditional block-by-block clearance. In the course of these clearances, the Golani Brigade's 51st Battalion was ambushed and a company commander and twelve soldiers were killed. In all, the Israeli Defence Force lost twenty-three personnel in the battle: 'The professed effortless "smoothness" of the raids on Balata and Nablus must be compared with difficulties, "striation" and physical destruction that IDF attack brought on Jenin.'[33] The illusions of fractal manoeuvre were further exposed during the Second Lebanon War. Then, the IDF initially deployed small, light infantry forces that tried to manoeuvre against Hezbollah strongholds. They were easily repulsed in almost every case. For instance, at Bint Jbeil, an important town near the border, Hezbollah defenders employed advanced weaponry against the IDF infantry from fortified positions; they killed nine Israeli soldiers, wounded many more, and repelled the attacks.

Israeli experiences in Jenin in 2002 and Southern Lebanon, especially at Bint Jbeil, demonstrate a vital point about urban manoeuvre in the twenty-first century. It may be possible to engage in sophisticated urban infiltrations when the enemy is weak or surprised, or when the purpose of a mission is only to raid. Yet, when the objective has been to seize and clear an urban area, driving out the enemy in its entirety, the utility of swarming tactics has become extremely questionable. This is especially true when the enemy has been organized and well equipped. In recent urban battles, Sunni and Shia militias, Hezbollah and ISIS have used advanced weaponry. In Iraq, for instance, Shia insurgents eventually used explosive formed projectiles (EFPs) – IEDs that penetrated even the thickest armour of Abrams and Challenger tanks.[34] Some insurgents in Iraq were not mere guerrillas; they were hybrid, state-backed militias. The thunder runs in Baghdad in 2003, which have sometimes been taken as an ideal of urban manoeuvre, were successful only because the Iraqi defenders were so inept. They failed to fortify their positions, thereby exposing themselves to lethal American counterfire, and their marksmanship was atrocious; they were often poorly motivated. If the Iraqis had approached the standard 1:1 loss ratio that skilled urban defenders are normally able to inflict on even well-trained opponents, they 'would have produced thousands of friendly casualties' – the outcome of the thunder runs might then have been very different.[35]

Confronting a determined, well-equipped urban enemy like this, swarm tactics have become wholly impracticable; they have only exposed the attackers. In cities, swarms are vulnerable to being surrounded, cut off and defeated in detail, as well as being struck by their own supporting fires, and being impossible to support logistically. A US marine who fought in Fallujah in 2004 summarized the point eloquently: 'If we'd gotten sexy and tried to do some manoeuvre, we would have been more exposed to the enemy.'[36] In face of an entrenched enemy, the only way to advance without suffering heavy casualties has been to grind through cities, building by building.

Indeed, more recent experiences at Mosul and Marawi throw some doubt on the utility of swarming, in general, and CQB tactics in particular. CQB tactics, designed for hostage rescue, have been shown to work very well against lightly armed opponents, who are taken by surprise in unfortified buildings; then stacks can flow freely through corridors and rooms, clearing each in turn. They were very successful during Special Operations Forces raids in Iraq, Afghanistan and Syria. However, in the heavy urban battle of the twenty-first century, subtle manoeuvres of this type have become irrelevant and sometimes impossible. For instance, in Mosul and Marawi, conventional Iraqi and Filipino troops rarely fought in intact buildings, but in ruined structures, filled with rubble and detritus. It was simply impossible to advance in stack formation in this environment. Indeed, in some cases, these tactics become suicidal. In Marawi, for instance, Isnilon Hapilon's troops and its Maute group allies had observed American CQB tactics. They learnt that stacks gathered outside doorways before making an entry. Consequently, they adopted some lethal countermeasures. As Filipino soldiers stacked outside doorways, the defenders simply fired small arms, rockets and explosives through the walls near the door. Alternatively, defenders dug small firing pits just in front of the doorway inside rooms. Knowing that attacking Filipino soldiers aimed their weapon at their eye-line as they entered the doorway (in line with CQB drills), they would be extremely vulnerable to close-range fire from below. The result was that the Filipino forces took casualties precisely because they were employing CQB tactics.[37] The irrelevance of 'sexy' manoeuvre is likely to be even more self-evident against a genuinely equal force like Russia, China, Iran or North Korea.

The battle of Mosul demonstrates the point very well. The coalition attacked ISIS simultaneously on multiple axes, overwhelming ISIS commanders. However, while the attacks took different axes, each advance was slow and deliberate. The Iraqis did not engage in fractal manoeuvre. Indeed, on the only occasion they advanced rapidly, they suffered a terrible defeat. In December 2016, Iraqi forces pushed rapidly forward to take the Al-Salam hospital, but failed to clear all the terrain behind them: 'They captured Salam hospital by directing a focused offensive and pushing through for over a mile, not consolidating gains but using momentum to capture as much territory as possible.'[38] They were counterattacked by ISIS fighters hidden in uncleared rooms, reinforced by others who had infiltrated through tunnels or the rubble; about 100 Iraqi soldiers were surrounded. By the end of the day, at great loss, the Iraqi forces had lost all the ground they had gained, suffered heavy casualties as well as losing twenty vehicles.[39] The Iraqis consequently adopted a different approach:

> Iraqi assaults were linear: a block or two and then back-clear. Our fires destroyed Iraqi designated targets and allowed them to move forward with the support of joint fires. The approach was lineal on a micro-scale. Maybe we could get them to change their tactics? No. Once they decided to move in a certain way, we embraced them and supported what worked for them.[40]

In Western Mosul, where the streets were narrow and the topography complex, the Iraqi forces had to adapt their tactics again: 'It became a geometry exercise.' In particular, instead of attacking buildings frontally, it was necessary to attack the angles and the corners of the building obliquely.[41] Nevertheless, this refinement of Iraqi tactics did not alter the fundamental fact that the battle was a painstakingly slow process. In Mosul, the Iraqi forces engaged in slow attrition, seizing and clearing the city block by block in a series of limited operations, followed by a back-clear and fortification of the area they had just taken.

In urban warfare, manoeuvre is dead and positional warfare – the siege – has returned. The central military problem of urban warfare today is not how to move, still less how to swarm, but rather how to breach, clear and hold heavily fortified buildings and neighbourhoods. In place of a rapier thrust, urban warfare has become a process of long, slow boring. The use of tanks and heavy armour in recent urban battles convincingly demonstrates this reprise of positional warfare. The tank had originally been designed to break the shackles of positional warfare on the Western Front. It was the original and archetypical weapon of manoeuvre. In the 1930s, major military figures, such as J. F. C. Fuller, Mikhail Tukhachevksy and Heinz Guderian, advocated massing tanks for deep operational manoeuvre. Indeed, although it was more by accident than by design, the Wehrmacht demonstrated the potency of the mass armoured strike during the battle of France in 1940.[42] Twentieth-century military doctrine confirmed that tanks were designed for manoeuvre operations in the field, not combat in towns. From the 1930s to the very end of the Cold War, the tank retained its role as the shock arm of land forces, designed for and dedicated to manoeuvre and deep strike. The Gulf War represented the apotheosis of manoeuvre warfare. Against weak opposition, thousands of American and British tanks charged across the desert to outmanoeuvre Iraqi forces. The US 24th Mechanized Division, for instance, advanced more than 300 miles in four days, obliterating any Iraqi opposition in its path.

In the twentieth century, the tank was *the* weapon of the field. Although the infantry always claimed the title, armour became, in fact, the queen of the battle. In the twenty-first-century urban battle, it has retained its centrality. However, its role has been inverted. In cities, it is no longer the dominant weapon because of its speed; manoeuvre has become irrelevant. The tank has become indispensable in urban operations because its armour provides unique levels of protection, while its main gun and co-axial machines guns provide vital direct fire-support. Armour is no longer the modern equivalent of cavalry. On the contrary, it has become the siege engine of the postindustrial age. The tank – often paired with the armoured bulldozer – is the contemporary battering ram, siege tower, catapult, tortoise and mantlet combined in a single weapon.

In the mid-twentieth century, military forces were officially some-what sceptical about the use of tanks in urban environments. Narrow streets seemed to preclude their deployment. The US Army's 1939 and 1941 *Field Manual 100-5* discussed urban operations only briefly, suggesting a rather pessimistic view of the role of tanks in towns and cities. The urban battles of the 1940s demonstrated this to be false. Nevertheless, even in the twenty-first century, the urban utility of armour has often been severely underappreciated by the armed forces themselves. Distracted by the original function of the tank, some mili-tary personnel have continued to deny their importance in the urban battle, which they maintain is primarily an infantry fight; after all, only infantry can get into and clear rooms. Before the thunder runs of April 2003, for instance, US commanders were 'afraid of exposing tanks to street fighting'. Yet, on the first thunder run, on 5 April, although every single vehicle was struck by at least one rocket-propelled grenade, not one was put out of action.[43] Urban battles in the early years of this century confirm the absolute requirement for heavy armour against any significant enemy. In the first week of the battle of Sadr City in March 2008, US forces employed Stryker armoured vehicles, which, protected against small arms fire, some rockets and smaller IEDs, had proved effective in periods of lower intensity. In the first week of the battle for Sadr City, though, their vulnerability was demonstrated clearly: six were destroyed. They were replaced by Abrams tanks and Bradley armoured vehicles: 'Stryker armoured vehicles lacked lethality and survivability compared with available tank and mechanized forces . . . Strykers could not equal M1 tanks.'[44] The IDF made a similar discovery in their operations in Gaza. During Operation Protective Edge in 2014, when the IDF conducted a limited strike and clearance operation in Gaza against Hamas militants, even moderately armoured vehicles proved vulnerable. Seven Israeli soldiers were killed in an attack on an M113 armoured personnel carrier. The conclusion was clear: 'Thin-skinned vehicles have no place on or near today's urban battlefield.'[45]

Tanks have proved essential for the siege conditions of contemporary urban warfare because they fulfil four vital functions; mass, protection, firepower and mobility. As force numbers have shrunk, tanks have mitigated the reduction in mass. This is particularly the case in the urban attack. In the past, combat power was often provided by sheer weight of numbers. This is a major problem today because armies have shrunk dramatically. As the number of soldiers has diminished, the armed forces have sought to offset this loss through increasing the weight, firepower and effectiveness of the units they deploy. In the urban battle, although the sheer numbers of personnel have declined, the density of the remaining combat forces has increased. Small numbers of infantry are now supported by much more armour.

This rebalancing of the force has been very evident in recent urban operations. For instance, in Basra, the UK eventually deployed a tiny force into the city – a battalion of about 600 soldiers. They were able to survive only because they were mounted in heavy Warrior armoured vehicles and supported by Challenger tanks. The battle of Sadr City demonstrated a similar point. The 1st Battalion 68th Armor Regiment and 1st Battalion Stryker Regiment provided the direct combat power for this operation. This force consisted of about 2,000 combat troops, but it was a very heavy force of Abrams and Bradleys. It was able to execute the operation successfully, suffering minimal casualties. Armour has taken the place of numbers in the urban battle.

It is often argued that tanks are vulnerable in the urban environment. Tank armour is thickest at the front of the vehicle because, in the field, tanks attack enemy positions head-on. However, in cities, tanks are exposed to attack from above and the rear. This vulnerability was demonstrated very clearly at Grozny, when Chechen fighters destroyed many tanks and armoured personnel carriers from above. Recent footage from Syria shows that tanks remain vulnerable to vertical fire. Yet, despite this undoubted weakness, the tank still represents by far the best protection available and it has proved much more resilient than any equivalent vehicle in most urban battles. The tank played an important role in Mosul, protecting the Iraqi infantry from attack. As Iraqi forces advanced through the city, tanks were positioned on junctions in their flanks, physically blocking avenues of approach against counterattacks by ISIS fighters and, especially, suicide vehicles. Tanks have not been indestructible but, unlike almost any other vehicle, they have been able to remain in and, indeed, to dominate the open streets in urban combat. They have acted as semi-mobile strong points, around which attacks can be hinged. This quasi-static role has been a crucial function because, while infantry must stay off the streets, it is essential to occupy the streets so that the enemy's freedom to move is restricted.

The tank has also played a crucial role in recent urban battles as the optimal platform for direct fire support along with the artillery, as discussed in the last chapter. The modern tank is normally equipped with a 120mm gun, the equivalent of a light artillery piece. The length of the gun barrel has proved an occasional disadvantage in the urban fight since it has limited its traverse and elevation. Despite this, the tank has been recurrently able to provide heavy, accurate and rapid direct fire in support of infantry. The weapon has been employed to suppress enemy forces or to destroy specific strongholds. During the Iraq invasion, US Army tanks breached defences on a number of occasions. For instance, when the 101st Airborne Division seized An Najaf on 29 March 2003, Abrams tanks initiated the assault by breaching the walls of the Agricultural College for the air assault infantry. Unfortunately for the infantry, the tanks employed anti-tank sabot rounds, which are penetrative rather than explosive. The result was that the mousehole that they punched in the wall was far too small for soldiers to climb through. During the battle of Sadr City, American forces fired 800 tank rounds. In Mosul, the tank was constantly employed in a direct fire role.

The direct fire role is intimately related to a final tank function: mobility. Clearly, mobility here does not refer to genuine manoeuvre. Rather, it refers to the ability to breach through prepared defences in order to seize and clear an immediate objective. In the urban environment, this objective is normally a building or, perhaps, a block. In Mosul, one of the major problems was not only ISIS defences but also rubble, which obstructed any movement. It was impossible to continue the operation without clearing the streets for support vehicles and logistics. Tanks were employed extensively not only to breach defences with fire, but also to clear rubble and negotiate obstacles. Here, the armoured bulldozer, normally paired with an Abrams tank, played a crucial role. Bulldozers cleared rubble away from streets and, in some case, breached enemy defences with their blades. Indeed, so important did bulldozers become in the battle for Mosul that a senior commander claimed that they were the most useful and, perhaps, most important weapon in the coalition armoury.

The importance of tanks in the urban terrain highlights the character of the urban battle today. Tanks are no longer used in a roving role, charging *en masse* as armoured cavalry. Tanks have become the contemporary siege engine dedicated to the slow, close work of breaching and destroying fortifications, and suppressing enemy fighters so that strongpoints can be seized by infantry. Their redesignation as weapons of position demonstrates that the urban battle offers little opportunity for manoeuvre or penetration. On the contrary, the tank's role in recent battles shows that urban warfare has slowed and condensed into specific locales that are fought over intensely with massive firepower and extensive fortifications. The urban battle has concentrated into a localized war of position.

Beyond Manoeuvre

Most armed forces still aspire to manoeuvre; it has proved to be an efficient way of achieving military victory. Some scholars today would like to see flowing military manoeuvres, swarming intricately through the most complex urban terrain. Occasionally, dynamic, 'fractal' manoeuvre has been evident, when the opposition is weak and unprepared. Yet, as the urban battle has reached a higher level of intensity and enemy forces have been determined to hold a city, manoeuvre has become an illusion. It is no longer militarily possible, and attempts to manoeuvre have resulted only in heavy casualties and defeat. Once an opponent has secured an area, urban warfare has become positional. Siege conditions have set in.

At this point, manoeuvre has been replaced by the careful and difficult mission of working forward through positions in succession. Urban warfare has become a series of micro-sieges in which enemy lines have to be cleared and a small area secured, before the next assault. In the First World War, Allied forces on the Western Front had discovered by 1916 that the most effective way of attacking enemy lines was by limited bite-and-hold operations, supported by prodigious artillery bombardments. Urban warfare in the twenty-first century has assumed a similar pattern. Successful urban operations now consist of series of localized bite-and-hold operations, in which another line of defence, another building or stronghold, is taken. Unlike the First World War, these operations do not take place over a large front but, rather, in very narrow locales inside the city itself. The siege has become localized to specific neighbourhoods in the city, which are fought over in turn. In this way, urban manoeuvre – or rather the lack of it – reflects the wider topography of urban warfare today. As the previous discussions of airpower, fortifications and firepower showed, the urban battle has contracted onto small, fortified locales at which a vast panoply of weaponry from the air and ground is directed. This fire is used to support the grinding advance of heavy forces, consisting of relatively small numbers of infantry supported by increasing amounts of armour. The battlefronts of the twentieth century have been replaced by intense, localized micro-sieges on which aircraft, artillery, infantry, tanks and bulldozers now all congregate.

9

Partners

Traitors

In the twentieth century, when states were able to deploy mass armies, local partners were often of only limited utility in urban operations. In intense urban battles, state forces fought each other; they required little or no assistance from local, irregular militias or armed groups. Sometimes, especially in counterinsurgency campaigns, states employed local security forces to support their efforts. At the battle of Hué in 1968, three US Marine battalions fought alongside an Army of the Republic of Vietnam battalion. During Operation Anvil in Nairobi in 1954, when British forces cleared Mau Mau cells out of the city, local police units played an important supporting role. It was quite common in the twentieth century for armies to cooperate with indigenous security forces. However, these forces were formally recognized parts of the indigenous state apparatus. The strategy of actively partnering with an irregular militia or with other local political leaders in the city in order to prosecute a campaign was far less common. States were sufficiently powerful to secure cities by themselves or in conjunction with host states. By contrast, in the twenty-first century, partnerships with local militias as proxies or allies within the city have become all but unavoidable.

Of course, throughout history, besiegers have actively sought to exploit agents and proxies. Traitors or sympathetic citizens were frequently employed to overthrow cities. Indeed, in ancient Greece, while 'assault was rare and rarely successful', 'treason and intimidation were far more common'.[1] In his *Philippics*, Demosthenes emphasized the role of treachery in taking cities. Thus, traitors opened the gates of Mende to the Athenians in 432 BCE, and the gates of Torone to the Spartans in 424 BCE. Treachery was no less important in Roman sieges. At the siege of Syracuse during the Second Punic War in 212 BCE, Livy records how the Roman commander, Marcus Claudius Marcellus, inserted an agent into a Carthaginian delegation to bribe one of the Spanish mercenary commanders inside the city. This commander admitted Marcellus' troops through a side gate, which they were meant to be guarding.[2]

Armies have regularly sought to use partners to expedite their sieges, then. As armies have become smaller over the past few decades, it has become increasingly clear that military forces cannot besiege cities effectively. Mere arithmetic has compelled state forces to search the urban environment for partners in order to augment and amplify their own capabilities. They are simply not big enough to clear and secure metropolitan areas as they once were. At the same time, cities themselves have become far more heterogeneous. When the RAF and the USAAF bombed Germany during the Second World War, the German population was united politically and ethnically. Precisely because there was an indivisible relationship between the Nazi state and the people, the collective punishment of the people had a brutal logic; city, people and state were one unified entity. Thus, the strategy of air bombing was based on a concept of the people.[3] In this context, it was difficult to leverage a city through proxies, internal agents and partners. Yet, the globalized city of the twenty-first century is quite different. It consists of a diverse, heterogeneous population which is often closely inter-related with external diasporas and other cities. It is never isolated from these external connections. Consequently, not only do military forces increasingly depend upon informal, paramilitary or civilian partners to support them, but the extended, diverse metropolis of the twenty-first century presents them with extensive opportunities to find partners and allies. Proxies, agents, allies, partners – and traitors – have always played a role in urban warfare, but the special topography of the contemporary urban battlescape has invested them with renewed significance.

Twentieth-Century Partners

Proxies and agents may have been a less significant feature of urban warfare in the twentieth century. However, there were a number of highly pertinent examples when state forces relied on partnerships with local forces to achieve their goals. The siege of Beirut in 1982 involved an infamous case of partnering of this type. After the Six Days' War in 1967, the Palestinian Liberation Organization (PLO) was initially forced to relocate to Jordan until, in 1970, King Hussein expelled the organization. The PLO moved to Lebanon and settled in the Beirut area, mainly in urbanized refugee camps at Sabra and Shatila; its headquarters remained in the city. The PLO became a major belligerent in the Lebanese civil war that started in 1975, fighting against Christian militias. The UN brokered peace in 1980, giving the PLO its own administrative area in the south of the country. However, the PLO began to mount a campaign against Israel from its southern territories, which escalated in 1981. On 3 June 1982, Shlomo Argov, the Israeli ambassador in London, was shot in the head by three terrorists, one of whom was a Syrian intelligence officer. This action precipitated a major intervention by Israel into Lebanon, against both the Syrian army and the PLO.

The IDF assaulted northwards along the coast against the PLO, and inland along the Lebanese Ridge and the Beqaa Valley against the Syrian Army. Although the terrain was difficult, the IDF defeated the Syrian Army in the east and the PLO on the coast so that, by late June, the IDF enveloped Beirut, in which the PLO was trapped. The IDF had no experience of urban warfare and depended upon the Christian Phalangist forces in Beirut, commanded by Bashir Gemayel, to force the PLO into surrender. The Phalangists refused to attack the PLO though. An assault would be resisted by the Druse and Muslim militias in the city. The IDF were forced to besiege the city instead. In August and September, they mounted intense artillery and airstrikes, followed by ground assaults on the airport in the south and across the Green Line in the east to squeeze the PLO. These bombardments caused heavy civilian casualties. The IDF also suffered significant casualties: 88 killed and 750 wounded. Nevertheless, the PLO were eventually expelled from Beirut. The siege was, in military terms, a success.

However, the entire campaign was marred by infamous massacres at the Sabra and Shatila refugee camps on 16 to 18 September 1982. Having initially refused to help the IDF, the Christian Phalangists retaliated against the PLO after their leader Bashir Gemayel had been assassinated. Their attacks allowed the IDF to enter west Beirut. At the same time, the Phalangists also entered the Palestinian refugee camps to carry out a revenge massacre of 700 Palestinian civilians. It is unlikely that the IDF colluded directly in this atrocity. Indeed, the Israeli cabinet was always anxious that the Christians would take revenge on Palestinian civilians. Nevertheless, the IDF had formed a partnership with the Phalangist militias and so, while they might not have been formally accountable for the massacre, they bore some responsibility for it. The fact that the Phalangists and the IDF were cooperating was widely known. The massacres severely tarnished the reputation of the IDF.[4]

The siege of Beirut in 1982 was a twentieth-century battle; it was conducted by a large conscript army consisting of eight and a half divisions (about 78,000 soldiers), using mass firepower. Yet, it also provided a pre-emptive insight into urban operations of the twenty-first century. Beirut was a large and heterogeneous city, which by the late 1970s was divided between the Christian Phalangists militias in the east and the Muslim and Palestinian factions in the west. These militias were themselves numerous. The Phalangists estimated there were ninety militias, mostly Druse and Muslim, in the city. The IDF's relationship with the Phalangists was an augury of the future. Yet it was not unique.

Proxies also played an important role in the second battle of Grozny in 1999–2000. As the Russians refined their approach to urban operations after the disaster of the first battle, they became attuned to the possibilities, and even the necessity, of partnering with local forces. In particular, the Russians employed a local warlord, Beslan Gantemirov, as a political ally in the 1999–2000 battle. Gantemirov had been nominated for the the Chechen presidency after the removal of Dudayev in 1996. However, he was found guilty of embezzling state funds and was given a six-year sentence. He was pardoned by President Yeltsin in 1999 and appointed as head of the Chechen State Council. His militia, many of whose backgrounds were dubious, subsequently played a crucial role in the second battle for the city. Although they were not entrusted with heavy weapons, they were armed by the Russians and often acted as the spearhead for the Russian offensive. Unlike the Russian troops, they had political legitimacy, local knowledge and hated the Islamicist rebels. Their high casualties of about 700 fighters demonstrated the important role they played.

Ramadi

Beirut and Grozny were the first indications of the renewed importance of partners in urban warfare. Almost every urban battle of this century has affirmed the role of local, indigenous, often irregular allies and partners. Partnering with local militias became very important to the US forces during the occupation of Iraq and especially as the campaign reached its crisis in 2006–7. There are several early examples of partnering in Iraq at this time. However, there is little doubt that the US operations in Ramadi in 2006, and specifically the Anbar Awakening, provide the most pertinent and decisive example of the use of proxy forces during this campaign.

The 1st Armored Brigade Combat Team (the Ready First) of the 1st Armored Division, under Colonel Sean MacFarland, was deployed to Iraq in early 2006, initially to Tal Afar. It was then redeployed to Ramadi: 'The Ready First Combat Team entered Ramadi with a confidence and optimism that flowed from their four months of success in Tal Afar following the city's famous turnaround by McMaster's unit.'[5] However, Ramadi was a far tougher prospect. It was a much larger city than Tal Afar and the insurgency was much worse there. From July 2005 to June 2006, the 2nd Brigade, 28th Infantry Division, a National Guard Unit from Pennsylvania, had had a torrid time in the city: eighty-two soldiers were killed during the tour. A police recruitment drive had started in January 2006, but this had stalled after a series of Al Qaeda strikes. In addition, following the assassination of Abu Masab al-Zarqawi, the Al Qaeda leader in Iraq, by a US airstrike on 7 June 2006, Al Qaeda retaliated against US and Iraqi forces. For instance, on 24 July 2006, they staged attacks against fifteen targets in the city in thirty-two minutes, one of which killed the Ready First Brigade's adjutant.[6]

Al Qaeda's July counterattack was a major threat to the US. However, it also proved to be an opportunity because it began to convince local Sunni leaders that they could not cooperate with Al Qaeda. The jihadists were murdering their people and undermining tribal hierarchies. For instance, in September, local tribesmen were killed defending Jazeera Police Station, when Al Qaeda detonated a massive fuel truck bomb. On the same day, Al Qaeda killed an important sheikh, who had been cooperating with the US forces and in whose area the police station was located. Al Qaeda had deliberately hidden the sheikh's body so that he could not be buried within twenty-four hours, according to Islamic custom. It was the final insult for Sunni sheikhs and an immediate catalyst for the Awakening.

Sheikh Sattar Abu-Risha was the first Sunni leader to decide to break with Al Qaeda and realign himself and his militias with the US. He was followed by others. Colonel MacFarland recognized the importance of the Sunni tribes and leaders like Sheikh Sattar to the success of his operations in Ramadi. He simply did not have enough troops to secure the city alone, and the Iraqi security forces were similarly insufficient in number or reliability. Consequently, and in the face of considerable

American consternation, MacFarland made a momentous decision in September 2006: 'Let's pick a horse and back it ... Let's back the sheikhs in Anbar. They're all we've got to work with.'[7]

Although MacFarland, as commander, took the leading role, he worked closely with a small group of subordinates in his brigade. There were a number of officers in the Ready First Brigade who played an important role here. Lieutenant Colonel Tony Deane, one of the battalion commanders, and the deputy brigade commander, Lieutenant Colonel Jim Lechner, were vital in cultivating this relationship with the tribes. Lechner, for instance, procured the money and authorizations from the Ministry of the Interior to train and equip the Awakening fighters. Lieutenant Commander Jocko Willinck of SEAL Team 3 helped with the training and support of these auxiliaries. One of the brigade's interpreters, Sterling Jensen, also had a close relationship with the Sheikhs. Finally, much has also been made of a junior staff officer in the headquarters, Captain Travis Patriquin. Officially, Patriquin was initially assigned an important but minor staff role. However, a fluent Arabic speaker with extensive operational experience having served in Afghanistan and in Tal Afar under Colonel McMaster, he also made an important contribution to the Awakening.[8] MacFarland, Deane, Lechner, Willinck, Jensen and Patriquin formed a very close relationship with Sheikh Sattar and the other sheikhs in Ramadi.

Colonel MacFarland and his subordinates quickly realized that the Iraqi police were the crux of the problem in Ramadi – and in Iraq more generally. Although there were many Al Qaeda terrorists operating in Ramadi, the most serious challenge was everyday crime, corruption and uncertainty. The insurgency and Al Qaeda's terrorism thrived in this environment. Al Qaeda could be defeated and the insurgency quelled most effectively by the introduction of a reliable police force in Ramadi. Yet, the establishment of a legitimate and competent police force had proved impossible. The young men in the Sunni tribes, many of whom were in the militias, actively opposed the police, whom they saw, not unreasonably, as an arm of the Shia-dominated Iraqi state. Al Qaeda also targeted police recruitment, and any volunteers placed themselves and their families at great risk. In addition, once they had been recruited, policemen were normally deployed away from their local area. Because they did not know these new districts, they were less effective and they worried for their safety of their now unprotected families.[9] A possible solution for Ramadi lay in encouraging sheikhs to allow their young men to volunteer for a local police force, in their own neighbourhoods. These recruits had every interest in securing their own streets

This is the Sheik with his militia. Militias are bad.. "But they just protect my
family and tribe.." Says the Sheik. "Let's have Chai.." (In order to protect their
families, many young men have resisted joining the Iraqi Army, because they
might be sent elsewhere in Iraq while the security suffers in their home areas.
Iraqis hate even the thought of their family suffering while they're gone. Come
to think of it, Joe feels exactly the same way..)

Figure 9.1: Captain Patriquin's stick-man presentation
Source: Selected slide from Captain Travis Patriquin's
PowerPoint presentation
(https://abcnews.go.com/images/US/how_to_win_in_anbar_v4.pdf).

since their families lived there. Moreover, precisely because they were
already members of their own communities, they had an incompara-
ble understanding of the neighbourhood. Locals identified foreign Al
Qaeda fighters instantly. In effect, Sheikh Sattar and MacFarland's plan
was to convert tribal militiamen, some of whom had been responsible
for the deaths of US soldiers, into local policemen.

It was a risky plan. Multinational Command-Iraq, under General
Casey, had formally rejected the proposal. However, MacFarland
continued to develop and promulgate a local Ramadi police plan. He
sought to explain the strategy to his own commanders at the Marine
Expeditionary Force Headquarters and the higher chain of command
in Baghdad; some officers 'were adamantly opposed to building new
police stations in tribal areas, fearing it would lead to generating de
facto tribal militias'.[10] As MacFarland began to get permissions from his

superiors, Patriquin was given the job of trying to explain the new strategy to his staff counterparts in other units in Anbar. MacFarland had
humorously suggested that Patriquin's presentation had to be simple
enough so that marines could understand it. To this end, Patriquin
developed a now famous power-point presentation consisting of seventeen slides (see Figure 9.1). The stick-men cartoon depicted a complex
process.

The presentation documented the difficulties that US troops faced;
they did not know Ramadi and were weighed down with 80 pounds of
equipment. They could not be helped by Iraqi soldiers, who were hated
locally as part of Prime Minister Maliki's Shia regime. Consequently,
normal local people were being intimidated by terrorists and radicals,
whom the coalition forces found it impossible to identify. The slide
show then introduced the local sheikhs who had been excluded by the
coalition up to that point. It was recommended that the militiamen be
retrained and redesignated as local police, under the authority of the
sheikhs. The presentation concluded with a slide showing all the sheiks,
US and American soldiers, local Sunnis and local policemen happy
– with only the insurgents sad: 'Everyone wins! Except the terrorist
(which is ok because terrorists suck).' The slide show is a rather evoca-
tive artefact from a difficult period. However, it proves the importance
of the partnering strategy that MacFarland's brigade enacted in Ramadi.

On 24 September 2006, MacFarland and the sheikhs approved a
charter they had been negotiating, announcing a change of strategy publicly. The new alliance was demonstrated in the following months. Al
Qaeda fighters had been mortaring one of the US Army's main forward
operating bases in Ramadi, Camp Corregidor, for weeks. However,
after the Awakening announcement, Sheikh Jassim, an important tribal
leader in Ramadi and close associate of Sheikh Sattar, declared war on
the mortar teams on 28 September, after they had kidnapped some of
his tribesmen. He erected four checkpoints to interdict the Al Qaeda
mortars. Later, on 25 November, Al Qaeda mounted a major and final
assault against Sheikh Jassim and his Abu Soda tribal militia in Sufiyah,
a district located on a blunt peninsula south of the Euphrates, known as
the shark's fin. Al Qaeda broke through two checkpoints in the south
of the area before encircling Jassim and his fighters at his own house,
who, in danger of being overrun, radioed 1st Brigade's Headquarters
at Corregidor. The headquarters immediately assigned drones, F-18s,
armour and riverine forces to relieve Jassim. As night fell, it became
difficult to distinguish Abu Soda militia from Al Qaeda, since the fighting was at such close quarters. It consequently became impossible to

support Jassim with airpower; they were in immediate danger of being massacred. However, Captain Patriquin, who was watching the battle from the Tactical Operations Centre, suggested to Jassim in Arabic that they wave rags, cloths or flags above their heads so that the surveillance drones could see them. These were picked up by the UAVs. Hornets were instructed to fly low over them and strikes from Paladin howitzers were called in on Al Qaeda positions. Al Qaeda began to retreat as US armour arrived. The battle of Sufiyah cemented the Awakening, leading to the defeat of Al Qaeda in Ramadi.

Following the battle of Ramadi, the Bush administration agreed to the now famous surge in Iraq. General David Petraeus was appointed as Commander of Multinational Force-Iraq and was charged with implementing the population-centric counterinsurgency strategy laid out in *Field Manual 3-24*. There is little doubt that the new techniques outlined in this volume played an important role in ending the conflict in Iraq (at least temporarily). However, the Anbar Awakening and the alliance of US forces with local Sunni militia played a pivotal role in the US successes in 2007. Indeed, this partnership strategy was disseminated across Iraq in 2007 as a central element of the surge. Later, General Petraeus, for instance, declared that he was willing to negotiate even with leaders who had American blood on their hands.[11] It was a comment that would probably have been impossible without actions of the Ready First in Ramadi.

Operation Inherent Resolve

Ramadi was the first time in Iraq when the US formally partnered with local, irregular forces in order to secure a city. The battle against ISIS in Mosul has only affirmed the centrality of partnered and proxy forces to the urban warfare, though the form it took there was quite different from Ramadi. In Mosul, the US Army did not primarily partner irregular forces but, rather, the Iraqi Army itself, which provided almost all the ground forces. By chance, Lieutenant General Sean MacFarland was the Commander of Operation Inherent Resolve until August 2016. Having experienced their significance in Ramadi in 2006, he affirmed the indispensability of proxy forces in the fight against ISIS. The US Army was simply not big enough to commit itself to every urban operation:

> In Mosul, there were two million people in the city. The US Army has 1.2 million soldiers in it. How much of that do you want to consume, when you have so many other battles? It makes sense for us to provide

support air, fire, counter-fires, intelligence. That is much better than providing the infantry.[12]

Clearly, there were some obvious advantages to partnering with the Iraqi Army. It minimized US casualties, gave the operation political legitimacy, and strengthened and improved the Iraqi Army. However, a partnered operation of this sort was also intricately complicated. The combat and local political advantages that might accrue from the use of partnered forces could be exploited only by careful negotiation and diplomacy. These difficulties were compounded in Mosul by the sheer size and complexity of the battle.

Before Mosul, MacFarland had commanded the recapture of Ramadi from ISIS in early 2016. He contrasted the operations. Ramadi was a much smaller city on which there was little intelligence. Ramadi was a difficult fight, but Mosul was a 'horse of a different colour': 'It was three times larger, was very diverse and it had an old and a new part.'[13] Significantly, the location of Mosul immediately created political difficulties for the US partnership with the Iraqi Army. Mosul was close to the Green Line, north of which the Kurdish Peshmerga forces held sway: 'There was no love between the Peshmerga and Iraqi Security Forces.'[14] Consequently, 'bringing the Iraqi Security Forces into play required much negotiation with Barzani [Masoud Barzani, President of Kurdistan Region]'; 'I assured the Kurds that there would be Americans with every ISF unit north of the Green Line.'[15]

Because of its complexity and size, Mosul had to be a deliberate operation: 'In Ramadi, we had taken what we had and built the airplane in flight. In Mosul, we knew this would not work. We could mount the operation only after we had trained the Iraqis in combined armed tactics and equipped them.' Experienced primarily in counterinsurgency, the Iraqi Security Forces struggled to get into the city; 'they lacked the training and the equipment'.[16] Consequently, the Iraqis were trained by US mentors and reinforced with bulldozers, tanks, line-charges, air support and obscuration fire to clear paths through the minefields. In addition, US mentors physically accompanied their Iraqi units into battle. They were able not only to encourage them morally but improve their liaisons with coalition airpower, artillery and casualty evacuation. Accompanied Iraqi troops were far more combat effective: 'The key was accompanying ISF at battalion level. That was a game changer. When you talk about advise and assist, if you add *accompany* to that, you also get assurance.' Indeed, the process of increased combat power was self-reinforcing:

Once we had the authority to accompany, the coalition forces on the ground had to be well-protected. And so we were authorized to provide more protection, like artillery support. So we established US and French Firebases near Mosul and we were able to use Attack Helicopters – all of which added to the combat multiplying effect. All of these enablers became available once we had the authority to accompany.[17]

At the same time, American mentors embedded within units in Mosul itself were able to supervise and report upon their activities in the city. So the coalition was protected from the kind of dangers that the IDF discovered in Beirut in 1982. However, the coalition was not divested of all difficulties in this area. The Iraqi Army was a formally partnered force; it was the Iraqi state's official military. There were many other irregular militias in Mosul though, some of which were loosely allied to the coalition and acted as quasi-proxies for them. Kurdish forces, Shia militias, the Iranian Republican Guard Corps and the Badr Brigade all fought in the battle: 'Some of these were doing the right thing.' Others were 'shades of grey'.[18] There were further complexities. The federal police were nominally an official state security force. Yet, the influence of Shia or pro-Iranian forces was not always clear. 'Were they truly Iraqi? They were led by figures connected to the Badr Organisation', a semi-sectarian force in which 'militia-men could don police uniforms and mix in'.[19] The result was a delicate, political and diplomatic problem. General MacFarland had to manage partner, proxy and independent military forces: 'Trying to minimize the effect of Shia militias in Sunni cities required a lot of engagement with other actors.'[20] The coalition sought to harness these militias in a very loosely coupled alliance dedicated to the defeat of ISIS in the city. The relationship between unrecognized, nonstate militias was carefully bounded and required constant vigilance. For instance, although the coalition might cooperate at a distance with these forces, they could not offer fire support to them:

In regards to the Shia militias, I couldn't provide them with fire support. However, I could support the Iraqi Army and, even if a militia were near them, they might benefit. The bottom line is that we developed a process to ensure the enemy was not protected by the proximity of a Shia militia group, while remaining true to our guidance not to support them.[21]

The battles of Ramadi and Mosul are directly pertinent to the question of partnering and urban warfare. They usefully illustrate the increasing indispensability of both partner and proxy forces in urban warfare for the United States. American forces are simply not big enough to clear whole cities or to bring them under control. They have had to share their mission with local state forces, militias or proxies of some kind. However, they also show the range that partnering can take and that it is often fraught with political difficulties.

Other Proxies

In the twenty-first century, proxies have not been a uniquely American strategy. On the contrary, partnering has become a widespread, necessary, even preferred, practice in urban operations. Indeed, since the 1980s, Iran has 'perfected the use of human surrogates'.[22] The Iranian Republican Guard Corps and its Quds Force, originally conceived as a multinational Islamicist force dedicated to the liberation of Jerusalem, have played a key role in Iran's proxy policy. For instance, the Quds Force established Hezbollah in 1982, the Badr Corps in Iraq in 1983, and consolidated Muqtada al-Sadr's Shia Jaysh al-Mahdi in Iraq in 2005.[23] Each of these militias has participated in major urban battles over the last two decades.

In Syria, for instance, the Assad regime has relied very heavily on allies and proxy forces; Russian airstrikes saved the regime in 2015. Furthermore, in all the major battles to retake the cities of western Syria, proxy ground forces have played a vital role. In particular, Hezbollah and the Iranian Republican Guard Corps, and especially the Quds Force, have constituted a major part of the force. The Syrian Army consisted of about 70,000 reliable troops. It was also supported by the National Defence Forces, numbering some 50–60,000, and the sectarian militia, Shabbihah. Hezbollah, Iran and Iraqi Shia militias, like the Abu Al Fadl al-Abbas Brigade, provided about 30,000 additional forces. The regime's irregular forces were larger than the Syrian Army contingent. Indeed, by 2013, the opposition was claiming that the commander of the Quds Force, Qassem Soleimani, had more power than Assad in Syria. It was noticeable that Soleimani himself declared that 'the Syrian Army is useless'. He tried to improve its capabilities with the creation of the National Defence Forces, which may have been trained in Iraq. Because of their experience, training and motivation, these external forces from Lebanon and Iran have been engaged in some of the heaviest urban fighting. At Al-Qusayr, Hezbollah fighters led the assault.[24] Soleimani was a central figure in all this. There is little doubt that Soleimani played a major role in planning some of the ground offences. By the time of the battle of Al-Qusayr, Soleimani was directing operations. With his forces, he continued to play a significant role in the Syrian civil war until his own assassination on 3 January 2020 in a US drone strike in Baghdad. His forces performed a very similar function to what the Kurdish Peshmerga, Iraqi Army and Shia militias did for the US in its campaign against ISIS.

In the Donbas, Russia has also relied heavily on proxies. In the spring of 2014, the Donetsk and Luhansk declared themselves as separatist republics from Ukraine, as Russia seized control of Crimea. Ukrainian forces counterattacked the Donbas in July, concentrating especially on the Donetsk region. The separatist forces there were a strange amalgam of fighters from post-Soviet Russian republics. Some of these militias were effective. For instance, the Vostok Battalion from Chechnya was experienced and had potent firepower. In many cases, though, the Donetsk People's Republic Army consisted of 'ragtag volunteers, criminals and misfits'.[25] The separatist forces were commanded, and often funded, by dubious businessmen such as Igor Strelkov, Konstantin Malofeev and Alexander Khodakovsky. Consequently, facing a badly trained, ill-disciplined and disorganized militia force, the first weeks of the Ukrainian offensive were successful. Donetsk Airport fell in May in a disastrous battle for the separatists in which fifty of them were killed; other towns, such as Sloviansk, Kramatorsk and Mariupol, were also threatened.[26] By August 2014, a wedge was appearing between Donetsk and Luhansk.[27] Moscow became concerned. Although he denied doing so, Putin deployed additional Spetsnaz ('little green men'), artillery and ground forces; in all, 12,000 Russian troops augmented a local force of some 45,000. Even then, these forces struggled to regain some of the territory lost to Ukrainian forces, as the battles for Donetsk Airport showed. However, although a final political settlement has not been reached, the lines have now substantially stabilized and, in effect, Russia has annexed the Donbas. In the Donbas, a combination of Russian special forces, regular troops and heavy artillery fighting, together with irregular, local militias, has been successful.

Since the early 2000s, partnered local state, militia or irregular forces have played an increasingly important role in urban warfare. There are obvious reasons why. Urban warfare is labour-intensive and costly; while casualties have often been much less than in the most intense battles of the Second World War, they are still high. States have struggled to generate enough personnel to conduct a major urban battle on their own. As a result, they have been forced to draw upon additional support. Weaker states fighting for their own sovereignty, such as Iraq, Syria and Ukraine, have been forced to mobilize irregular troops. However, even for major powers, like the US or Russia, the use of proxy forces has become more or less the norm. Not only do even these powers lack personnel, but proxy forces have become particularly useful on operations, for which there may be limited public support. Against ISIS and in the Donbas, the US and Russia both also employed a radical model in which they provided the more sophisticated military support, such as airpower, while indigenous forces, of more or less regularity, conducted ground operations. Irregular forces have become a critical element of urban battle today. However, although they have become indispensable partners for state forces, proxies have also complicated the conduct of war very considerably, as the different interests, agendas and ethics of partners and allies have to be negotiated or mitigated. Consequently, they have actually contributed to the deceleration of urban warfare and to the rise of the localized siege. In many cases, proxy forces have their own local agendas and interests, which they prioritize; they become focused on particular objectives in the city. Moreover, even when they are capable and share the strategic interests of their patron states, their use requires extensive political negotiation. These negotiations necessarily slow the pace of urban operations. Partner forces have become an increasingly necessary part of the urban battle. They have reaffirmed its evolution towards slower, more localized sieges.

10

Rumour

The First Casualty of War

Fortification, fire, armour, and combat forces, be they regular, irregular or partnered, remain utterly central to the prosecution of urban operations. Nevertheless, while brute combat power plays the dominant role in street fighting, it would be quite wrong to ignore other less physical elements of urban warfare. In particular, in the globalized urban conflicts of the twenty-first century, the appropriation, dissemination and exploitation of information have been major concerns for all protagonists.

Information and, above all, intelligence have always been central to warfare. Commanders have to know the terrain, the location and the intentions of the enemy. Information has played an especially important role in urban warfare. Unlike campaigns in the field, urban warfare, by its very definition, necessarily involves large civilian populations. Sometimes, in the case of an insurgency or civil war, this civilian population is actively engaged in the struggle, but, at the very least, it constitutes a more or less passive actor in the fighting. In Stalingrad and Hamburg, civilians were little more than victims, but, in other urban battles, such as the Paris Commune, they became a potent agent in the struggle. The civilian population of the city is always an important audience for the belligerents. Precisely because there are so many civilians present in urban conflict, they can become critical to the outcome of the fighting. Protagonists have sought to pacify, intimidate, co-opt, recruit and mobilize them to their own advantage. Information has been an essential means of engaging with the civilian population.

Plainly, the military use of information to influence, demoralize or encourage civilians is not novel. On the contrary, besiegers and besieged have always employed information, both true and false, to leverage civilian populations in towns and cities under attack. Rumour has, in short, always been an intrinsic weapon of urban warfare. Indeed, in classical antiquity, some military commanders became adept at communicating with the civilian population. For instance, during the Peloponnesian War, Brasidas, a Spartan general, became known as a master of intimidation. He repeatedly persuaded the defenders of cities to surrender. He successfully talked Acanthus, Stagirus, Amphipolis and other cities into capitulating without the inconvenience of actually besieging them; his threats alone sufficed.[1] At the siege of Jerusalem in 70 CE, both the Romans and the Jewish partisans inside the city employed information to persuade or coerce the civilian population. For instance, having been repulsed in his first attempt to take the Second Wall, Titus called a temporary suspension of the siege, 'in the hope that they [the Jews] would be inclined surrender in view of the demolition of the second wall or through fear of starvation'. While the civilians inside Jerusalem starved, they had to watch as Titus paraded his entire army in front of the walls:

> Every yard of ground before the City shone with silver and gold, a spectacle which filled the Romans with delight, their enemies with terror. Spectators crowded the whole length of the Old Wall and the north side of the Temple and behind the walls eyes could be seen peering from every window – nowhere in the City was there an inch of ground not hidden by crowds. Utter consternation seized even the boldest when they saw the entire army assembled, the splendour of their armour and the perfect discipline of the men.[2]

However, while there is nothing absolutely new about the use of information to influence the civilian population, the role of rumour and propaganda has evolved in the global era. Some commentators and military practitioners have rightly emphasized the salience of information operations in urban warfare. They are correct to highlight its increased importance in the early twenty-first century. As cities have exploded in size and their populations diversified, the recruitment of the population has become absolutely vital to the success of any operation. Precisely because there is now an even larger civilian audience, it is essential for military forces to expend more effort in explaining the purpose and benefits of an urban operation to them. Moreover, since military forces have become so small, they are dwarfed by this civilian population. In Stalingrad, the civilian population of about 900,000 at the start of the battle was either ignored or actively targeted by German and Russian forces, which eventually outnumbered the civilians. In recent urban battles in Syria, Iraq, Gaza, Yemen, Libya and the Donbas, civilian populations have far outnumbered the armed forces fighting the battles. Consequently, as military forces have shrunk to the extent that they are unable to inundate the entire city or overwhelm the civilian population by mere mass, they have had to pay increasingly close attention to the perspectives and interests of civilians. Their interactions with the civilian population have become deeply operationally significant. Indeed, some commentators have stated that 'operational reach is proportional to popular support': 'Attackers and defenders should employ resources in the physical environment to mobilize individuals and groups to achieve operational objectives.'[3] As military forces have diminished, they have increasingly used information operations to amplify their influence in those neighbourhoods where they are no longer physically present, and to recruit civilian populations there. The informational domain has, therefore, become a salient element of the urban battlescape.

Winning the Narrative

The armed forces continue to enjoy a monopoly on the legitimate use of lethal violence. They alone have the naked combat power to attack and destroy cities. Nevertheless, a striking, if ironic, feature of military thinking over the past two decades has been the tendency of some senior personnel to diminish and even disparage the importance of traditional combat power. Instead, they have talked about the 'narrative'. Military operations are no longer primarily about seizing physical objectives, but more about 'winning the narrative': 'Strategic narratives must be fought. Defence's actions, images and words must consistently align with the relevant strategic narrative to build and maintain credibility. Maintaining the initiative will require a proactive and innovative approach. Hard-earned credibility with audiences must be protected.'[4] The armed forces can prevail not by killing, but merely by attaining informational dominance over their opponents.

Consequently, in the last decade, Western armed forces have become especially interested in the concept of 'cognitive manoeuvre' in the virtual domain. The aim of cognitive manoeuvre is not to march on the enemies' positions, but to manoeuvre in informational space,

promulgating narratives that are irresistible not only to enemy fighters but, above all, to third parties. This approach has generated some
very striking assertions: 'In the Urban Environment, the will of the
people will often be the Centre of Gravity.'[5] Winning over the civilian
population, not the destruction of enemy forces in a city, has become
the military priority. As a result, cities are now understood to consist
not only of enemy forces but also of 'audiences, actors, adversaries
and enemies'.[6] Operations in Iraq and Afghanistan demonstrated that
some enemy forces are implacable; they are irreconcilable and cannot
be persuaded by any amount of information operations. They must be
killed or captured. However, in a complex, heterogeneous city, enemy
forces will comprise only a small part of the population. The vast
majority of the inhabitants of any urban area will be far more pliable.
These population elements can be seen on a spectrum from the potentially opposed (adversaries), to the more or less neutral (actors and
audiences). Information operations and the efforts to win the narrative
aim to recruit the support – or at least the tolerance – of these large
population groups.

Of course, the emergence of digitalized global social media has
amplified the significance of information operations. It would be unwise
to underestimate the significance of news, information or rumour in
previous eras, disseminated by word of mouth, proclamation or publication in the form of notices or newspapers. Nevertheless, digital social
media (Facebook, WhatsApp, YouTube, Instagram, Twitter, Snapchat,
etc.) have plainly altered the informational landscape. In particular,
liberated from government regulation or the mediation of news companies, social media has increased the velocity of news; information
flows instantaneously from private citizen to private citizen. At the
same time, the reach of social media is unprecedented; it has become
potentially – and sometimes actually – global in its range. Social media
seems to be the purest embodiment of globalization, therefore. It has
eliminated borders and united disparate and dispersed viewers into vast,
interconnected transnational audiences.

Plainly, urban warfare has been affected by these developments.
The informational terrain has changed. This transformation has not
been lost on various commentators. Indeed, some have claimed that
warfare itself has been revolutionized by social media. These writers
adopt a cataclysmic position. David Patrikarakos's popular book, *War
in 140 Characters*, is one of the most obvious works in this emerging genre. The title of the book refers to the number of characters
originally allowed on a Twitter post. Patrikarakos is an established

journalist, who has covered a number of wars. He was working in the Donbas in 2014 when he experienced an epiphany about the contemporary character of warfare. Even as he listened to rockets and bombs striking targets in Donetsk, he was simultaneously following the war on Twitter feeds:

> I woke up and, as always, immediately checked my phone. What I saw astonished me: Twitter was reporting that Ukrainian forces had driven pro-Russia separatists from their strong hold in the nearby town of Sloviansk. The rebels were now fleeing to Donetsk, the self-proclaimed capital of the separatist enclave. Tweeted photos of the escaping convoy taken by passers-by confirmed the story. I checked the BBC and other traditional news outlets for coverage but found nothing.[7]

The experience was disorienting and forced him to reconsider his understanding of conflict. As a result, Patrikarakos declared the appearance of *Homo digitalis*, a globalized society transformed by digital social media. *Homo digitalis* has been engaged in a new kind of conflict:

> I began to understand that I was caught up in two wars; one fought on the ground with tanks and artillery, and an information war fought largely, though not exclusively, through social media. And perhaps counter-intuitively, it mattered more who won the war of words and narratives than who had the most potent weaponry.[8]

For Patrikarakos, war has become hyperreal; the prime theatre is no longer the field, but the screen. It is fought out in the hyperspace of the internet, beyond the control of states, armed forces and news agencies: 'Social media has irretrievably changed the way that wars are fought.'[9]

Patrikarakos is not alone. US political scientist P. W. Singer co-authored a book, called *LikeWar*, with Emerson Brooking that affirmed Patrikarakos's fundamental thesis: social media has transformed war. A physical ordeal has mutated into ideational struggle for narratives. Singer and Brooking certainly identify some impressive examples of the application of social media to urban conflict. For instance, in response to the attempted Turkish coup of July 2016, the Mayor of Ankara tweeted a message to his citizens: 'Retweet: everyone hit the street.'[10] The result was a mass mobilization of the inhabitants of Ankara and other Turkish cities that helped suppress the coup. Similarly, ISIS have conducted brilliant information campaigns on social media with their hashtag, #AlleyesonISIS.[11] ISIS have exploited international events, like the World Cup in 2014, partly through the use of their mobile app 'Dawn of Glad Tidings'.[12] Indeed, Singer and Brooking pointedly claimed that ISIS's psychological campaign in Mosul was a 'new sort of blitzkrieg' in which, operating in virtual space, they 'moved faster than the truth'[13] – 'viral marketing thus became Islamic State's greatest weapon'.[14] ISIS's Junaid Hussain, in particular, took the lead here, acting as a 'superspreader'.

The Israeli Defence Force is also very relevant here. During Operation Pillar of Defence in 2012, when the IDF executed a series of counterstrikes against Hamas in Gaza, they tweeted about their assassination of the Hamas leader, Ahmed al-Jabari: 'We recommend that no Hamas operative, whether low level or senior leaders, show their faces above ground in the days ahead.'[15] The IDF calibrated their campaign around the social media response to it. When support for Hamas increased on social media, the IDF reduced the number of airstrikes, while increasing their propaganda efforts.[16] According to Singer and Brooking, the narrative has become a primary objective in war, especially since 'bots', generating messages by algorithm, have multiplied the possibility for fraud, lies and misinformation.

For the armed forces and for these commentators, rumour is no longer just an inevitable element of urban warfare, but has become the prime medium and, even, the objective of conflict. Above all, unlike conventional weaponry, social media is unconstrained. It is ubiquitous, freed from the laws of physics. At the same time, it is unmediated; there is no divide between the sender, the message and the receiver. The message is injected into the target population, hypodermically and with instantaneous effects. Singer and Brooking, Patrikarakos and other writers in this genre all describe a utopian – or dystopian – war of the future in which the message has become the very medium of conflict. If the messages are convincing, numerous and fast enough, informational dominance and, thus, victory are assured.

A Sceptical Sociology of Information Operations

The image of an individualized, infinitely manipulable media audience is a troubling one. It has become particularly worrying as a result of the increasing role that 'bots' have played in disseminating false news stories in the last few years. 'Bots' refer to fake accounts linked to computers programmed with algorithms. They have rightly engendered deep concern. The fear is that bots have so colonized certain news stories with misinformation and fake news that computers are now influencing human behaviour autonomously. There is, in fact, very good evidence that the Russian state, for instance, has become adept at the exploitation of bots to influence public debate in the West. It tried to influence the US presidential election of 2016, for instance. Yet, the problem is much wider. Up to 15 per cent of Twitter accounts may be bots.[17] The concern about bots is well-founded. It is disturbing that major political processes might be subverted by artificial intelligence.

Yet, in fact, although bots have been heavily exploited by various political actors in the past decade, social media has in no way been automated. On the contrary, social media campaigns consist of three elements: leaders, bots and believers. At the apex, any social media campaign requires a committed activist group, dedicated to the cause, which has clear political goals. This core group develops a communication strategy, programs its bots, and initiates and changes the storylines in order to manipulate public perceptions. States – and their secret services – have often been involved in this process; both Russia and China have been exposed on a number of occasions. However, nonstate groups, like ISIS, have also become adept here. These human leaders have accounts with large numbers of followers. Having established a strategy, the activists have then normally employed bots to replicate, multiply and disseminate their message. The spread of bots is worrying, precisely because they have proved to be effective in their function. Yet, 'bot accounts themselves can only bridge the structural hold between networks, not completely change a narrative'.[18] Bots can only amplify, not autonomously initiate, a message.

Finally, and equally importantly, a successful information campaign requires networks of true believers who accept and promulgate the message – not only on social media but within their own faith communities on a face-to-face basis: 'Below the bot network is a group consisting of true believers without a large following.'[19] Although individuals within this network often only have a small number of followers, they have a number of weak connections to mutual contacts. The result is that a bigger network is mobilized, comprising localized communities. They are united into a homophily, which can also integrate more isolated, dispersed individuals. The weak links between the networks of believers also facilitate the communication of propaganda to external nonbelievers. Successful information campaigns rely on faith communities: 'The cohesiveness of the group indicates how a coordinated effort can create a trend in a way that a less cohesive network could not accomplish.'[20]

A sociological understanding of information operations is immediately relevant to the question of urban warfare. As forces decline and cities become larger, more heterogeneous and interconnected, information operations have certainly become more important. However, cities and their citizens are not powerless against the hypnotism of the social media. The effects of even the most aggressive propaganda have been mediated through existing social affiliations. Individuals and communities may be mobilized by messaging only insofar as the message is consistent with their collective beliefs and is then actively reinforced and enacted in immediate face-to-face interactions. The Arab Spring provides an excellent example of how established social commitments have inevitably mediated the reception narratives emanating from social media. The protests and uprisings took almost all commentators by surprise. In their enthusiasm for the movement, some commentators quickly assumed that unregulated social media had played a decisive part; it had mobilized citizens virtually. The 2011 protests in Tahrir Square in Cairo or at the clock tower in Homs, Syria, were effectively very large flash-mobs, consisting of anonymous individuals, each reacting to internet posts.

It is true that most individuals who congregated in these very large crowds did not know each other. It is also true that social media played a useful role in advertising the events and encouraging people onto the streets. Yet, it is a mistake to think that the crowds that precipitated the Arab Spring consisted of isolated individuals who simply spontaneously gathered, individually and separately, in response to posts on Facebook. On the contrary, in every case, pre-existing social groups played a leading role in mobilizing their members into action. Crowds did not primarily consist of autonomous individuals, congregating randomly, but of a conglomeration of already cohesive social groups. This pattern was very clear in the town of Dar'a where the Syrian uprising began. The rebellion in Dar'a was surprising, as this town was known for its support for the Assad regime. However, the citizens of the town rose up in 2011. Antiregime graffiti had appeared at the end of February and on 6 March pupils were arrested when more graffiti was found at a local school. Major protests followed the arrest and torture of these children; protestors were attacked by security forces and some killed. On 18 March, there was a major protest in which four more were killed and the Baath Party Headquarters was burned down.

How did a regime-supporting town turn so quickly into the first rebel city? Social media facilitated communications. Yet, the explanation of this transformation lies in the social constitution of Dar'a, which consisted of 'dense social networks, partly interlinked but not wholly overlapping with clan solidarities'.[21] In particular, four interlocking communities facilitated the protests: clan affiliations, labour migration, cross-border traffic and criminal enterprises. Most citizens of Dar'a were members of one or other of its seven major clans; discontent disseminated down through clan links. These links were themselves reinforced by the new horizontal networks that had developed between citizens who lived and worked away from the city. Because of the dire situation in Dar'a, many inhabitants had been forced to work abroad from where they could see the shortcomings of the Assad regime at first hand alongside fellow Dar'ans. Working together away from home created new groups of discontentment. These constituencies were further reinforced by emergent communities engaged in cross-border trade, which, in many cases, also involved highly integrated criminal gangs. The result was a city whose inhabitants were members of up to four overlapping, self-reinforcing social networks, each increasingly aware of the ineptness of the Assad government. For instance, when a local MP, Nasser Al-Hariri, went to see the city's intelligence chief Atef Najib to ask for the release for the imprisoned schoolchildren in March 2011, he removed his scarf. In Muslim culture, this signifies that the request cannot be refused; Najib simply threw the scarf in the bin. The story quickly disseminated across the city along the clan and economic networks, provoking widespread fury. The locus of the Syrian uprising was not, then, in social media but, instead, in the urban communities of Syria's cities, which responded collectively to events. Social media merely helped to articulate the various networks.

The role played by football fan groups, ultras, in Tunisia and other countries during the Arab Spring was the most striking example of the communal – rather than media – basis of urban action. The Tunisian uprising began in December 2010 but Tunisian ultras had already clashed with security forces in November. These ultras had cooperated with Takriz, a cyber think-tank and resistance network, for over a decade and, in street battles against President Ben-Ali, the football fans and Takriz formed the fighting core of the resistance. The ultras were well adapted to play a leading role in an urban revolution. They were a highly cohesive group with a stable membership. During the football season, they met every week to support their team. In addition, the ultras were extremely familiar with crowd dynamics; indeed, they regularly clashed with the police. Consequently, they possessed the unity, the practical skill and the boldness to initiate major street protests: 'the ultras' street battle experience helped other protestors break down barriers of fear'.[22] These ultras – not a random anonymous population – formed the urban vanguard of the Arab Spring in many countries. Their role was confined not only to Tunisia. For instance, on 25 January 2011, Mohamed Hassan, the leader of the Egyptian Ultras White Knights, led a march from the Cairo neighbourhood of Shubra; it eventually grew to 10,000 participants.[23]

The Battle of Mosul

Although the battle of Mosul involved brutal, attritional combat, information operations played an important role too. Throughout the battle, ISIS and the coalition adopted two interrelated information strategies. Both belligerents sought simultaneously to encourage, coerce or intimidate local populations, while also mobilizing international and global support for their campaign. Consequently, two narratives were observable during the battle: a local narrative for Moslawis involved in or immediately affected by the battle, and a global narrative addressing ethnic diasporas and the international community and its institutions. It is very useful to look at each informational strategy in turn.

ISIS was at the forefront of information operations in 2010s, although they always lacked military mass; between 2014 and 2017, they had a small army with no armour, little heavy weaponry and no air force. However, they offset their military weakness by intense information campaigns, which, of course, exploited the shocking potential of their humanitarian outrages. Indeed, there is evidence to show that ISIS deliberately broadcast the most gruesome methods of torture and execution, in order to intimidate local populations while inspiring would-be supporters.[24] Consequently, although outrageous, footage of drowning captives or a Jordanian pilot being burned to death had a strategic purpose.

ISIS's extraordinary seizure of Mosul, when some 48,000 Iraqi security personnel capitulated to about 1,500 ISIS fighters, cannot be solely attributed to its information operation. The Iraqi army units in the city were utterly demoralized by appalling leadership and, in most cases, were severely short of personnel. At the same time, significant numbers of Sunni Moslawis were sympathetic to ISIS, if not outright supporters of them, because of the depredations of the Shia government in the city, especially by Lieutenant General Mahdi al-Gharawi, who was accused of killing and torturing Sunnis.[25] However, ISIS's information campaign in Mosul was very influential. By the time ISIS mounted an attack on Mosul in June 2014, they had become adept at exploiting social media, and used it heavily in Mosul. There is little doubt that the notoriety of ISIS preceded them, terrifying Iraqi soldiers and Moslawis before the first ISIS fighters even arrived there. ISIS were like a twenty-first-century Brasidas. Indeed, their information campaign against Mosul seemed to have been carefully planned. In June 2012, ISIS launched a video on the internet called *The Clanging of the Swords Part 1*. An hour long, the video interspersed lectures from jihadi ideologues and violent scenes. In the next two years, Parts 2 and 3 were released, and in May 2014, just before the attack on Mosul, Part 4 was broadcast. It marked a major development in ISIS's skill: 'ISIS's media team could no longer be considered students; they were now fully professional.'[26] The video included some clever messaging that explicitly targeted Shia Iraqi soldiers in Mosul. It displayed ISIS's unstoppable power and its mercilessness towards its enemies. Yet, it also welcomed anyone who joined the jihad, including its former enemies, such as Iraqi soldiers, and foreign recruits. The sixty-minute video began with aerial footage of Fallujah, which ISIS had just conquered. As the narrator boasted about ISIS's conquests, masked jihadi columns marched past. The film then displayed ISIS fighters shooting and killing individuals in civilian dress, whom they claimed were Shia soldiers. It then switched to clips of suicide bombings, executions, sniper killings and, notably, Iraqi soldiers digging their own graves to accompanying chants: 'The Islamic State has been established by the blood of the truthful. No one will ever stand between the mujahideen and their people in Iraq after this day.'[27] At the end, the video showed hundreds of graphic murders. *The Clanging of the Swords Part 4* was watched by millions. Its message was plainly for the global Muslim *ummah*. Yet, it seemed also to be cleverly constructed to demoralize Iraqi soldiers in Mosul itself. Their fate was certain: unless they joined ISIS, they were digging their own graves, as their comrades had before them.

In addition to these psychological pressures, as its fighters approached Mosul, ISIS also activated sleeper cells in the city which informed the population of their approach, while, at the same time, they attacked and executed some state officials. It was too much for Iraqi soldiers, who stripped off their uniforms and fled. Once they had taken control of the city, ISIS imposed strict Sharia (Islamic) law on the population. Although undoubtedly brutal, the caliphate was organized and administered effectively. Much of this rule involved direct control of the population, but information, relayed through social media, was very important in ensuring ISIS's hegemony over the city. Above all, footage of executions continued to feature as a central element of its communications strategy, intimidating any possible civilian opposition. ISIS also employed traditional means of disseminating information to civilians, by means of graffiti, street signs and flags. In this way, they physically signified their dominance on every street by public symbols.

ISIS employed an information campaign to sustain its control of Mosul. As coalition forces began to retake Mosul from October 2016, they too began to engage in information operations, exploiting the potential of social media. An American officer emphasized the importance of this dimension of the battle: 'You have got to fight in the information environment as much as the fight itself.'[28] Others concurred: 'It was an integral part of the fight.'[29] This was challenging:

> For US forces to compete on the battlefield of perceptions, commanders and staffs need to go beyond traditional intelligence preparation of the operational environment and develop human matrixes that explore the demographics, cultural differences, and values of the inhabitants. Information operations must be nested in the populaces' needs and desires in the area of operations.[30]

As a result, the coalition found that traditional leaflet drops, which were favoured in the twentieth century, were simply not effective; they did not target a specific audience. Instead the coalition turned to messaging through media. Here, ISIS's own propaganda was easily turned against itself: 'ISIS really were their own worst enemy.'[31] The coalition conducted extensive information operations against ISIS, seeking to undermine its leadership and encourage civil resistance.[32] Much of this work, especially the attempts of the coalition to influence ISIS leaders themselves, remains classified. It is also difficult to know how effective these information operations were in the battle. As one commander noted, 'it is hard to tell how much the information operations achieved'.[33] However, senior US generals have suggested that aggressive information operations did influence and help undermine the ISIS leadership: 'I was very confident we were living in their commanders' minds rent free.'[34] Above all, the Iraqi security services and the coalition made a systematic attempt to divide Iraqi ISIS fighters from foreign ones, suggesting that, if Iraqis gave themselves up, they might, as nationals, be offered clemency. Here, the coalition's strategy echoed ISIS's own messaging of Iraqi troops in Mosul in 2014.

As it targeted ISIS leadership, the coalition also sought to incite the civil population. It exercised great care here, since any resistance potentially put the entire civilian population at risk. It began to communicate with resistance cells working in Mosul itself. The Mosul Battalion and the Men of Mim were the most important groups. As the battle developed, these two groups engaged in covert strikes against ISIS fighters, assassinating a number of them. Graffiti was one of the most striking methods by which they sought to undermine ISIS hegemony. The Men of Mim, for instance, sprayed the letter 'M' in Arabic script on walls. The 'M' stood for the Arabic words: Muqawama (resistance). Muaarada (opposition), and Muwajaha (confrontation). The graffiti was intended to show to the people of Mosul that ISIS could be defied. At the same time, these resistance groups defaced existing ISIS graffiti and signs. Information operations were certainly not decisive in Mosul and could not compare with the effect of 94,000 Iraqi troops supported by a fleet of airpower, artillery and tanks. Yet, it was certainly an interesting innovation.

During the battle of Mosul, both ISIS and the coalition sought to incite the support and compliance of the civilian population through the use of information. However, the information campaigns of both protagonists extended far beyond the city limits of Mosul across the global urban archipelago that has now emerged.[35] While both belligerents certainly sought to message the local population, they also sought to communicate with the international community in general and with specific constituencies in other cities across the world. Of course, ethnic diasporas have often been important here, but so have other potential allies, supporters or enemies abroad.

ISIS, of course, became highly adept at messaging a global Islamicist diaspora and in recruiting and mobilizing jihadists across the world. Consequently, while they were establishing their caliphate, they were also committed to a deep battle against hostile Islamic and Western states. They incited a series of terrorist attacks across Europe from 2014, including the attacks in Paris on the *Charlie Hebdo* offices (January 2015) and the Bataclan theatre (November 2015), the Berlin Christmas Market (December 2016) and the Manchester Arena in the UK (May 2017). In some cases, they had actively supported the attackers. The recruitment of young European Muslim women as 'ISIS brides' was one of the most interesting and, perhaps, surprising examples of its successful use of information. Despite its extreme patriarchalism, some European females were so attracted by ISIS's representation of the caliphate that they travelled to Syria in order to join the movement. They seem to have been inspired by a concept of feminine duty and submission, which, while denying them Western freedoms, offered them a social purpose and a community that they craved. In the UK, Shemima Begum was the most notorious and tragic case of this online recruitment. Born in 1999, Begum was radicalized on line and in February 2015, at the age of fifteen, she left her family home in Bethnal Green in the East End of London, a few miles north-west of the Docklands,[36] with three friends. In Syria, she married a Dutch jihadist, with whom she had three children. Her husband was subsequently killed by the coalition and all her children died of disease. She was eventually captured in a refugee camp in 2018 after the fall of the caliphate.

ISIS's deep informational battle across Europe and the West was striking. However, one of its most novel informational campaigns was directed elsewhere: the Philippines. The battle of Mosul started in October 2016 and was finally concluded in July 2017. Even as the coalition was completing operations in Mosul, it initiated a simultaneous assault on Raqqa beginning on 6 June 2017. These final battles of the caliphate became indivisibly linked to another major military operation occurring some 5,000 miles away in the southern Philippines at Marawi on the island of Mindanao. ISIS – and Al Qaeda – had been infiltrating the region for some years. Filipino security forces conducted a major operation against the Moro National Liberation Front after it had seized the airport at Zamboanga in 2013. By 2016, the ISIS-affiliated Abu Sayyaf group led by Isnilon Hapilon had formed an alliance with the Maute group. Commanded by Hapilon, militants from these groups attacked Marawi and seized important buildings in the centre of the city on 23 May 2017. The attack was deliberately intended as a global counterstrike by ISIS in response to the attacks on Mosul – and the group's imminent defeat there. The seizure of Marawi was a suicide operation whose prime purpose was to demonstrate a glorious ISIS action on global media, at the very moment of its liquidation in Iraq and Syria. Footage from the fighting at Marawi was exploited by ISIS to encourage its future supporters across the world that it was not defeated. Strikingly, combat operations in Marawi finished on exactly the same day as the fighting at Raqqa also ended: 17 October 2017. This was a coincidence, but it usefully highlighted the informational interconnectedness of these urban conflicts. In this case, ISIS actively sought to unite two urban battles in one global jihadist campaign through strategic communications.

It is easy to deplore ISIS's information campaigns, which have exploited grotesque depictions of violence, torture and murder. Nevertheless, the coalition that eventually crushed the caliphate adopted a similar informational strategy, albeit without the graphic content. While seeking to inform and mobilize some Moslawis inside the city, the coalition invested a major effort in messaging an international audience. The deputy commanding general of Operation Inherent Resolve was responsible for information and media activity during the Mosul and Raqqa operations. He described the great difficulty of orchestrating this global media campaign: 'It is a human story and there is a voracious demand. It totally changes the dynamic of the fight: the level of scrutiny you are under.'[37] Consequently, the coalition had to construct an effective narrative so that their military operations, in which large parts of both Mosul and Raqqa were ruined, were justified. It had to fight a military campaign that actually fitted this narrative. Thus, for instance, in order to mount an attack on Raqqa in the summer of 2017, the coalition had to breach the walls of the city. This was a problem: 'The ancient walls are a World Heritage site. The day we hit the wall, I went to the media to explain – "We broke it but we had to".'[38] The issue of civilian casualties was also a constant concern. The coalition had to try to minimize unnecessary deaths and collateral damage, but it also had to explain how and why such casualties were unavoidable: 'Civilian casualties matter enormously. We had to retain international legitimacy in order to have the freedom to operate. If we lost the civilian casualty argument in the media, we lost freedom of manoeuvre.'[39] One of the ways in which the coalition sought to achieve this legitimacy was by arguing that a city does not primarily consist of its buildings; they are just structures. A city is its people and, in order to liberate Moslawis from the predations of ISIS, it was necessary to fight for and therefore destroy some of the city's physical infrastructure. It was a creative but not implausible narrative. The global information campaign, explaining what the coalition was doing to states and their citizens, was critical to the operation. Wider international support, or at least consent, was vital. Consequently, it was not just a question of doing 'some information and outreach activities and then getting back to some proper chaps' warfare'.[40] The informational campaign was an integral part of the fight from the start.

This was complicated because the battle was so long. The coalition had to construct a narrative that was sustainable in the long term, despite changing conditions and many reversals in the course of the battle.

> [In Mosul], the story ebbs and flows. The battle starts, then we hit the city. Then it starts with liberation, civilian casualties, destructions, humanitarian suffering, and victory. The narrative will veer and haul

through the battle. However do you manage the media in that context? As the story evolves, you cannot go silent.[41]

In order to sustain their narrative, the coalition formed strategic relations with international media corporations: 'You've got to hit the French, Germans, Iraqis and regional – and do so all the time. You had to get all the outlets a voice. The scale is immense.'[42] Information management in Mosul was an industrial operation, therefore. Yet, despite the scale, a successful campaign also relied on personal relationships between the coalition commanders and specific journalists. These relations were cemented when the credibility of the narrative being promulgated by the coalition commanders was supported by evidence.

Mosul was not unique in recent years. Urban battles have almost always involved an important informational element. Yet, Mosul stands as a pertinent example of information operations in urban warfare in the twenty-first century. Information operations are not new; rumour, lies and propaganda have always played a vital role in siege warfare going back to Bronze Age Mesopotamia. However, a new informational battlescape is now emerging. At one level, messaging has become increasingly localized in cities, addressing specific communities and neighbourhoods most involved in the fight. At the same time, narratives have been simultaneously radiated outwards to an international audience and a transnational diaspora that are enrolled in the fight virtually. The informational geography of the urban battle today has become highly unusual therefore. Like other aspects of urban warfare, it has both concentrated on specific locales in the city and also transnationalized across the globe. When Titus tried to intimidate Jerusalem in 70 CE, he paraded his troops in front of the walls so that the despairing Jews inside could physically see them. He had one message for a single, united, captive audience. Things are now quite different. Messaging has concentrated on selected groups inside the city itself, while other narratives have addressed the global diaspora. Information operations are as much a part of the inner-urban siege of the twentieth century as the concrete walls and firepower that have defined it.

11

Armageddon

A Tale of Two Cities

Stalingrad, 13 November 1942: the German Army's 305th Infantry Division began its final assault on the Barrikady Gun Factory in the north of the city.[1] The attack began with a huge bombardment. Then the infantry advanced, supported by ten short-barrelled armoured assault guns. As part of the operation, the specialist assault engineers of Storm Company 44 from 50th Regiment attacked the Commissar's House (see Map 11.1). This building lay just east of the factory and represented a formidable obstacle. In the style of a mock castle with thick high walls and additional improvised fortifications, the Commissar's House was a U-shaped building, whose courtyard faced the German positions across the street. Surprising the Russian defenders, the storm company charged the main door in the middle of the building. They correctly surmised that not only would the flanks of the building be subjected to enfilading fire from other Russian positions, but that the occupants had also blocked the windows and doors of the wings, presuming that the Germans would assault through them:

> The pioneers and grenadiers of Storm Company 44 dashed past the entrances of the southern keep and worked their way along the inner wall of the practically enclosed forecourt, hurling grenades through windows as they went. This daring move caught Klyukin (the Russian officer commanding the defence of the Commissar's House) and his men off guard, for there were now precious few defenders positioned at

the windows overlooking the courtyard. The pioneers swiftly formed up outside the portico of the central entrance. Others, kneeling down, covered the main group by aiming their weapons at the many leering windows.[2]

The storm company broke in and, once again surprising the Russians, made their way immediately to the first floor, seeking to clear the building from top to bottom.[3] The fighting was fierce but, eventually with significant casualties, the Commissar's House was seized. However, the offensive itself had stalled and, by 25 November, the German attack into the city had culminated.

Fallujah, 13 November 2004: sixty years to the day after the attack on the Commissar's House in Stalingrad, Kilo Company, 3rd Battalion, 1st Regiment Marines (3/1 Marines) were holding the mansion complex in an area in the south-western sector of Fallujah, known as Queens, half a kilometre west of Phase Line Henry. Third Platoon were clearing through apparently quiet streets in the area, when they reached the final house on the block, a building that would become known as the Hell House (see Map 11.2). One of the corporals in the platoon described it as 'a pretty small, nondescript light yellow cement house, with a dome-shaped roof and a small second storey. In the centre of the house there was a large rotunda with a catwalk that ran around the inside.'[4] The rotunda and balcony would play a crucial role in the subsequent fight. One of the platoon's fire-teams, led by Sergeant Christopher Pruitt, approached the building. As they entered the courtyard, they found fresh human faeces in the outhouse, so they knew the building was occupied. Cautiously, the four marines in the fire-team stacked by the door and entered the foyer, to be confronted by an armed insurgent whom they shot. However, as they continued into the next room, they were attacked by an insurgent with an AK-47; Pruitt was wounded, staggering out into the street bleeding.

Reinforcements from the platoon converged on the house and another squad, led by Sergeant Bradley Kasal, re-entered the house. They reached the centre of the house, which consisted of a 'large open space with stairs on the left leading up two walls to a rooftop balcony'. The centre of the room was dominated by a skylight under the rotunda. Although the marines threw grenades into this room before entering, two insurgents 'sprayed the large room with AK fire from the skylight above'. Two marines were wounded; one was trapped in the room. The rest of the platoon attempted a rescue, but two more were wounded by a grenade. 'By now all of Third Platoon had converged on the fight,

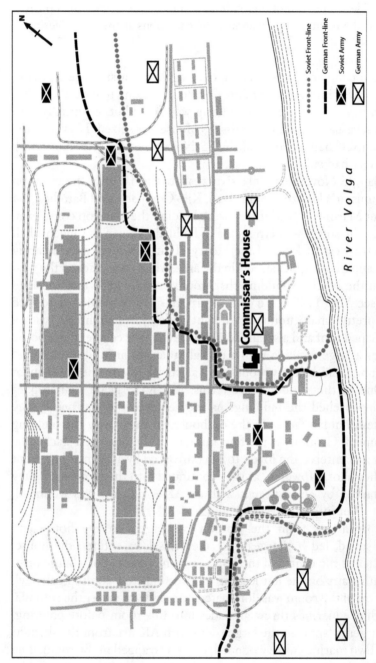

Map 11.1: The battle of Stalingrad, attack on the Commissar's House, November 1942
Source: Map courtesy of Army University Press, *Stalingrad: The Commissar's House* (2018):
www.youtube.com/watch?v=deXzTPe_TF4.

along with their CAAT [Combined Anti-Armour Team] support.'[5] Sergeant Kasal and some other marines continued to try and clear the house. They killed one insurgent but another marine was killed, while Kasal and three other marines were wounded. Under intense suppressive fire, all the wounded marines were eventually extracted from the building. The platoon commander then ordered the building to be demolished. The company's combat engineer planted a satchel charge by the propane tanks in the kitchen and, when all the marines were clear, lit the fuse: 'The explosion raised a giant cloud of dust and debris high into the air . . . the building and even the outer courtyard wall had been reduced to a pile of smoking rubble.'[6] One insurgent was dead, but a second, who, with dark hair and beard, may have been a Chechnyan, threw a grenade that detonated without causing any casualties.[7] He was killed by a final hail of rifle-fire. The Hell House was secure.

Although the battle for the Commissar's House was part of a total interstate war and the Hell House a civil insurgency, the continuities between the urban fighting in Stalingrad in November 1942 and Fallujah in November 2004 are evident. In the assaults on the Commissar's House at the Barrikady Gun Factory and on the Hell House in the Queens District, troops attacked a fortified enemy position. The fighting was carried out at close quarters, with German and American troops clearing rooms with grenades, charges and small arms fire. Their tactics were similar. The realities of urban combat at the small unit level endure. Small groups of soldiers have to force their way into fortified buildings and rooms today, just as they did in the 1940s. Doorways, balconies and roofs offer excellent protection for defenders; every room and corridor is a potential killing zone.

These continuities are undeniable and should never be forgotten. Yet, just because the close fight is similar, it does not mean that urban warfare itself has remained the same. On the contrary, if the fights for the Commissar's House and the Hell House are situated in a wider operational context, it becomes difficult to assert that the urban battle remains unchanged in the twenty-first century. The anatomy of urban warfare has evolved. Indeed, the transformation of the revised urban battlescape becomes even more apparent when Fallujah is put alongside Aleppo, Marawi or Mosul. In the twentieth century, as Stalingrad showed, interstate urban battles were typically part of a larger campaign fought primarily on a front. Alternatively, on counterinsurgency campaigns, state forces typically drove insurgents out of the city altogether. In either case, the field was the dominant theatre of operations then. In this century, by contrast, combatants have converged on each other

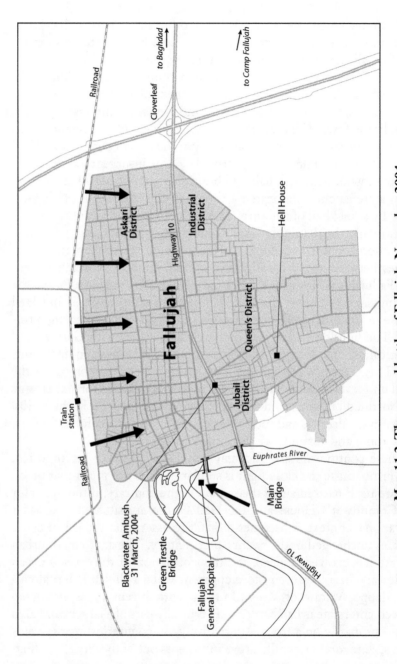

Map 11.2: The second battle of Fallujah, November 2004

Source: Based on map from General Stanley McChrystal, *My Share of the Task: A Memoir* (New York: Portfolio, 2014), 126.

inside cities themselves. The battles have taken place within cities, coalescing into a series of inner-urban micro-sieges. Why has the urban battle condensed into these signature localized sieges?

Three interrelated reasons explain this urban migration and have been repeatedly stressed throughout this book. First, cities have grown so big that it is difficult for forces to avoid them, especially since they are political, economic and social hubs. Second, weapons are more accurate; as the field has become more lethal, state and nonstate forces have sought refuge in cities. Third, military forces are much smaller. Consequently, standing state armies can no longer envelop or inundate cities. Today, urban battles no longer encompass the whole city. Combatants have, therefore, converged onto specific locales inside the city. Even when they are confronting insurgents, state forces are no longer numerous enough to drive them out of cities; insurgents have themselves become too powerful. Battles have, therefore localized into a series of intense interior engagements. Once inside cities, forces have fought for decisive neighbourhoods, blocks, specific buildings and structures.

Not only have battles localized but, in these contested locations, the fighting has assumed a very particular morphology. It has decelerated into punctuated siege operations. Of course, in the twentieth century, urban battles involved intense fights for particular objectives, such as the Barrikady Gun Factory or the Commissar's House. Yet these local attacks were normally part of much wider operations mounted across the city. The Commissar's House assault, for instance, was part of LI Army Corps' attack across the whole city, involving five divisions from the Tennis Racket and Mamayev Kurgan sectors in the south to the Barrikady Gun Factory in the north of the city.[8] With reduced forces, the urban battle has become a series of localized bite and hold operations.

Moreover, once reduced forces have converged on decisive locales, the very tactics and methods that they have adopted in these fights have retarded the tempo of operations, reinforcing the tendency towards the micro-siege conditions. Although forces are now much smaller, they are also much better armed than in the twentieth century. Troops have far more firepower at their disposal. Heavily armed infantry soldiers and tanks have fired prodigious quantities of ammunition at each other, often at extreme close range. Fixed- and rotary-wing, piloted and remote aircraft and artillery have struck enemy positions from distance with increased lethality. Against this firepower, it has become very difficult for troops to move in the close urban fight, especially since combat forces are now so small that commanders need to avoid heavy casualties. A war of position has replaced a war of movement.

The process is mutually reinforcing. As a result of increased fire power and their reduced numbers, combatants have made extensive use of fortifications to protect themselves; walls, barriers and gabions have proliferated. These walls have substituted flesh for concrete, as some defence against increased firepower. These defences have been very necessary and highly effective. Yet, of course, they have themselves actively decelerated operations. Consequently, faced with increased firepower and more defensive fortifications, protagonists have been compelled to mount deliberate breaches, followed by the slow clearances of very limited objectives.

The urban battle has coagulated into slow, localized sieges within the city itself. Other factors have also contributed to the emergence of this battlescape. At Stalingrad, the German Army Group B included Hungarian, Romanian and Italian troops that fought as discrete, independent armies. By contrast, because state forces have shrunk, irregular and partnered forces have become increasingly prominent in urban battles. Sometimes, as in Fallujah or Mosul, the partnered forces have been the host nation's own security forces. Yet, in many cases, irregular militias have been employed in the urban fight. They were vital to the US campaign against ISIS. In Syria, they were in the vanguard of Assad's victories, and in the Donbas, Russia reinforced local forces with its own troops. The armed surrogate has emerged. The urban battle has become a melange of state, nonstate, irregular and hybrid military forces. States have found proxy warfare convenient. Yet, it has only consolidated the new topography of urban warfare. Partnered forces are often less well trained and equipped than their patrons' armies. Even when they are capable, their motivations and interests often deviate from their patrons' objectives. Consequently, the use of proxies requires extensive diplomacy and negotiation, all of which retards the speed of operations yet further. Reduced forces, and the increasing use of firepower, fortification and partners, have impelled the rise of urban positional warfare.

Siege warfare has returned. Yet, it has done so in a strange way. While adopting the methods of positional warfare, military forces have also increasingly employed information operations to recruit, encourage or intimidate the local population, which now outnumber them. Even as the urban battle has concentrated on specific locales inside the city, it has globalized outwards. As the battle rages in the streets, participants have communicated to a global urban archipelago by means of digital communications and social media. Cities miles away from the fight have been recruited into the combat in real time. Often, this global audience has been relatively passive. At other times, external states, international organizations or diasporas have been compelled to offer some support for protagonists or victims of the battle. Yet, sometimes, the connection is more immediate and military. The battle of Marawi in the summer of 2017 was an extension of the battles of Mosul and Raqqa; it was part of one ISIS campaign. Urban warfare has developed a definable anatomy in recent decades. It has localized and globalized; battles have imploded and exploded; they have condensed onto specific urban districts, while also simultaneously extrapolating outwards. It is vital that scholars, the armed forces, policymakers and humanitarians recognize the new urban battlescape and its strange morphology.

Megacity War

Since the early 2000s, urban warfare has coalesced into a recognizable pattern. The question is whether this military topography will continue into the future. If scholars, professionals and policymakers are interested in the evolution of urban warfare, it is substantially in order to develop some sense of its future as we move forward. It is, therefore, useful to consider the possible trajectories of urban warfare out to 2040. Today, commentators worry about three possible urban Armageddons: megacity war, autonomized urban warfare and nuclear holocaust. It is useful to conclude this book by considering the likelihood of these prognostications. What will urban warfare look like in the near future?

Military professionals and many military scientists are most troubled by the prospect of war breaking out not just in cities in the coming decades, but rather in megacities of more than 10 million inhabitants. These fears are certainly suggested by the demographics. In 1974, there were only two megacities in the world. There are now thirty-seven, mostly located in Asia. Megacities now cover such a large area and have become such strategic nodes, that some claim they will be physically and politically unavoidable: 'Megacities are rapidly becoming the epicenters of human activity on the planet and, as such, they will generate most of the friction which compels future military intervention.'[9] More people now live in these cities than in the past, very many of them in wretched conditions; they are, therefore, the ideal loci for future conflict. Many fear that Western forces will be forced to fight state and nonstate opponents in an environment of bewildering complexity.

The US will be drawn into megacities whether it wants it or not. In *Megacities and the United States Army*, it is argued that 'to ignore

megacities is to ignore the future'.[10] Many commentators have concurred, claiming that megacity war is all but inevitable:

> Due to their increasing political, economic, and social significance,
> megacities represent strategic key terrain interconnected to national
> and even international centers of gravity. Megacities, due to their
> increasing number, geographical locations, and crucial strategic impor-
> tance, are also the most likely environments where the US military will
> have to execute its missions.[11]

For Western forces, the prospect of fighting in this urban dystopia is
disturbing. They fear that they will be overwhelmed by the sheer scale
and complexity of the environment in which they will have to operate.

There is a broad consensus among military professionals about megacities. Yet, it is by no means unanimous. Michael Evans, for instance,
has dismissed the claim that armies will necessarily fight in megacities in the future at all: 'Megacities are not necessarily the principal
urban areas in which American forces may be called upon to fight in
the future.'[12] For Evans, the demographics do not support the megacity argument. Although no one can deny the rise of megacities since
the late twentieth century, most of the human population still live
in medium-size metropolitan areas; 'Urban growth in the developing
world is not centred on a few megacity "population bombs" but on a
far more dispersed grouping of diverse middle cities whose populations
range from between 150,000 to 10 million.'[13] By contrast, 'there are
over 200 cities of this size in China, 50 in Latin America and 39 in
Africa and the Middle East'. Evans has argued that, in reality, warfare is
more likely to occur in 'middleweight cities'.[14]

Evans's scepticism is understandable. Yet, it seems entirely conceiv-
able that state forces may have to conduct counterinsurgency operations
in megacities in the future. Indeed, it might be argued that in Latin
America, the security forces are already engaged in such operations
in their struggles against organized crime. It might be unpopular, but
US forces could easily be deployed abroad again to conduct the kind
of counterinsurgency operations that they did in Iraq and Afghanistan.
Some genuine megacities in Asia might also become the crucible of
urban insurgency. The battles of Marawi, Mosul or Mumbai might
be a presage of that future. It is even possible that insurgent urban
challenges could emerge in the United States or Europe in the future.
The global depression that will follow the 2020 coronavirus pandemic
could easily generate urban unrest not only in already fragile cities in

the global South, but also in the global North. Protests such as those engendered by Black Lives Matter after the murder of George Floyd in May 2020 might be forerunners of this difficult metropolitan future. The armed forces may be ordered to support civilian powers in maintaining civic order in the coming crises in North America and Europe.

Urban disorder and insurgencies are not unlikely in megacities in the next two decades. However, Western militaries are not only concerned that they might have to suppress urban insurgencies in the coming years; they are also worried that they might have to fight a near-peer, interstate war inside a megalopolis. This a truly dystopian vision. It is sensible to be concerned about such an eventuality. It would be a costly, risky and destructive enterprise. Clearly, the question of whether interstate war could occur in a megacity is complex. It depends on which states go to war with each other. For instance, China and India have many megacities but, if the tensions in the summer of 2020 were indicative, any confrontation between them is likely to take the form of a border clash high in the Himalayas, miles from any major town. However, although it is far from comprehensive, a brief survey of the theatres in which Western forces are preparing for possible military action might illustrate the prospects of genuine megacity war more clearly. Western armed forces are currently preparing for four possible interstate, near-peer scenarios against China, Russia, Iran and North Korea. Could megacity war happen in these theatres?

It seems unlikely that an American conflict with Iran would involve significant ground forces; an invasion seems improbable. It would probably consist of air and, maybe, some special operations strikes against specific facilities or against naval forces. Similarly, China seems to defy the prognostications about megacity war. Although China is urbanizing dramatically, and already has the largest number of megacities in the world, even if the US and China were to go to war, there is little realistic chance that they would fight in a megacity – or even on land at all. A land invasion of mainland China by the US is totally unfeasible and inconceivable. Theoretically, Chinese and American forces might fight in Tokyo or Taipei. Yet, this too is exceedingly unlikely. Any future war with China is almost certainly likely to be for maritime supremacy over the South and East China Seas and, ultimately, the Pacific Ocean. A major maritime confrontation is not inevitable, but it is possible. The outcome of that naval battle will probably predetermine the fate of Japan and Taiwan, independently of any land battle.

A future war between Russia and NATO is likely to involve a land battle in the Baltics. Certainly, NATO is preparing to defend the Baltic states territorially. The Donbas suggests that any such confrontation against Russia is likely to be urban. In the Donbas, reduced Ukrainian and Russian forces converged on urban areas. A similar dynamic seems probable in the Baltics. The era of the Cold War with engagements between the massed Soviet and NATO divisions is over. Fronts are likely to be replaced by dispersed battles and it is most likely that those battles will converge on the cities and towns of the Baltics, as they did in eastern Ukraine. Neither Russia nor NATO have the forces to mount a lineal defence. It would probably be unwise for NATO to try to deploy into the field in a traditional way because Russian long-range artillery presents a major danger to alliance formations located there, as the war in the Donbas so clearly shows. In the summer of 2014, Ukrainian forces mounted an operation to retake Donetsk and the surrounding areas. On 11 July 2014, Russian drones identified elements of the Ukrainian 24th, 72nd Mechanized and 79th Airmobile Brigades in the open, near the town of Zelenopillya, launching a long-range artillery strike on it. Within minutes, two of the Ukrainian mechanized battalions were destroyed.[15] Although the strike at Zelenopillya now seems to have been the result of Ukrainian military incompetence rather than Russian skill, NATO forces in the Baltics would be exposed to Russia's target acquisition systems and long-range artillery. It seems probable, then, that NATO forces will try to defend the eastern Baltics from inside fortified positions in urban areas. If they lose these urban areas, they will be compelled to attack Russian forces in them. Urban warfare is highly likely in any war with Russia, therefore. However, although there is a significant urban population in the Baltics, there are no megacities, so the fear of having to fight Russian forces in a vast urban area is quite unfounded. Megacity war cannot happen in this theatre.

North Korea is the fourth theatre in which Western forces might be engaged in high-intensity interstate war in the next decade. Here, the conditions are present for a major interstate battle in a megacity. In 1950, during the Korean War, Seoul was a city of approximately 1 million inhabitants; today, 10 million people live in the city. It is a true megacity only forty miles south of the 38th Parallel. On demographic grounds, it might be assumed that any war between North and South Korea must involve megacity fighting. It is certainly possible. However, while there has been a reduction of forces in most other theatres, the opposite is the case in Korea. It is the one region in which mass armies still exist. On the Korean Peninsula, for instance, approximately 700,000 North Korean soldiers and 400,000 Republic of Korea troops confront each other along an 80-mile frontier.[16] In order to protect themselves, the Republic of Korea (ROK) has constructed extensive tunnel networks, bunkers and field fortifications. ROK forces aim to hold a North Korean assault on a series of defensive lines just south of the demilitarized zone – well before they reach Seoul – until American reinforcements arrive.[17] It is, of course, possible that the North Korean forces could breach these defences and that subsequent battles could take place in Seoul itself. This is precisely what happened in 1950. However, in 1950, the South Korean and American forces were poorly prepared. Today, it would be very difficult to breach ROK defences quickly, even with the massive forces the North has at its disposal.

The Korean theatre has some ironies then. It is the only theatre in which Western forces are preparing to fight a near-peer opponent on the ground, where there is actually a megacity. Yet, because of the very size of the forces that would be involved, urban fighting is less likely in Korea than in the Baltics, where combat densities are low. It is not wrong for Western forces to be concerned about the prospect of fighting in megacities. However, entranced by the sheer scale of these cities, they have exaggerated the likelihood of this doomsday scenario. Western armies will almost certainly have to fight in cities in the future. It is possible that they might have to conduct a counterinsurgency campaign in one, but interstate warfare in megacities is actually rather unlikely.

The Smart City

Military professionals are troubled by megacities. By contrast, academics, especially social and political scientists on the left, are more concerned about a different kind of Armageddon: the rise of autonomous weapons, robots and artificial intelligence. They are deeply worried by the implications of advanced military technology for citizens, in cities that have themselves already been digitalized. For instance, in his critical assessment of the militarization of cities, geographer Stephen Graham is deeply disturbed by the proliferation of new security technologies. He believes that the security forces are actively seeking to submit cities to total control. They are apparently obsessed with 'technophilic desire and fetishistic urges for mastery and control, adjusted to the new imperatives of urban counter-insurgency warfare'.[18] Graham is not alone in this view. Paul Scharre fears that military forces are developing autonomous weapons systems that will be able to identify and engage targets, independently of human control:

Militaries around the globe are racing to deploy robots at sea, on the ground, and in the air – more than ninety countries have drones patrolling their skies. These robots are increasingly autonomous and many are armed. They operate under human control for now, but what happens when a Predator drone has as much autonomy as a Google car?[19]

His fear is that, 'in future wars, machines may make life and death engagement decisions'.[20] At the moment, urban conflict remains a profoundly human phenomenon. The fear is that a state security force might be able to monitor city streets ubiquitously, targeting civilians identified as enemies at will.

The fear is not absurd. Autonomous weapon systems, robotics and artificial intelligence are becoming increasingly important to the armed forces. However, the vision depicted by these writers is more closely related to science fiction than to reality. There is a precedent for this. In the 1920s and 1930s, a proliferation of futurist literature extrapolated from the experience of air raids in the First World War. This chimed with airpower theory of the time, promulgated by Giulio Douhet, Billy Mitchell and Hugh Trenchard. H. G. Wells, for instance, imagined a future in which entire cities might be obliterated in a single air bombardment. Hiroshima and Nagasaki notwithstanding, the Second World War and subsequent strategic air campaigns showed that these fears were exaggerated; it is actually quite difficult to destroy cities with conventional weapons, especially when they are defended. Yet, by the late twentieth century, popular millenarian fantasies obsessed about the threat posed by robots, cyborgs and computers. Intelligent machines seemed to represent a danger to humankind.

Two films in the early 1980s captured these anxieties graphically. In 1982, Ridley Scott released *Blade Runner*, based on Philip K. Dick's 1968 novel, *Do Androids Dream of Electric Sheep?* The film was located in a dystopian Los Angeles in 2019 in which a private detective attempts to track down murderous androids in the city. The themes of *Blade Runner* were directly repeated in one of the most popular films of this era: James Cameron's 1984 film, *Terminator*. This film begins with a vision of Los Angeles in 2029 after the super-computer, Skynet, has tried to annihilate the human species in a massive nuclear holocaust. Drones fly above the urban ruins, firing their lasers at the last human survivors, while vast robotic tanks crush human skulls beneath their tracks. The film itself follows the attempts of an android, sent back from the future, to ensure humanity's extinction. They are memorable visions, like those depicted by H. G. Wells in the 1930s, which play brilliantly on common fears of a nuclear Armageddon initiated by a computer error.

Concerns about the automation of weaponry are well-founded, especially in urban warfare. In recent decades, remote weapons have become commonplace in urban conflict. Drones have proliferated. States have employed their existing drone fleets for urban operations, but they are also experimenting with nano-drones that might be deployed in swarms to monitor streets, buildings or even rooms. Nonstate combatants are increasingly procuring and employing drones to watch their enemies or drop munitions on them. Partly autonomous weapons have also begun to appear. These weapons have taken – and will take – many different forms, but some prototypes are already operational. For instance, both the US Army and the British Army have successfully trialled an autonomous vehicle manufactured by MILREM Robotics, called the Type-X Robotic Combat Vehicle. Trials have shown that it is possible to tether two robotic vehicles to a single tank. These vehicles have been programmed to operate autonomously on instruction of the tank commander. They are able to reconnoitre routes and engage targets independently, in line with their algorithms. When they have completed their missions, the autonomous vehicles are programmed to follow behind the mother tank.

The British Army has also tested a remote-controlled, six-rotor armed drone. This vehicle, the prototype of which his called the 'i9', has been specifically designed for urban warfare and will be able to drop grenades or shoot firearms inside buildings and rooms. Up till now, it has been difficult for drones to fire weapons inside buildings. They have been unable to manage the recoil, crashing into the walls as a result. However, by means of artificial intelligence, the stabilization problem seems to have been resolved and the potential for employing such drones in urban combat is high.[21] Paired tanks and tracked robots or drones are only two examples of the emergence of remote and quasi-autonomous weapons today.

Insurgents have also tried to exploit the potential of autonomous weapon systems. For instance, David Kilcullen has repeatedly emphasized the way in which insurgents have innovated with digital equipment procured online.[22] Thus, in Aleppo, rebels downloaded software from the web onto their tablets to range their mortars. In an even more striking example, he claimed that some ISIS sniper rifles in Mosul were operated by activists from a cyber-café in Brussels. These examples suggest that, in the future, insurgents might be able to conduct urban warfare remotely or even autonomously, just as effectively as states.

These short examples show the potential of robotics and autonomous weapons for urban warfare in future conflict.

The inexorable rise of autonomous weapons may change urban tactics and, perhaps, some aspects of warfare over the next couple of decades. Certainly, these weapons have captured the public's imagination and fears. However, autonomous weapons have emerged as armed forces have radically shrunk in size. They have been developed to compensate for the lack of mass. Tethered, robotic vehicles multiply the capability of a human tank crew; they do not replace them. ISIS's automated sniper rifle in Aleppo was effective only because it was sited in an area defended by actual ISIS fighters. The sniper rifle augmented human fighters; it did not substitute for them. As fewer forces are deployed, human combatants will exploit remote, robotic or autonomous weapons systems. Yet, it seems unlikely that their introduction will radically alter urban warfare today. An extension of current trends, documented in this book, seems more probable. It would seem that, in the future, urban warfare will continue to exist in the form of slow, deliberate sieges in which intense firepower is concentrated on specific objectives. Even with robots, there are too few combatants to fight otherwise. It is likely simply that the military forces operating on the ground will consist of ever diminishing human combatants, each augmented by robots and autonomous weapons. Yet, the urban battle will still be organized around human protagonists, assisted by technology, rather than determined by autonomous systems.

Nuclear Holocaust

There is a final future for urban combat. This pathway leads urban warfare not so much forward to the future, but back to the past. It is closer to a genuine Armageddon. As we have seen, the topography of urban warfare has changed in recent decades. As a result of the expansion of cities, the reduction of armies and the introduction of precision weaponry, battles have condensed into discrete locales within the city itself. There, the fighting is as intense as ever – but is typically much slower than it was in the twentieth century. Mass fighting across the city has been displaced by discrete, localized battles within it. Yet, it is possible that mass, attritional warfare might return to the city. A genuine repeat of battles like Stalingrad or Berlin is unlikely, simply because states do not have the troops. Nevertheless, states could resort to massive air bombardment of urban areas with strategic bombers or missiles. Air raids of this type have not been seen since the Americans engaged in their Rolling Thunder and Linebacker operations in Vietnam. Yet, US B-52 heavy bombers were used against rural targets in Afghanistan. Russian TU-95s bombed targets in Syria away from cities. These bombers could be used against urban targets. In a high-intensity war between the countries, Russia, China, the US or North Korea might target whole cities, as the RAF, USAAF and Luftwaffe did in the Second World War. These scenarios should not be dismissed. They are not impossible.

Yet, urban air raids would not return urban warfare directly to the bombing campaigns of the past. Even heavy bombers today employ some precision weaponry, and it seems unlikely that they would not try to target with some degree of precision – not out of humanity, but out of military expediency. Area bombing is simply an inefficient way to conduct war. Moreover, because of advanced air defence systems, it would be extremely difficult to mount a strategic bombing attack of this type against a peer enemy. A strategic air raid on a city would require a sustained and systematic attack on air defences first. That operation would be difficult and costly. It would seem irrational to invest so much effort to degrade enemy air defences only to bombard a city randomly from above. Yet, area bombing remains a possibility. Indeed, a conventional missile attack is possible and, perhaps, more likely than the return of the air raid, although such an attack would aim at destruction of particular targets rather than whole swathes of the city.

In reality, if states did want to destroy each other's cities, a nuclear exchange is more likely than a return to conventional, strategic bombing. In this situation, cities would become very vulnerable to general destruction. Indeed, while it must be hoped that a nuclear exchange is improbable, there are currently nine nuclear states. In the next decade, other states may also develop a nuclear capability; indeed, it is probable. As a result of this proliferation, a nuclear exchange could break out between a number of states: India and Pakistan, India and China, Israel and Iran, the US and Russia, the US and China, North Korea and the US, China and Japan, etc. At this point, a future nuclear urban war might resemble the last days of the Second World War with the destruction of Hiroshima and Nagasaki. Nuclear weapons could be used by any one of these states to destroy enemy cities and kill citizens, as they were in 1945. Seoul would be an obvious target in any war in Korea. Baltic cities might also be incinerated if a conflict between Russia and NATO escalated. Yet, in other future conflicts, Delhi, Islamabad, Jerusalem, Tehran, Tokyo, Taipei, Washington and Beijing could all be targeted by nuclear weapons.

Three urban Armageddons are possible in the next two decades: war in a megacity, automated war in a smart city, or a return of mass air attack with conventional or nuclear weapons. The armed forces, policymakers and military scientists must be aware of these three pathways. However, the most likely future for urban warfare is not a cataclysm or a revolution but, rather, a continuation of the trends evident in the early twenty-first century. The urban battlescape of the near future is most likely to replicate Mosul, Marawi and Aleppo. Brutal, intense but slow-moving, attritional urban battles involving state, nonstate and hybrid forces are likely to coalesce on specific locales inside cities, as they have done since the end of the twentieth century. Urban warfare will continue to consist of a sequence of micro-sieges for objectives within urban areas. This is a future for which we might pessimistically hope. Yet, a genuine urban Armageddon is possible, when cities are incinerated not by divine intervention, like the fabled Sodom and Gomorrah, but by deliberate human intention. Humans will determine which future it is to be.

Notes

Chapter 1   Gomorrah

1 James Verini, *They Will Have to Die Now: Mosul and the Fall of the Caliphate* (London: Oneworld 2019), 16.

2 General Stephen Townsend, Multidomain Battle in Megacities Conference, Fort Hamilton, New York, 3 April 2018: https://www.youtube.com/watch?v=ARz0l_evGAE.

3 Colonel Pat Work, US Army, MWI Podcast: 'The battle for Mosul', 14 February 2018: https://mwi.usma.edu/mwi-podcast-battle-mosul-col-pat-work/.

4 Gareth Brereton, *I Am Ashurbanipal: King of the World, King of Assyria* (London: Thames and Hudson, 2019), 281.

5 Townsend, Multidomain Battle in Megacities Conference.

6 Townsend, Multidomain Battle in Megacities Conference.

7 Robert Postings, 'An analysis of the Islamic State's SVBIED use in Raqqa', *International Review* 11 May 2018: https://international-review.org/an-analysis-of-islamic-states-svbied-use-in-raqqa/; 'A guide to the Islamic State's way of urban warfare', Modern War Institute, 7 September 2018: https://mwi.usma.edu/guide-islamic-states-way-urban-warfare/.

8 Postings, 'An analysis of the Islamic State's SVBIED use in Raqqa'.

9 Townsend, Multidomain Battle in Megacities Conference.

10 Townsend, Multidomain Battle in Megacities Conference.

11 Stephen Graham, *Cities under Siege: The New Military Urbanism* (London: Verso, 2010), 16.

12 Timothy Thomas, 'The 31 December 1994 – 8 February 1995

battle for Grozny', in William Robertson (ed.), *Block by Block: The Challenges of Urban Operations* (Ft Leavenworth, KS: US ACGS College Press, 2003), 170–1.

13 Major-General Rupert Jones, OF-7, British Army, Deputy Commander, Operation Inherent Resolve, personal interview, 3 August 2018.

14 Amos Harel and Avi Issacharoff, *34 Days: Israel, Hezbollah and the War in Lebanon* (London: Palgrave Macmillan, 2008), 191.

15 Raphael Marcus, 'Learning "under fire": Israel's improvised military adaptation to Hamas tunnel warfare', *Journal of Strategic Studies* 42(3–4) 2019, 357.

16 Paul Quinn-Judge, 'Ukraine's meat grinder is back in business', *Foreign Policy*, 12 April 2016.

17 Virgil, *The Aeneid*, trans. David West (London: Penguin 2003), 37.

18 *The Bible*, Joshua 6:21.

19 Wayne Lee, *Waging War: Conflict, Culture and Innovation in World History* (Oxford: Oxford University Press, 2016), 15.

20 Edward Soja, *Postmetropolis* (Oxford: Blackwell, 2000), 32.

21 Lee, *Waging War*, 16.

22 Soja, *Postmetropolis*, 64.

23 Brereton, *I Am Ashurbanipal*, 109.

24 Richard Norton, 'Feral cities', *Naval War College Review* 56(4) 2003, 1.

25 Kevin M. Felix and Frederick D. Wong, 'The case for megacities', *Parameters* 45(1) 2015, 19–32.

26 John Spencer 'The city is not neutral: why urban warfare is so hard', Modern War Institute, 4 March 2020: https://mwi.usma.edu/city-not-neutral-urban-warfare-hard/.

27 David Betz and Hugh Stanford-Tuck, 'The city is neutral', *Texas National Security Review* 2(4) 2019, 60–87.

28 Alice Hills, *Future Wars in Cities: Rethinking a Liberal Dilemma* (London: Frank Cass, 2004), 153.

29 I take the word battlescape from Arjan Appadurai, *Modernity at Large* (Minneapolis: University of Minnesota Press, 1996).

30 The word 'siege' is derived from the Latin word *sedicum*, meaning a seat. *Sieger* in French means to sit.

Chapter 2   Numbers

1 Louis Wirth, *On Cities and City Life: Selected Papers* (Chicago, IL: Chicago University Press, 1964).

2 Headquarters, Department of the Army, *ATP 3-06: Urban Operations* (December 2017), 1–3.

3 Carl von Clausewitz, *On War*, trans. Michael Howard and Peter Paret (Princeton, NJ: Princeton University Press, 1989), 87.

4 Clausewitz, *On War*, 75.

5 Antonio Sampaio, *Illicit Order: The Military Logic of Organized Crime and Urban Security in Rio de Janiero* (London: IISS, 2019), 8.

6 Mike Davis, *Planet of the Slums* (London: Verso), 1–11.

7 Russell Glenn, *Combat in Hell: A Consideration of Constrained Urban Warfare* (Santa Monica, CA: Rand Arroyo Centre, 1996), 2.

8 Ralph Peters, 'Our soldiers, their cities', *Parameters* 26(1) 1996, 43.

9 E.g., Gregory Ashworth, *War and the City* (London: Routledge, 1991); Michael C. Desch, 'Why MOUT now?' in Michael C. Desch (ed.), *Soldiers in Cities: Military Operations on Urban Terrain* (Carlisle PA: Strategic Studies Institute, 2001), 1–16; Sean Edwards *Mars Unmasked: The Changing Face of Urban Operations* (New York: Rand Arroyo Centre, 2000); Paul Hirst, *Space and Power* (Cambridge: Polity, 2005); Louis DiMarco, *Concrete Hell: Urban Warfare from Stalingrad to Iraq* (Oxford: Osprey, 2012).

10 Gian Gentile, David E. Johnson, Lisa Saum-Manning, Raphael S. Cohen, . . . James L. Doty, III, *Reimagining the Character of Urban Operations for the US Army* (Santa Monica, CA: Rand Arroyo Centre, 2017), 8–9.

11 Michael Evans, 'Lethal genes: the urban military imperative and Western strategy in the early twenty-first century', *Journal of Strategic Studies* 32(4) 2009, 516.

12 Michael Evans, *City without Joy: Military Operations in the 21st Century* (Canberra: Australian Defence College, Occasional Series no. 2, 2007), 14.

13 David Kilcullen, *Out of the Mountains: The Coming of Age of the Urban Guerrilla* (London: Hurst and Company, 2013), 74–6.

14 Frank Hoffman, 'Complex irregular warfare: the next revolution in military affairs', *Orbis: A Journal of World Affairs* 50(3) 2006, 395–411.

15 See Chapter 3 for an explanation of the rise of urban insurgencies.

16 Alec Wahlman, *Storming the City* (Denton: University of North Texas Press, 2015), 1–2.

17 Alice Hills, *Future Wars in Cities: Rethinking a Liberal Dilemma* (London: Frank Cass, 2004), 16–26; Kilcullen, *Out of the Mountains*, 18–40.

18 Saskia Sassen, 'When the city itself becomes a technology of

war', *Theory, Culture and Society* 27(6) 2010, 37; Warfare Branch, Headquarters Field Army, *Operations in the Urban Environment* (Warminster: Land Warfare Centre, 2018), 13.

19 Hans Delbrück, *History of the Art of War within the Framework of Political History*. Vol. 1: *Warfare in Antiquity*, trans. Walter Renfroe, Jr. (London: Greenwood Press, 1975), 33.

20 Delbrück, *History of the Art of War*.

21 Delbrück, *History of the Art of War*. See also Gordon Craig, 'Hans Delbrück: military historian', in Peter Paret (ed.), *The Makers of Modern Strategy* (Princeton, NJ: Princeton University Press, 1986), 333, 336.

22 Christopher Duffy, *The Fortress in the Age of Vauban and Frederick the Great, 1660–1789*, vol. II (London: Routledge & Kegan Paul, 1985), 292.

23 Duffy's argument is consistent with the debates about the early modern military revolution, a major element of which involved a discussion of the increasing size of European armies after 1500.

24 Jeremy Black, *Fortifications and Siegecraft* (London: Rowman & Littlefield, 2018), 236.

25 Clausewitz, *On War*, Book Six, chs 10 and 11, 'Fortresses' and 'Fortresses – continued', and Book Seven, ch. 17, 'Attack on fortresses'.

26 E.g., Karl Haltiner, 'The definite end of the mass army in Western Europe?' *Armed Forces and Society* 25(1) 1998, 7–36.

27 Relative to the size of the Israel population, the IDF has, in fact, shrunk by about half in the same era.

28 Matt Matthews, *We Were Caught Unprepared: The 2006 Hezbollah–Israel War* (Ft Leavenworth, KS: US Army Combined Arms Centre, Combat Studies Institute, 2008), 50; David Johnson, *Hard Fighting: Israel in Lebanon and Gaza* (Santa Monica, CA: Rand Arroyo Centre, 2011), 69.

29 S. L. A. Marshall, 'Notes on urban warfare', Army Material Systems Analysis Agency, Aberdeen Proving Ground, Maryland, April 1973, 8–11.

30 S. J. Lewis, 'The battle of Stalingrad', in William Robertson (ed.), *Block by Block: The Challenges of Urban Operations* (Ft Leavenworth, KS: US ACGS College Press, 2003), 30.

31 David Glantz, with Jonathan House, *The Stalingrad Trilogy, Volume 2: Armageddon in Stalingrad: September–November 1942* (Lawrence: University of Kansas Press, 2009).

32 Lewis, 'The battle of Stalingrad', 31.

33 Glantz, *The Stalingrad Trilogy*, 33, 719–20; Antony Beevor, *Stalingrad* (London: Penguin 1999), 433–5.

34 Glantz, *The Stalingrad Trilogy*, 609; Beevor, *Stalingrad*, 242–3; Lewis, 'The battle of Stalingrad'.

35 Beevor, *Stalingrad*, 435–7.

36 Alexander McKee, *Caen: Anvil of Victory* (London: Souvenir, 1984), 247.

37 John Mearsheimer, 'Maneuvre, mobile defence and the NATO central front', *International Security* 6(3) 1982, 116, 118; also John Mearsheimer, 'Why the Soviets can't win quickly in Central Europe', *International Security* 7(1) 1982, 33.

38 E.g., Army Field Manual, vol. IV, part 5, *Fighting in Built-up Areas* (1983), 1–2.

39 Headquarters, Department of the Army, *Field Manual 90-10: Military Operations on Urbanized Terrain* (Washington, DC: US Government Printing Office, 1979), 1-1.

40 Christopher R. Gabel, '"Knock 'em all down": the reduction of Aachen, October 1944', in Robertson (ed.), *Block by Block*, 60–90.

41 Kevin Benson, 'Manila, 1945', in John Antal and Bradley Gericke (eds), *City Fights: Selected Histories of Urban Combat from World War II to Vietnam* (New York: Ballantine, 2003), 230–50.

42 Rick Andres, Craig Wills and Thomas Griffith, 'Winning the allies: the strategic value of the Afghan Model', *International Security* 30(3) 2005/6, 124–60; Steven Biddle, 'Allies, airpower and modern warfare: the Afghan model in Afghanistan and Iraq', *International Security* 30(3) 2005/6, 161–76.

43 Andrew Cordesman, *The Iraq War: Strategy, Tactics and Military Lessons* (London: Praeger, 2003), 16, 130; Kenneth Estes, *Marine Corps Operations in Iraq 2003–2006* (Quantico, VA: USMC History Division).

44 Cordesman, *The Iraq War*, 44.

45 Cordesman, *The Iraq War*, 46–7.

46 Walter L. Perry, Richard E. Darilek, Laurinda L. Rohn and Jerry M. Sollinger (eds), *Decisive War, Elusive Peace* (Santa Monica, CA: Rand Arroyo Centre), 205.

47 Perry et al., *Decisive War, Elusive Peace*, 205.

48 Perry et al., *Decisive War, Elusive Peace*, 86.

49 Perry et al., *Decisive War, Elusive Peace*, 90–3.

50 Perry et al., *Decisive War, Elusive Peace*, 205–6.

51 Stephen Biddle, 'Speed kills: reassessing the role of speed, precision

and situation awareness in the fall of Saddam', *Journal of Strategic Studies* 30(1) 2007, 27.

52 Biddle, 'Speed kills', 29.

53 Perry et al., *Decisive War, Elusive Peace*, 65, 67–78; Gregory Fontenot, E. J. Degen and David Tohn, *On Point: The US Army in Operation Iraqi Freedom* (Ft Leavenworth, KS: Combat Studies Institute Press, 2004), 89; Gary Livingston, *An-Nasiriyah: The Fight for the Bridges* (Open Library: Caisson Press, 2017); Ray Smith and Bing West, *The March Up* (London: Pimlico, 2003), 31–48; Rod Andrew, Jr., *US Marines in Battle: An-Nasiriyah, 23 March – 2 April 2003* (CreateSpace Independent Publishing Platform, 2014).

54 Tim Pritchard, *Ambush Alley* (Novato, CA: Presidio, 2007), 341.

55 http://www.geonames.org/IQ/largest-cities-in-iraq.html.

56 Michael Dewar, *War in the Streets* (London: BCA, 1992), 81–4.

57 Anthony Cordesman and Abraham Wagner, *The Lessons of Modern War, Volume IV: The Gulf War* (Boulder, CO: Westview, 1996), 116, 118.

58 Fontenot et al., *On Point*, 100.

59 Kevin Wood, *The Mother of All Battles* (Annapolis, MD: Naval Institute Press, 2008).

60 Fontenot et al., *On Point*, 2.

61 https://www.abc.net.au/news/2015-06-09/ukrainian-rebels-have-army-the-size-of-small-european-state/6530828.

62 Amos Fox, '"Cyborgs at Little Stalingrad": a brief history of the battles of the Donetsk airport, 26 May 2014 to 21 January 2015', May 2019: https://www.ausa.org/sites/default/files/publications/LWP-125-Cyborgs-at-Little-Stalingrad-A-Brief-History-of-the-Battle-of-the-Donetsk-Airport.pdf, 10.

63 Paul Quinn-Judge, 'Ukraine's meat grinder is back in business', *Foreign Policy*, 12 April 2016: http://foreignpolicy.com/2016/04/12/ukraines-meat-grinder-is-back-in-business/.

Chapter 3   The Urban Guerrilla

1 David Kilcullen, *Out of the Mountains: The Coming of Age of the Urban Guerrilla* (London: Hurst and Company, 2013), 29.

2 ATP-99, *Urban Tactics* (NATO, February 2017), 2.9

3 Karl Hack, 'The Malayan emergency as counter-insurgency paradigm', *Journal of Strategic Studies* 32(3) 2009, 383–414.

4 David Anderson, *Histories of the Hanged: Britain's Dirty War in*

Kenya and the End of Empire (London: Weidenfeld and Nicolson, 2005), 201.

5 Anderson, *Histories of the Hanged*, 202–5.

6 Anthony Burton, *Urban Terrorism: Theory, Practice and Response* (London: Leo Cooper, 1975), 169.

7 Robert Taber, *War of the Flea: A Study of Guerrilla Warfare Theory and Practice* (Washington, DC: Potomac Books, 2002), 127.

8 Burton, *Urban Terrorism*, 175–6.

9 Mark Bowden, *Hué 1968* (London: Grove, UK, 2017)

10 Ernesto Che Guevara, *Guerrilla Warfare* (BN Publishing, 2007), 8

11 Régis Debray, *The Revolution in the Revolution?* (Harmondsworth: Penguin, 1972), 66.

12 Carlos Marighella, *Minimanual of the Urban Guerrilla* (Spade, 1969), 21.

13 Marighella, *Minimanual*, 3–4.

14 Marighella, *Minimanual*, 17.

15 Marighella, *Minimanual*, 41.

16 David Hodges, *The Philosophy of the Urban Guerrilla: The Revolutionary Writings of Abraham Guillén* (New York: William Morrow and Company, 1973), 30.

17 Hodges, *The Philosophy of the Urban Guerrilla*, 234.

18 Hodges, *The Philosophy of the Urban Guerrilla*, 237.

19 Hodges, *The Philosophy of the Urban Guerrilla*, 250.

20 Hodges, *The Philosophy of the Urban Guerrilla*, 250.

21 Hodges, *The Philosophy of the Urban Guerrilla*, 250.

22 Hodges, *The Philosophy of the Urban Guerrilla*, 257.

23 E.g. Tim Pat Coogan, *The IRA* (London: Fontana/Collins, 1987); Patrick Bishop and Eammon Mallie, *The Provisional IRA* (London: Corgi, 1988); Richard English, *Armed Struggle: The History of the IRA* (London: Macmillan, 2003); Frederick Boal (ed.), *Ethnicity and Housing: Accommodating the Differences* (London: Routledge, 2018).

24 *The Sunday Times* Insight Team, *Ulster* (Harmondsworth: Penguin 1972), 126–43; English, *Armed Struggle*, 101–2.

25 E.g., Ciarán De Baróid, *Ballymurphy and the Irish War* (London: Pluto, 2000), 42; Rod Thornton, 'Getting it wrong: the crucial mistakes made in the early stages of the British Army's deployment to Northern Ireland', *Journal of Strategic Studies* 30(1) 2007, 73–107; Frank Burton, *Politics of Legitimacy* (London: Routledge and Kegan Paul, 1978), 113.

26 Tony Geraghty *The Irish War: A Military History of a Domestic Conflict* (London: HarperCollins, 2000), 33–40; Nick van der Bijl,

Operation Banner: The British Army in Northern Ireland 1969–2007 (Barnsley: Pen and Sword, 2017), 35; David Barzilay, *The British Army in Ulster* (Belfast: Century Service Ltd, 1973), 11–16.

27 English, *Armed Struggle*, 105–7, 160.

28 M. L. R. Smith and Peter Neumann, 'Motorman's long journey', *British Contemporary History* 19(4) 2005, 419.

29 Smith and Neumann, 'Motorman's long journey', 419; M. L. R. Smith, *Fighting for Ireland: The Military Strategy of the Irish Republican Movement* (London: Routledge, 1995), 97.

30 Patrick Webb, 'The battles for Divis Flats: a study in community power', PhD thesis, Ulster University, 2016.

31 Patrick Radden Keefe, *Say Nothing: A True Story of Murder and Memory in Northern Ireland* (London: William Collins, 2018), 7.

32 Radden Keefe, *Say Nothing*, 33.

33 Geraghty, *The Irish War*, 22.

34 Radden Keefe, *Say Nothing*, 34.

35 Michael Barthorp, *Crater to the Creggan: The History of the Royal Anglian Regiment 1964–1974* (London: Leo Cooper, 1976), 108.

36 Steven Bowns, *Aden to Afghanistan: Fifty Years of the Royal Anglian Regiment 1964–2014* (Oxford: Osprey, 2014), 167.

37 Barthorp, *Crater to the Creggan*, 108, 110.

38 Bowns, *Aden to Afghanistan*, 168–9.

39 Alan Parkinson, *1972 and the Ulster Troubles: 'A Very Bad Year'* (Portland, OR: Four Courts Press, 2010), 207.

40 Andrew Sanders, 'Operation Motorman (1972) and the search for a coherent British counter-insurgency strategy in Northern Ireland', *Small Wars and Insurgencies* 24(3) 2013, 465–492.

41 Huw Bennett, 'From direct rule to Motorman', *Studies in Conflict and Terrorism* 33(6) 2010, 522; Barzilay, *The British Army in Ulster*, 47.

42 Frederick Boal, 'Integrating and division: sharing and segregating Belfast', *Planning Practice and Research* 11(2) 1996, 151–8; Frederick Boal, 'Territoriality on the Shankill-Falls Divide, Belfast', *Irish Geography* 41(3) 2008, 349–66; Frederick Boal, Paul Doherty and Dennis Pringle, *Social Problems in the Belfast Urban Area: An Exploratory Analysis*, Occasional Paper, no. 12 (London: Queen Mary College, 1978).

43 Robert Thompson, *Defeating Communist Insurgency: Experiences from Malaya and Vietnam* (London: Chatto & Windus, 1974), 47–8.

44 David Galula, *Counterinsurgency Warfare* (Westport, CT: Praeger, 2006), 21.

45 Lieutenant General Sir Richard Shirreff, Evidence to Chilcot Inquiry: https://webarchive.nationalarchives.gov.uk/20110119122 500/http://www.iraqinquiry.org.uk/.

46 Warren Chin, 'Why did it all go wrong? Reassessing British counterinsurgency in Iraq', *Strategic Studies Quarterly*, Winter 2008, 128.

47 John Spencer, 'Stealing the enemy's urban advantage: the battle of Sadr City', Modern War Institute, 31 January 2019: https://mwi.usma.edu/stealing-enemys-urban-advantage-battle-sadr-city/.

48 http://luminocity3d.org/WorldCity/#6/34.715/31.157.

49 Christopher Phillips, *The Battle for Syria: International Rivalry in the New Middle East* (New Haven, CT: Yale University Press, 2018), 47–8; Mouna Al-Sabouni, *The Battle for Homs: Memoir of a Syrian Architect* (London: Thames and Hudson, 2016); Robin Yassin Kassab and Leila Al-Shami, *Burning Country: Syrians in Revolution and War* (London: Pluto Press, 2016), 43–4, 56, 82; Stephen Starr, *Revolt in Syria: Eye-Witness to the Uprising* (London: Hurst and Co, 2015); Nicholas van Dam, *Destroying a Nation: The Civil War in Syria* (London: I. B. Tauris, 2017); Jonathan Little, *Syrian Notebook: Inside the Homs Uprising* (London: Verso, 2015).

50 Phillips, *The Battle for Syria*, 120.

51 van Dam, *Destroying a Nation*, 106–8; Phillips, *The Battle for Syria*, 161.

52 Janice Perlman, *Favela* (Oxford: Oxford University Press, 2010), 24.

53 Antonio Sampaio, *Illicit Order: The Military Logic of Organized Crime and Urban Security in Rio de Janeiro* (London: IISS, 2019), 9.

54 Ioan Grillo, *Gangster Warlords: Drug Dollars, Killing Fields, and the New Politics of Latin America* (London: Bloomsbury, 2017), 72–6.

55 Grillo, *Gangster Warlords*, 77; Perlman, *Favela*, 178.

56 Misha Glenny, *Nemesis: One Man and the Battle for Rio* (London: Bodley Head, 2015); Desmond Enrique Arias, *Drugs and Democracy in Rio de Janeiro* (Chapel Hill: University of North Carolina Press, 2006); Desmond Enrique Arias, 'The dynamics of criminal governance: networks and social order in Rio de Janeiro', *Journal of Latin American Studies* 38(2) 2006, 293–325; Desmond Enrique Arias, 'Trouble en route: drug trafficking and clientelism in Rio de Janeiro shantytowns', *Qualitative Sociology* 29(4) 2006, 427–45.

57 Kees Koonings and Dirk Kruijt, 'The rise of megacities and the urbanization of informality, exclusion and violence', in Kees Koonings and Dirk Kruijt (eds), *Megacities: The Politics of Urban*

Exclusion and Violence in the Global South (London: Zed Books, 2009), 8–28.

58 Alverado De Souza Pinheiro, *Irregular Warfare: Brazil's Fight against Criminal Urban Guerrillas* (Hurlbert Field, FL: JSOU Press, 2009), 10.

59 Perlman, *Favela*, 105.

60 Sampaio, *Illicit Order*, 24.

61 De Souza Pinheiro, *Irregular Warfare*, 2.

62 De Souza Pinheiro, *Irregular Warfare*, 14.

Chapter 4   Metropolis

1 Stephen Graham, *Vertical: The City from Satellites to Bunkers* (London: Verso, 2018), 161.

2 Graham, *Vertical*, 161.

3 Graham, *Vertical*, 6.

4 Mike Davis, *City of Quartz* (London: Vintage, 1990), 233.

5 Neil Brenner and Christian Schmid, 'Towards a new epistemology of the urban?', *City* 19(2–3) 2015, 152

6 Brenner and Schmid 'Towards a new epistemology of the urban?', 172.

7 Ash Amin and Nigel Thrift, *Cities: Re-imagining the Urban* (Oxford: Blackwell, 2001), 26.

8 Brenner and Schmid, 'Towards a new epistemology of the urban?', 170.

9 Peter Hall, *Cities in Civilization* (London: Weidenfeld & Nicolson, 1998), 928.

10 Hall, *Cities in Civilization*, 930–1.

11 Dov Tamari, 'Military operations in urban environments: the case of Lebanon, 1982', in Michael C. Desch (ed.), *Soldiers in Cities: Military Operations on Urban Terrain* (Carlisle, PA: Strategic Studies Institute, 2001), 46.

12 John Spencer, 'The city is not neutral: why urban warfare is so hard', Modern Warfare Institute, 4 March 2020: https://mwi.usma.edu/city-not-neutral-urban-warfare-hard/.

13 Michael Evans, 'Lethal genes: the urban military imperative and Western strategy in the early twenty-first century', *Journal of Strategic Studies* 32(4) 2009, 544.

14 John Spencer and John Amble, 'A better approach to urban operations: treat cities like human bodies', Modern War Institute, 13 September 2017: https://mwi.usma.edu/better-approach-urban-operations-treat-cities-like-human-bodies/.

15 Spencer and Amble, 'A better approach to urban operations'.
16 Abel Wolman, 'The metabolism of cities', *Scientific American* 213, September 1965, 179–90.
17 Jane Schneider and Ida Susser, *Wounded Cities* (Oxford: Berg, 2003), 33–4.
18 David Kilcullen, *Out of the Mountains: The Coming of Age of the Urban Guerrilla* (London: Hurst and Company, 2013), 43.
19 Kilcullen, *Out of the Mountains*, 46.
20 Kilcullen, *Out of the Mountains*, 50.
21 Chief of Staff of the Army, *Megacities and the US Army: Preparing for an Uncertain Future* (Arlington, VA: Office of the Chief of Staff of the Army, Strategic Studies Group, 2014), 10.
22 Chief of Staff of the Army, *Megacities and the US Army*, 11.
23 Louis Wirth, *The Ghetto* (Chicago: Chicago University Press, 1956), 6.
24 David Harvey, *Social Justice and the City* (London: Edward Arnold, 1973), 59.
25 Harvey, *Social Justice and the City*, 59.
26 Harvey, *Social Justice and the City*, 59–60.

Chapter 5   Walls
 1 James Scott, *Against the Grain: A Deep History of the Earliest States* (New Haven, CT: Yale University Press, 2017), 119.
 2 James D. Tracy (ed.), *City Walls: The Urban Enceinte in Global Perspective* (Cambridge: Cambridge University Press, 2000), 1.
 3 John Spencer, 'The most effective mechanism on the modern battlefield is concrete', Modern Warfare Institute, 14 November 2016: https://mwi.usma.edu/effective-weapon-modern-battlefield-concrete/.
 4 Wayne Lee, *Waging War: Conflict, Culture and Innovation in World History* (Oxford: Oxford University Press, 2016), 223.
 5 Lee, *Waging War*, 222.
 6 Lee, *Waging War*, 228.
 7 David Eltis, *The Military Revolution in Sixteenth Century Europe* (London: I. B. Tauris, 1998), 77.
 8 Christopher Duffy, *Siege Warfare* (London: Routledge & Kegan Paul, 1979), 15.
 9 Duffy, *Siege Warfare*, 21.
10 Jeremy Black, *Fortification and Siegecraft: Defence and Attack Through the Ages* (London: Rowman & Littlefield, 2018), 66.
11 Duffy, *Siege Warfare*, 34.

12 Martha Pollak, *Cities at War in Early Modern Europe* (Cambridge: Cambridge University Press, 2010), 11.

13 M. S. Anderson, *War and Society in Europe of the Old Regime 1618–1789* (Stroud: Fontana, 1988), 40.

14 Anderson, *War and Society in Europe of the Old Regime*, 88.

15 Christopher Duffy, *The Fortress in the Age of Vauban and Frederick the Great* (London: Routledge & Kegan Paul, 1985), 154.

16 Duffy, *The Fortress in the Age of Vauban and Frederick the Great*, 156.

17 Alastair Horne, *The Fall of Paris* (London: Macmillan, 1965), 325–6.

18 Black, *Fortification and Siegecraft*, 198.

19 Alexander Watson, *The Fortress: The Great Siege of Przemyśl* (London: Allen Lane, 2019), 6–8.

20 Watson, *The Fortress*, 106.

21 Watson, *The Fortress*, 200.

22 See, for instance, the Divis Flats, Belfast (Chapter 3).

23 Paul Virilio, *Bunker Archaeology* (New York: Princeton Architectural Review, 2008), 40; See also Kevin Mallory and Arvid Ottar, *Architecture and Aggression: A History of Military Architecture in North West Europe, 1900–1945* (London: Architectural Press, 1973).

24 Oscar Newman, *Defensible Space: People and Design in the Violent City* (London: Architectural Press, 1972), 2.

25 Newman, *Defensible Space*, 2–3.

26 Peter Marcuse 'The "war on terrorism" and life in cities after September 11, 2001', in Stephen Graham (ed.), *Cities, War and Terrorism* (London: Verso, 2004), 271.

27 Jon Coaffee, *Terrorism, Risk and the City* (Farnham: Ashgate, 2009), 122.

28 Jon Coaffee, 'Recasting the ring of steel: designing out terrorism in the city of London?', in Graham (ed.), *Cities, War and Terrorism*, 278.

29 Eyal Weizman, 'Strategic points, flexible lines, tense surface and political volumes', in Graham (ed.), *Cities, War and Terrorism*, 179.

30 Eyal Weizman, *Hollow Land: Israel's Architecture of Occupation*. (London: Verso, 2007), 131.

31 Teresa Caldiera, *City of Walls* (Los Angeles: University of California Press, 2000), 231.

32 For the most comprehensive analysis of this battle, see David Johnson, M. Wade Markel and Brian Shannon, *The 2008 Battle for Sadr City: Reimagining Urban Combat* (Santa Monica, CA: Rand Arroyo Centre, 2013).

33 General Joseph Martin, personal interview, 16 November 2018.

34 Lieutenant-General Danilo Pamonag, Filipino Army, personal email, 25 May 2019.

Chapter 6   Air

1 Ralph Peters, 'Our soldiers, their cities', *Parameters*, 26(1) 1996, 43–50.
2 Eyal Weizman, 'Introduction to the politics of verticality', Open Democracy, 2002: http://www.opendemocracy.net/ecology-poli ticsverticality/article_801.jsp.
3 Stephen Graham, *Cities under Siege: The New Military Urbanism* (London: Verso, 2010), 31.
4 Stephen Graham, *Vertical: The City from Satellites to Bunkers* (London: Verso, 2018), 13–14.
5 Stuart Elden, 'Secure the volume: vertical geopolitics and the depth of power', *Political Geography* 34, 2013, 49; See also Peter Adey, Michael Whitehead and Alison Williams, *From Above: War, Violence and Verticality*. (London: Hirst and Co., 2013); Daphné Richemond-Barak, *Underground Warfare* (Oxford: Oxford University Press, 2018).
6 Ralph Sawyer, *Fire and Water: The Art of Incendiary and Aquatic Warfare in China* (Cambridge, MA: Westview Press, 2004), 123–4.
7 Alexander Watson, *The Fortress: The Great Siege of Przemyśl* (London: Allen Lane, 2019), 137.
8 B. H. Liddell Hart, *Paris: or The Future of War* (London: Kegan Paul, Trench, Trubner & Co., 1923), 44.
9 Liddell Hart, *Paris*, 45.
10 Giulio Douhet, *The Command of the Air* (Tuscaloosa: University of Alabama Press, 2009), 8–9.
11 Douhet, *The Command of the Air*, 55.
12 Douhet, *The Command of the Air*, 18.
13 Martin Coward, *Urbicide* (London: Routledge, 2009).
14 Douhet, *The Command of the Air*, 22.
15 Douhet, *The Command of the Air*, 61.
16 Liddell Hart, *Paris*, 46.
17 Richard Overy, *The Bombing War* (London: Penguin, 2014), 53.
18 Overy, *The Bombing War*, 267.
19 Arthur Harris, *Bomber Offensive* (London: Collins, 1947), 77.
20 Harris, *Bomber Offensive*, 77.
21 Conrad Crane, *Bombs, Cities, and Civilians: American Airpower Strategy in World War II* (Kansas: University of Kansas Press, 1993).

22 Keith Lowe, *Inferno: The Devastation of Hamburg* (London: Hamburg, 2007), 192–3.
23 Martin Middlebrook, *The Battle of Hamburg* (London: Cassell and Co., 1980), 84.
24 Middlebrook, *The Battle of Hamburg*, 137.
25 Middlebrook, *The Battle of Hamburg*, 245.
26 Middlebrook, *The Battle of Hamburg*, 240–1, 245–7.
27 John A. Warden, III, 'The enemy as a system', *Airpower Journal*, 9(1) 1995, 40–55.
28 AJP 3-3, *Allied Joint Doctrine for Air and Space Operations* (NATO, April 2006), 1–4.
29 William Head, 'The battles of Al-Fallujah: urban warfare and the growth of air power', *Air Power History* (2013), 40.
30 Head, 'The battles of Al-Fallujah', 35.
31 Kenneth Estes, *Marine Corps Operations in Iraq 2003–2006* (Quantico: VA: USMC History Division), 63–4.
32 Head, 'The battles of Al-Fallujah', 35.
33 Dick Camp, *Operation Phantom Fury* (Minneapolis: Zenith: 2009), 133.
34 Camp, *Operation Phantom Fury*, 132.
35 David Johnson, M. Wade Markel and Brian Shannon, *The 2008 Battle for Sadr City: Reimagining Urban Combat* (Santa Monica, CA: Rand Arroyo Centre, 2013), 53.
36 Johnson et al., *The 2008 Battle of Sadr City*, 57.
37 Mosul Study Group, *What the Battle for Mosul Teaches the Force*, US Army, 2017: https://www.armyupress.army.mil/Portals/7/Primer-on-Urban-Operation/Documents/Mosul-Public-Release1.pdf, 60.

Chapter 7   Fire

1 Wayne Lee, *Waging War: Conflict, Culture and Innovation in World History* (Oxford: Oxford University Press, 2016), 17.
2 Gareth Brereton, *I Am Ashurbanipal: King of the World, King of Assyria* (London: Thames and Hudson, 2019), 281.
3 Paul Bentley Kern, *Ancient Siege Warfare* (London: Souvenir, 1999), 182.
4 Thucydides, *The Peloponnesian War* (Harmondsworth: Penguin, 1967), 143.
5 Barry Strauss, 'Naval battles and sieges' in Philip Sabin, Hans van Wees and Michael M. Whitby (eds), *The Cambridge History of Greek and Roman Warfare, Volume 1* (Cambridge: Cambridge University Press, 2007), 245.

6 Ralph Sawyer, *Fire and Water: The Art of Incendiary and Aquatic Warfare in China* (Cambridge, MA: Westview Press, 2004), 7.

7 Strauss, 'Naval battles and sieges', 239.

8 Kern, *Ancient Siege Warfare*, 112.

9 Lee, *Waging War*, 92.

10 Alice Hills, *Future Wars in Cities: Rethinking a Liberal Dilemma* (London: Frank Cass, 2004), 64, 142.

11 War Department, *FM 31-50: Attack on a Fortified Position and Combat in Towns* (Washington, DC: US Government Printing Office, 1944), 19.

12 Headquarters, Department of the Army, *FM 31-50: Combat in Fortified and Built-up Areas* (Washington, DC: US Government Printing Office, 1964), 33.

13 Alec Wahlman, *Storming the City* (Denton: University of North Texas Press, 2015), 44.

14 Wahlman, *Storming the City*, 44.

15 Warfare Branch, Headquarters Field Army, *Urban Tactical Handbook* (Warminster: Land Warfare Development Centre, 2013), 98.

16 Warfare Branch, *Urban Tactical Handbook*, 30.

17 Warfare Branch, *Urban Tactical Handbook*, 30.

18 Warfare Branch, *Urban Tactical Handbook*, 98.

19 General Joseph Martin, US Army, Land Component Commander, Operation Inherent Resolve, personal interview, 16 November 2018.

20 James Verini, *They Will Have to Die Now* (London: Oneworld, 2019), 14.

21 Lieutenant General Danilo Pamonag, Filipino Army, personal email communication, 25 May 2019.

22 Lester Grau, 'Changing Russian urban tactics: the aftermath of the battle from Grozny', *INSS Strategic Forum*, 28 July 1995.

23 Tim Pritchard, *Ambush Alley* (Novato, CA: Presidio, 2007), 253.

24 Pritchard, *Ambush Alley*, 189.

25 Martin, personal interview, 16 November 2018.

26 Mosul Study Group, *What the Battle for Mosul Teaches the Force*, US Army, 2017: https://www.armyupress.army.mil/Portals/7/Primer-on-Urban-Operation/Documents/Mosul-Public-Release1.pdf, 56.

27 Pamonag, personal email communication, 25 May 2019.

28 ATP-99, *Urban Tactics* (NATO, February 2017), 2–4.

29 Warfare Branch, Headquarters Field Army, *Operations in the Urban*

Environment (Warminster: Land Warfare Development Centre, Doctrine Note 15/13), 61.

30 Wahlman, *Storming the City*, 152.

31 Wahlman, *Storming the City*, 152–4.

32 Wahlman, *Storming the City*, 164.

33 Wahlman, *Storming the City*, 165.

34 David Johnson, M. Wade Markel and Brian Shannon, *The 2008 Battle for Sadr City: Reimagining Urban Combat* (Santa Monica, CA: Rand Arroyo Centre, 2013), 54.

35 Mosul Study Group, *What the Battle for Mosul Teaches the Force*, 12.

36 Mosul Study Group, *What the Battle for Mosul Teaches the Force*, 14.

37 Robert Postings, 'An analysis of the Islamic State's SVBIED Use in Raqqa', *International Review*, 11 May 2018: https://international-review.org/an-analysis-of-islamic-states-svbied-use-in-raqqa/.

38 Martin, personal interview, 16 November 2018.

39 Maarten Broekhof, Martijn Kitzen and Frans Osinga, 'A tale of two Mosuls: the resurrection of the Iraqi armed forces and the military defeat of ISIS', *Journal of Strategic Studies*, 12 December 2019: https://doi.org/10.1080/01402390.2019.1694912.

40 Mosul Study Group, *What the Battle for Mosul Teaches the Force*, 15.

41 Tim Ripley, *Operation Aleppo: Russia's War in Syria* (Lancaster: Telic-Herrick Publications, 2018), 49.

42 Pavel Baev, 'Russia's airpower in the Chechen war: denial, punishment and defeat' *Journal of Slavic Military Studies* 10(2) 1997, 8.

43 Tom Cooper, *Moscow's Game of Poker: Russian Military Intervention in Syria, 2015–17* (Warwick: Helion and Co, 2018), 26.

44 Ripley, *Operation Aleppo*, 52.

45 Ripley, *Operation Aleppo*, 110.

46 Ripley, *Operation Aleppo*, 190.

47 Ripley, *Operation Aleppo*, 50.

48 For a superb discussion of the enduring importance of firepower in urban warfare, see Doug Winton, 'Is urban combat a great equalizer?', PhD Thesis, John Hopkins University, 2018.

49 Mike Boden, 'Berlin, 1945', in John Antal and Bradley Gericke (eds), *City Fights: Selected Histories of Urban Combat from World War II to Vietnam* (New York: Ballantine, 2003), 265.

50 Boden, 'Berlin, 1945', 279.

51 William Robertson (ed.), *Block by Block: The Challenges of Urban Operations* (Ft Leavenworth, KS: US ACGS College Press, 2003), 184.

52 Winton, 'Is urban combat a great equalizer?', 167.

53 Scott Huesing, *Echo in Ramadi* (Washington, DC: Regnery, 2018), 90

54 Huesing, *Echo in Ramadi*, 90.

55 Mosul Study Group, *What the Battle for Mosul Teaches the Force*, 70.

56 Mosul Study Group, *What the Battle for Mosul Teaches the Force*, 70.

57 Colonel, OF-5, US Army, J5, Operation Inherent Resolve, personal interview, 30 September 2019.

58 Colonel, OF-5, personal interview, 30 September 2019.

59 Charles Knight and Katja Theodarakis, *Special Report: The Marawi Crisis – Urban Conflict and Information Operations* (Barton, ACT: Australian Strategic Policy Institute Ltd, 2019), 13. SLICE stands for strategize, locate, isolate, constrict, eliminate.

60 James Lewis, 'The battle of Marawi: small team lessons learned from the close fight', *The Cove*, 26 November 2018.

61 Warfare Branch, Headquarters Field Army, *Operations in the Urban Environment*, 68.

62 Janice Perlman, *Favela* (Oxford: Oxford University Press, 2010), 105,

63 https://www.benning.army.mil/infantry/doctrinesupplement/atp3-21.8/.

64 I am grateful to Patrick Bury for this point.

65 Warfare Branch, Headquarters Field Army, *Operations in the Urban Environment*, 66.

66 See Winton, 'Is urban combat a great equalizer?'.

67 Colonel, OF-5, US Army, email correspondence, 16 April 2020.

68 This figure is based on an estimate that the US employed a unit of 155mm (18 guns), a unit of 105mm (18 guns), a High Mobility Rocket Artillery System Battery (6 or 8 launchers), and a French battery (8 Guns).

69 David Vergun, 'Task force commander recalls assisting Iraqi troops in drive on Mosul', US Army, 6 May 2017: https://www.army.mil/article/187097/task_force_commander_recalls_assisting_i.

Chapter 8   Swarms

1 Eyal Weizman, *Hollow Land: Israel's Architecture of Occupation* (London: Verso, 2007), 188.

2 Weizman, *Hollow Land*, 188.

3 Although the word 'fractal' has become established in the social sciences to mean broken or divided, this is a misnomer. Fractal formally refers to a mathematically conceived curve, any part of which has the same statistical qualities as the original; see *The*

Compact Oxford English Dictionary (Oxford: Clarendon, 1992), 630. The word that should be used is 'fracted'.

4 Weizman, *Hollow Land*, 171.

5 Sahera Bleibeh, 'Walking through walls: the invisible war', *Space and Culture* 18(2) 2015, 156–70.

6 Weizman, *Hollow Land*, 193.

7 Lieutenant General Paul van Riper, *A Concept for Future Military Operations on Urbanized Terrain* (Quantico, VA: Department of the Navy, Marine Corps Combat Development, 1997), III-7.

8 Eyal Ben-Ari, Zeev Lerer, Uzi Ben-Shalom and Ariel Vainer, *Rethinking Contemporary Warfare* (New York: SUNY Press, 2010), 124.

9 Zygmunt Bauman, *Liquid Modernity* (Cambridge: Polity, 2000).

10 Benjamin Runkle, 'Jaffa, 1948' in John Antal and Bradley Gericke, *City Fights: Selected Histories of Urban Combat from World War II to Vietnam* (New York: Ballantine, 2003), 297.

11 Runkle, 'Jaffa, 1948', 298.

12 Michael Dewar, *War in the Streets* (London: BCA, 1992), 30–1.

13 Thomas-Robert Bugeaud, *La Guerre des rues et des maisons* (Paris: Jean-Paul Rocher, 1997), 130.

14 Bugeaud, *La Guerre des rues et des maisons*, 138.

15 Thucydides, *The Peloponnesian War* (Harmondsworth: Penguin, 1967), 98.

16 Headquarters, Department of the Army, FM 90-10-1, *An Infantryman's Guide to Combat in Built-up Areas* (Washington, DC: US Government Printing Office, 1995), B-13.

17 Jonathan House *Combined Arms Warfare in the Twentieth Century* (Lawrence: University of Kansas Press, 2006), 257–8.

18 Headquarters, Department of the Army, FM 3-06, *Urban Operations* (Washington, DC: US Government Printing Office, 2006), 2.2–3.

19 Commando Training Centre Royal Marines, *Close Quarters Battle Instructor* (2011), 12.2–3.

20 This process is known as initiative-based tactics (IBT).

21 For a longer discussion of close-quarters battle, see Anthony King, *The Combat Soldier: Infantry Tactics and Cohesion in the Twentieth and Twenty-first Centuries* (Oxford: Oxford University Press, 2013), 237–65, 315–32.

22 David Arquilla and John Ronfeldt, *Swarming and the Future of Conflict* (Santa Monica, CA: Rand Arroyo Centre, 1999), 44.

23 David Johnson, *Hard Fighting: Israel in Lebanon and Gaza* (Santa Monica, CA: Rand Arroyo Centre, 2011), 42.

24 David Zucchino, *Thunder Run: The Armored Strike to Capture Baghdad* (London: Atlantic Books, 2004), 237.

25 Paul Virilio and Sylvère Lotrine, *Pure War* (New York: Semiotext(e), 1997); Paul Virilio, 'The state of emergency', in James Der Derian (ed.), *The Virilio Reader* (Oxford, Blackwell, 1998), 48–57.

26 Amos Fox, 'The re-emergence of the siege: an assessment of the trends in modern land warfare', *Association of the US Army*, 3 July 2018: https://www.ausa.org/publications/reemergence-siege-assessment-trends-modern-land-warfare.

27 David Glantz, with Jonathan House, *The Stalingrad Trilogy, Volume 2: Armageddon in Stalingrad: September–November 1942* (Lawrence: University of Kansas Press, 2009), 716.

28 Barry Posen, 'Urban operations: tactical realities and strategic ambiguities', in Michael C. Desch (ed.), *Soldiers in Cities: Military Operations on Urban Terrain* (Carlisle, PA: Strategic Studies Institute, 2001), 153.

29 Doug Winton, 'Is urban combat a great equalizer?', PhD thesis, John Hopkins University, 2018; Alec Wahlman, *Storming the City* (Denton: University of North Texas Press, 2015).

30 Wahlman, Alec *Storming the City*, 104.

31 Dick Camp, *Operation Phantom Fury* (Minneapolis: Zenith, 2009), 299.

32 Robert Postings, 'A guide to the Islamic State's way of urban warfare', Modern War Institute, 7 September 2018: https://mwi.usma.edu/guide-islamic-states-way-urban-warfare/.

33 Weizman, *Hollow Land*, 201.

34 Tim Ripley, *Operation Telic: The British Campaign in Iraq 2003–2009* (Lancaster: Telic-Herrick Publications, 2016), 260.

35 Stephen Biddle, 'Speed kills: Reassessing the role of speed, precision and situation awareness in the fall of Saddam', *Journal of Strategic Studies* 30(1) 2007, 36.

36 Camp, *Operation Phantom Fury*, 180.

37 Major, OF-3, US Army, personal interview, 9 January 2019.

38 Maarten Broekhof, Martijn Kitzen and Frans Osinga, 'A tale of two Mosuls: the resurrection of the Iraqi armed forces and the military defeat of ISIS', *Journal of Strategic Studies*, 12 December 2019: https://doi.org/10.1080/01402390.2019.1694912, 14

39 Postings, 'A guide to the Islamic State's way of urban warfare'.

40 General Joseph Martin, US Army Land Component Command, Operation Inherent Resolve, personal interview, 16 November 2018.

41 Martin, personal interview, 16 November 2018.
42 Karl-Heinz Frieser, *The Blitzkrieg Legend* (Annapolis, MD: Naval Institute Press, 2005).
43 Biddle, 'Speed kills', 13.
44 David Johnson, M. Wade Markel and Brian Shannon, *The 2008 Battle for Sadr City: Reimagining Urban Combat* (Santa Monica, CA: Rand Arroyo Centre, 2013), 58.
45 Russell W. Glenn, *A Short War in a Perpetual Conflict: Implications of Israel's 2014 Operation Protective Edge for the Australian Army* (Commonwealth of Australia: Directorate of Future Land Warfare, 2016), 103.

Chapter 9   Partners

1 Barry Strauss, 'Naval battles and sieges', in Philip Sabin, Hans van Wees and Michael M. Whitby (eds), *The Cambridge History of Greek and Roman Warfare, Volume 1* (Cambridge: Cambridge University Press, 2007), 244.
2 Philip De Souza, 'Naval battles and sieges', in Philip Sabin, Hans van Wees and Michael M. Whitby (eds), *The Cambridge History of Greek and Roman Warfare, Volume 1* (Cambridge: Cambridge University Press, 2007), 449, 457.
3 Thomas Hippler, *Governing from the Skies: A Global History of Aerial Bombing* (London: Verso, 2017); also Thomas Hippler, *Bombing the People: Giulio Douhet and the Foundation of Air-Power Strategy, 1884–1939* (Cambridge: Cambridge University Press, 2013), 19.
4 Richard Gabriel, *Operation Peace for Galilee: The Israeli–PLO War in Lebanon* (New York: Hill and Wang, 1984). See also Sara Fregonese, *War and the City: Urban Geopolitics in Lebanon* (London: I. B. Tauris, 2019)
5 William Doyle, *A Soldier's Dream: Captain Travis Patriquin and the Awakening of Iraq* (New York: NAL Caliber, 2012), 107.
6 Doyle, *A Soldier's Dream*, 117.
7 Doyle, *A Soldier's Dream*, 99.
8 Doyle, *A Soldier's Dream*, 81.
9 Doyle, *A Soldier's Dream*, 123–4.
10 Doyle, *A Soldier's Dream*, 125.
11 Nick Hopkins, 'Inside Iraq: "We had to deal with people who had blood on their hands"', *Guardian*, 6 July 2012: https://www.theguardian.com/world/2012/jul/16/inside-iraq-emma-sky.
12 Lieutenant General Sean MacFarland, Commander, Operation Inherent Resolve, personal interview, 23 July 2019.

13 MacFarland, personal interview, 23 July 2019.
14 MacFarland, personal interview, 23 July 2019.
15 MacFarland, personal interview, 23 July 2019.
16 MacFarland, personal interview, 23 July 2019.
17 MacFarland, personal interview, 23 July 2019.
18 MacFarland, personal interview, 23 July 2019.
19 MacFarland, personal interview, 23 July 2019.
20 MacFarland, personal interview, 23 July 2019.
21 MacFarland, personal interview, 23 July 2019.
22 Andreas Krieg and Jean-Marc Rickli, *Surrogate Warfare* (Washington, DC: Georgetown University Press, 2019), 164.
23 Krieg and Rickli, *Surrogate Warfare*, 176.
24 Christopher Phillips, *The Battle for Syria: International Rivalry in the New Middle East* (New Haven: Yale University Press, 2018), 161.
25 Michael Kofman, Katya Migacheva, Brian Nichiporuk, Andrew Radin, Olesya Tkacheva and Jenny Oberholtzer, *Lessons from Russia's Operations in Crimea and Eastern Ukraine* (Santa Monica, CA: Rand Arroyo Centre, 2017), 56.
26 Kofman et al., *Lessons from Russia's Operations*, 43.
27 Kofman et al., *Lessons from Russia's Operations*, 44.

Chapter 10   Rumour

1 Barry Strauss, 'Naval battles and sieges', in Philip Sabin, Hans van Wees and Michael M. Whitby (eds), *The Cambridge History of Greek and Roman Warfare, Volume 1* (Cambridge: Cambridge University Press, 2007), 245.
2 Josephus, *The Jewish War* (Harmondsworth: Penguin, 1967), 283.
3 Thomas Arnold and Nicholas Fiore, 'Five operational lessons from the battle of Mosul', *Military Review*, January–February 2019: https://www.armyupress.army.mil/Journals/Military-Review/English-Edition-Archives/Jan-Feb-2019/Arnold-Mosul/.
4 Joint Doctrine Note 2/19, *Defence Strategic Communication: An Approach to Formulating and Executing Strategy* (Swindon: Ministry of Defence, 2019): https://assets.publishing.service.gov.uk/govern ment/uploads/system/uploads/attachment_data/file/804319/2019 0523-dcdc_doctrine_uk_Defence_Stratrategic_Communication_jdn_2_19.pdf, 6.
5 Warfare Branch, Headquarters Field Army, *Operations in the Urban Environment* (Warminster: Land Warfare Development Centre, Doctrine Note 15/13), 19.
6 Warfare Branch, *Operations in the Urban Environment*, 19.

7 David Patrikarakos, *War in 140 Characters* (New York: Basic Books, 2017), 1.

8 Patrikarakos, *War in 140 Characters*, 4.

9 Patrikarakos, *War in 140 Characters*, 9.

10 P. W. Singer and Emerson T. Brooking, *LikeWar: The Weaponization of Social Media* (Boston, MA: Houghton Mifflin Harcourt, 2019), 91.

11 Singer and Brooking, *LikeWar*, 5.

12 Jarrad Prier, 'Commanding the trend: social media as information warfare', *Strategic Studies Quarterly* 11(4) 2017, 60.

13 Singer and Brooking, *LikeWar*, 8.

14 Singer and Brooking, *LikeWar*, 149.

15 Singer and Brooking, *LikeWar*, 194.

16 Singer and Brooking, *LikeWar*, 196.

17 Prier, 'Commanding the Trend, 54.

18 Prier, 'Commanding the Trend, 55.

19 Prier, 'Commanding the Trend, 55.

20 Prier, 'Commanding the Trend, 73.

21 Reinoud Leenders, 'Collective action and mobilization in Dar'a: anatomy of the onset of Syria's popular uprising', *Mobilization* 17(4) 2012, 424.

22 James Dorsey, 'Pitched Battles: the role of ultra soccer fans in the Arab Spring', *Mobilization* 17(4) 2012, 414.

23 Dorsey, 'Pitched battles', 413.

24 Singer and Brooking, *LikeWar*, 152.

25 Fawaz A. Gerges, *ISIS: A History* (Princeton, NJ: Princeton University Press), 127.

26 Jessica Stern and J. M Berger, *ISIS: The State of Terror* (London: William Collins, 2016), 110.

27 Stern and Berger, *ISIS*, 111–12.

28 Colonel, OF-5, US Army, J5, Operation Inherent Resolve, personal interview, 30 September 2019.

29 General Joseph Martin, Land Component Command, Operation Inherent Resolve, personal interview, 16 November 2019.

30 Mosul Study Group, *What the Battle for Mosul Teaches the Force*, US Army, 2017: https://www.armyupress.army.mil/Portals/7/Primer-on-Urban-Operation/Documents/Mosul-Public-Release1.pdf, 67.

31 Lieutenant General Sean Macfarland, Commander, Inherent Resolve, personal interview 23 July 2019.

32 Colonel, OF-5, US Army, personal interview, 30 September 2019.

33 Macfarland, personal interview, 23 July 2019.
34 Martin, personal interview, 16 November 2019.
35 See Chapter 4 pp. 69–71.
36 See the discussion of this area in Chapter 4 pp. 71–2.
37 Major-General Rupert Jones, OF-7, British Army, Deputy Commander, Operation Inherent Resolve, personal interview, 3 August 2018.
38 Jones, personal interview, 3 August 2018.
39 Jones, personal interview, 3 August 2018.
40 Jones, personal interview, 3 August 2018.
41 Jones, personal interview, 3 August 2018.
42 Jones, personal interview, 3 August 2018.

Chapter 11   Armageddon

1 David Glantz with Jonathan House, *The Stalingrad Trilogy, Volume 2: Armageddon in Stalingrad* (Lawrence: University of Kansas Press, 2009), 665.
2 James Mark, *Island of Fire* (Sydney: Leaping Horseman Books, 2006), 173.
3 Mark, *Island of Fire*, 173–4.
4 Dick Camp, *Operation Phantom Fury* (Minneapolis: Zenith, 2009), 262; Richard Lowry, *New Dawn* (New York: Savas Beattie, 2009), 190.
5 Lowry, *New Dawn*, 192.
6 Lowry, *New Dawn*, 197.
7 Camp, *Operation Phantom Fury*, 268.
8 Glantz, *The Stalingrad Trilogy*, 615.
9 Chief of Staff of the Army, *Megacities and the US Army: Preparing for a Complex and Uncertain Future* (United States Army, 2014), 4.
10 Chief of Staff of the Army, *Megacities and the US Army*, 4.
11 Kevin Felix and Frederick Wong, 'The case *for* megacities', *Parameters*, 45(1) 2015, 20.
12 Michael Evans, 'The case against megacities', *Parameters*, 45(1) 2015, 34.
13 Evans, 'The case against megacities', 34.
14 Evans, 'The case against megacities', 35.
15 Janne Matlary and Tormod Heier (eds), *Ukraine and Beyond: Russian's Strategic Security Challenge to Europe* (London: Palgrave Macmillan, 2010), 164.
16 Global Security Organization Korea: https://www.globalsecu rity.org/military/ops/oplan-5027.htm; International Institute for

Strategic Studies, *The Military Balance, 2017* (London: IISS, 2020), 287.

17 Global Security Organization Korea.

18 Stephen Graham, *Cities under Siege: The New Military Urbanism* (London: Verso, 2010), 162.

19 Paul Scharre, *Army of None: Autonomous Weapons and the Future of War* (New York: W. W. Norton and Company, 2019), 4.

20 Sharre, *Army of None*, 4.

21 Lucy Fisher, 'Armed drone is a real street fighter', *The Times*, 29 September 2020, 20.

22 David Kilcullen, 'Emerging patterns of adversary urban operations: insights from the NATO Urbanization Program', RUSI Urban Warfare Conference Session 3, 2 February 2018: https://rusi.org/rusi-urban-warfare-conference-presentations.

Bibliography

Adamson, William, 'Megacities and the US Army', *Parameters*, 45(1) (2015), 45–54.

Adey, Peter, Whitehead, Michael and Williams, Alison, *From Above: War, Violence and Verticality* (London: Hirst and Co., 2013).

Allied Joint Publications, AJP 3–3: *Allied Joint Doctrine for Air and Space Operations* (NATO, April 2006).

Al-Sabouni, Mouna, *The Battle for Homs: Memoir of a Syrian Architect* (London: Thames and Hudson, 2016).

Amin, Ash and Thrift, Nigel, *Cities: Re-imagining the Urban* (Cambridge: Polity, 2002).

Anderson, David, *Histories of the Hanged: Britain's Dirty War in Kenya and the End of Empire* (London: Weidenfeld & Nicolson, 2005).

Anderson, M. S., *War and Society in Europe of the Old Regime 1618–1789* (Stroud: Fontana, 1988).

Andres, Rick, Wills, Craig and Griffith, Thomas, 'Winning the allies: the strategic value of the Afghan model', *International Security*, 30(3) (2005/6), 124–60.

Andrew, Rod, Jr., *US Marines in Battle: An-Nasiriyah, 23 March – 2 April 2003* (CreateSpace Independent Publishing Platform, 2014).

Antal, John and Gericke, Bradley, *City Fights: Selected Histories of Urban Combat from World War II to Vietnam* (New York: Ballantine, 2003).

Appadurai, Arjun, *Modernity at Large* (Minneapolis: University of Minnesota Press, 1996).

Arias, Enrique Desmond, *Drugs and Democracy in Rio de Janeiro* (Chapel Hill: University of North Carolina Press, 2006).

Arias, Enrique Desmond, 'The dynamics of criminal governance: networks and social order in Rio de Janeiro', *Journal of Latin American Studies*, 38(2) (2006), 293–325.

Arias, Enrique Desmond, 'Trouble en route: drug trafficking and clientelism in Rio de Janeiro shantytowns', *Qualitative Sociology*, 29(4) (2006), 427–45.

Arnold, Thomas and Fiore, Nicholas, 'Five operational lessons from the battle of Mosul', *Military Review*, January–February 2019: https://www.armyupress.army.mil/Journals/Military-Review/English-Edition-Archives/Jan-Feb-2019/Arnold–Mosul/.

Arquilla, John and Ronfeldt, David, *In Athena's Camp* (Santa Monica, CA: Rand Arroyo Centre, 1997).

Arquilla, John and Ronfeldt, David, *Swarming and the Future of Conflict* (Santa Monica, CA: Rand Arroyo Centre, 1999).

Army Field Manual, vol. IV, part 5, *Fighting in Built-up Areas* (1983).

Ashworth, Gregory, *War and the City* (London: Routledge, 1991).

Baev, Pavel, 'Russia's airpower in the Chechen war: denial, punishment and defeat', *Journal of Slavic Military Studies*, 10(2) (1997), 1–18.

Barthorp, Michael, *Crater to the Creggan: The History of the Royal Anglian Regiment 1964–1974* (London: Leo Cooper, 1976).

Barzilay, David, *The British Army in Ulster* (Belfast: Century Service Ltd, 1973).

Bauman, Zygmunt, *Liquid Modernity* (Cambridge: Polity, 2000).

Beall, Jo, *Cities, Terrorism and Urban Wars of the 21st Century* (London: Frank Cass, 2007).

Ben-Ari, Eyal, Lerer, Zeev, Ben-Shalom, Uzi and Ariel Vainer, *Rethinking Contemporary Warfare* (New York: SUNY Press, 2010).

Bennett, Huw, 'From direct rule to Motorman', *Studies in Conflict and Terrorism*, 33(6) (2010), 511–31.

Benson, Kevin, 'Manila, 1945, in John Antal and Bradley Gericke, *City Fights: Selected Histories of Urban Combat from World War II to Vietnam* (New York: Ballantine, 2003), 230–50.

Betz, David, 'Webs, walls, and wars', *Global Crime*, 17(3–4) (2016), 296–313.

Betz, David and Stanford-Tuck, Hugh, 'The city is neutral', *Texas National Security Review*, 2(4) 2019, 60–87.

Biddle, Steven, 'Allies, airpower and modern warfare: the Afghan Model in Afghanistan and Iraq', *International Security*, 30(3) (2005/6), 161–76.

Biddle, Stephen, 'Speed kills: reassessing the role of speed, precision and situation awareness in the fall of Saddam', *Journal of Strategic Studies*, 30(1) (2007), 3–46.

Bishop, Patrick and Mallie, Eamonn, *The Provisional IRA* (London: Corgi, 1988).

Bishop, Ryan, 'The problem of violence: megacities and violence special section', *Theory, Culture and Society*, 27(6) (2010), 3–10.

Bishop, Ryan and Roy, Tania, 'Mumbai: city as target' *Theory, Culture and Society*, 26(7–8) (2009), 263–77.

Black, Jeremy, *Fortifications and Siegecraft: Defence and Attack Through the Ages* (London: Rowman & Littlefield, 2018).

Bleibeh, Sahera, 'Walking through walls: the invisible war', *Space and Culture*, 18(2) (2015), 156–70.

Boal, Frederick, (ed.), *Ethnicity and Housing: Accommodating the Differences* (London: Routledge, 2018).

Boal, Frederick 'Integrating and division: sharing and segregating Belfast', *Planning Practice and Research*, 11(2) (1996), 151–8.

Boal, Frederick, 'Territoriality on the Shankill-Falls divide, Belfast', *Irish Geography*, 41(3) (2008), 349–66.

Boal, Frederick and Livingstone, David. 'The frontier in the city: ethnonationalism in Belfast', *International Political Science Review*, 5(2) (1984), 161–79.

Boal, Frederick, Doherty, Paul and Pringle, Dennis, *Social Problems in the Belfast Urban Area: An Exploratory Analysis*, Occasional Paper, no. 12 (London: Queen Mary College, 1978).

Boden, Mike, 'Berlin, 1945', in John Antal and Bradley Gericke. *City Fights: Selected Histories of Urban Combat from World War II to Vietnam* (New York: Ballantine 2003), 251–88.

Bowns, Steven, *Aden to Afghanistan: Fifty Years of the Royal Anglian Regiment 1964–2014* (Oxford: Osprey, 2014).

Brenner, Neil, *New State Spaces* (Oxford: Oxford University Press, 2004).

Brenner, Neil (ed.), *Implosions/Explosions* (Berlin: Jovis, 2013).

Brenner, Neil and Schmid, Christian, 'Towards a new epistemology of the urban?', *City*, 19(2–3) (2015), 151–82.

Brenner, Neil and Schmid, Christian, 'The "urban age" in question', *International Journal of Urban and Regional Research*, 38(3) (2014), 731–55.

Brereton, Gareth, *I Am Ashurbanipal: King of the World, King of Assyria* (London: Thames and Hudson, 2019).

Broekhof, Maarten, Kitzen, Martijn and Osinga, Frans, 'A tale of two Mosuls: the resurrection of the Iraqi armed forces and the military defeat of ISIS', *Journal of Strategic Studies*, 12 December 2019.

Bugeaud, Thomas-Robert, *La Guerre des rues et des maisons* (Paris: Jean-Paul Rocher, 1997).

Burton, Anthony, *Urban Terrorism: Theory, Practice and Response* (London: Leo Cooper, 1975).

Burton, Frank, *Politics of Legitimacy* (London: Routledge and Kegan Paul, 1987).

Caldiera, Teresa, *City of Walls* (Los Angeles: University of California Press, 2000).

Camp, Dick, *Operation Phantom Fury* (Minneapolis, MT: Zenith, 2009).

Castells, Manuel, *The Informational City* (London: John Wiley and Sons, 1991).

Castilla, Sean M., 'On the likelihood of large urban conflict in the 21st century', *Small Wars Journal*, 25 March 2017: https://smallwars journal.com/jrnl/art/on–the–likelihood–of–large–urban–conflict–in–the–21st–century.

Cavanaugh, M. L., 'Walls and counterinsurgency', Modern War Institute, 9 April 2014, https://mwi.usma.edu/201449walls–and–counterinsurgency/.

Chief of Staff of the Army, Strategic Studies Group, *Megacities and the United States Army: Preparing for an Uncertain Future* (Arlington, VA: Office of the Chief of Staff of the Army, Strategic Studies Group, 2014).

Chin, Warren, 'Why did it all go wrong? Reassessing British counter-insurgency in Iraq', *Strategic Studies Quarterly*, 128 (Winter 2008), 119–35.

von Clausewitz, Carl, *On War*, trans. Michael Howard and Peter Paret (Princeton, NJ: Princeton University Press, 1984).

Coaffee, Jon, 'Recasting the Ring of Steel: designing out terrorism in the city of London?' in Stephen Graham (ed.) *Cities, War and Terrorism* (London: Verso 2004), 276–96.

Coaffee, Jon, *Terrorism, Risk and the City* (Farnham: Ashgate, 2009).

Coaffee, Jon and Lee, Peter, *Urban Resilience* (London: Palgrave, 2016).

Cohen, Raphael S., Johnson, David E., Thaler, David E., Allen, Brenna, ... Efron, Shira, *From Cast Lead to Protective Edge: Lessons from Israel's Wars in Gaza* (Santa Monica, CA: Rand Arroyo Centre, 2017).

Commando Training Centre Royal Marines, *Close Quarters Battle Instructor* (2011).

Coogan, Tim Pat, *The IRA* (London: Fontana/Collins, 1987).

Cooper, Tom, *Moscow's Game of Poker: Russian Military Intervention in Syria, 2015–17* (Warwick: Helion and Co, 2018).

Cordesman, Anthony, with Sullivan, George and Sullivan, William, *Lessons of the 2006 Israeli–Hezbollah War* (Washington, DC: CSIS Press, 2007).

Cordesman, Andrew, *The Iraq War: Strategy, Tactics and Military Lessons* (London: Praeger, 2003).

Cordesman, Andrew and Wagner, Abraham, *The Lessons of Modern War, Volume IV: The Gulf War* (Boulder, CO: Westview, 1996).

Coward, Martin, *Urbicide* (London: Routledge, 2009).

Craig, Gordon, 'Hans Delbrück: military historian', in Peter Paret (ed.), *The Makers of Modern Strategy* (Princeton, NJ: Princeton University Press, 1986).

Daniel, Jan, 'Criminal governance and insurgency: the Rio de Janeiro experience', *Central European Journal of International Security*, 9(4) (2015), 86–106

Daniel, Tommy, 'Concrete barriers: a false counterinsurgency idol', Modern War Institute, 23 March 2017: http://mwi.usma.edu/con crete–barriers–false–counterinsurgency–idol/.

Davis, Mike, 'The urbanization of empire: megacities and the laws of chaos', *Social Text*, 22(4) (2004), 9–15.

Davis, Mike, *Planet of the Slums* (London: Verso, 2006).

Davis, Mike, *City of Quartz* (London: Vintage, 1990).

De Baróid, Ciarán, *Ballymurphy and the Irish War* (London: Pluto, 2000).

Delbrück, Hans, *History of the Art of War within the Framework of Political History*. Vol. 1: *Warfare in Antiquity*, trans. Walter Renfroe, Jr. (London: Greenwood Press, 1975).

De Souza, Philip, 'Naval Battles and Sieges', in Philip Sabin, Hans van Wees and Michael M. Whitby (eds), *The Cambridge History of Greek and Roman Warfare, Volume 1* (Cambridge: Cambridge University Press, 2007).

De Souza Pinheiro, Alverado, *Irregular Warfare: Brazil's Fight against Criminal Urban Guerrillas* (Hurlbert Field, FL: JSOU Press, 2009).

Dewar, Michael, *The British Army in Northern Ireland* (London: Arms and Armour, 1997).

Dewar, Michael, *War in the Streets* (London: BCA, 1992).

Dorsey, James, 'Pitched battles: the role of ultra soccer fans in the Arab Spring', *Mobilization*, 17(4) (2012), 411–18.

Douhet, Giulio, *The Command of the Air* (Tuscaloosa: University of Alabama, 2009).

Doyle, William, *A Soldier's Dream: Captain Travis Patriquin and the Awakening of Iraq* (New York: NAL Caliber, 2012).

Desch, Michael C., 'Why MOUT now?' in Michael C. Desch (ed.), *Soldiers in Cities: Military Operations on Urban Terrain* (Carlisle, PA: Strategic Studies Institute, 2001), 1–16.

Dilegge, David, Bunker, Robert J., Sullivan, John P. and Keshavarz, Alma (eds), *Blood and Concrete: 21st Century Conflict in Urban Centers and Megacities* (US: Xlibris, 2019).

DiMarco, Louis, *Concrete Hell: Urban Warfare from Stalingrad to Iraq* (Oxford: Osprey, 2012).

Duffy, Christopher, *The Fortress in the Age of Vauban and Frederick the Great, 1660–1789, Volume II* (London: Routledge & Kegan Paul, 1985).

Duffy, Christopher, *Siege Warfare* (London: Routledge & Kegan Paul, 1979).

Dumper, Mick, *Jerusalem Unbound* (New York: Columbia University Press, 2014).

Eade, John, *Living the Global City* (London: Routledge, 1997).

Edwards, Sean, *Mars Unmasked: The Changing Face of Urban Operations* (New York: Rand Arroyo Centre, 2000).

Elden, Stuart, 'Secure the volume: vertical geopolitics and the depth of power', *Political Geography* 34 (2013), 35–51.

Eltis, David, *The Military Revolution in Sixteenth Century Europe* (London: I. B. Tauris, 1998).

English, Richard, *Armed Struggle: The History of the IRA* (London: Macmillan, 2003).

Estes, Kenneth, *Marine Corps Operations in Iraq 2003–2006* (Quantico: VA: USMC History Division, 2009).

Evans, Michael, 'The case against megacities', *Parameters*, 45(1) (Spring 2015), 33–43.

Evans, Michael, 'Lethal genes: the urban military imperative and Western strategy in the early twenty–first century', *Journal of Strategic Studies*, 32(4) (2009), 515–52.

Evans, Michael, *City without Joy: Military Operations in the 21st Century* (Canberra: Australian Defence College, Occasional Series No. 2, 2007).

Felix, Kevin and Wong, Frederick, 'The case *for* megacities', *Parameters*, 45(1) (Spring 2015), 19–32.

Fisher, Lucy, 'Armed drone is a real street fighter', *The Times*, 29 September 2020, 20.

Fontenot, Gregory, Degen, E. J. and Tohn, David, *On Point: The*

US Army in Operation Iraqi Freedom (Ft Leavenworth, KS: Combat Studies Institute Press, 2004).

Fox, Amos, 'Precision fires hindered by urban jungle', *Association of the US Army*, 16 April 2018: https://www.ausa.org/articles/precision-fires–hindered–urban–jungle.

Fox, Amos, 'The re-emergence of the siege: an assessment of the trends in modern land warfare', *Association of the US Army*, 3 July 2018: https://www.ausa.org/publications/reemergence–siege–assessment–trends–modern–land–warfare.

Fox, Amos, '"Cyborgs at Little Stalingrad": a brief history of the battles of the Donetsk airport, 26 May 2014 to 21 January 2015', May 2019: https://www.ausa.org/sites/default/files/publications/LWP-125–Cyborgs-at–Little-Stalingrad-A–Brief-History-of–the-Battle-of–the–Donetsk–Airport.pdf.

Fregonese, Sara, *War and the City: Urban Geopolitics in Lebanon* (London: I. B. Tauris, 2019).

Friedrich, Jörg, *The Fire: The Bombing of Germany, 1940–1945* (Ithaca, NY: Cornell University Press, 2006).

Frieser, Karl-Heinz, *The Blitzkrieg Legend* (Annapolis, MD: Naval Institute Press, 2005).

Gabel, Christopher R., '"Knock 'em all down": the reduction of Aachen, October 1944', in William Robertson (ed.), *Block by Block: The Challenges of Urban Operations* (Ft Leavenworth, KS: US ACGS College Press, 2003), 60–90.

Gabriel, Richard, *Operation Peace for Galilee: The Israeli–PLO War in Lebanon* (New York: Hill and Wang, 1984).

Galula, David, *Counterinsurgency Warfare* (Westport, CT: Praeger, 2006).

Gentile, Gian, Johnson, David E., Saum–Manning, Lisa, Cohen, Raphael S., . . . Doty, James L. III, *Reimagining the Character of Urban Operations for the US Army* (Santa Monica, CA: Rand Arroyo Centre, 2017).

Geraghty, Tony, *The Irish War: A Military History of a Domestic Conflict* (London: HarperCollins, 2000).

Gerges, Fawaz A., *ISIS: A History* (Princeton, NJ: Princeton University Press).

Glantz David, with House, Jonathan, *The Stalingrad Trilogy, Volume 2: Armageddon in Stalingrad: September–November 1942* (Lawrence: University of Kansas Press, 2009).

Glenn, Russell, *Combat in Hell: A Consideration of Constrained Urban Warfare* (Santa Monica, CA: Rand Arroyo Centre, 1996).

Glenn, Russell, *A Short War in a Perpetual Conflict*: *Implications of Israel's 2014 Operation Protective Edge for the Australian Army* (Australian Army, 2016).

Glenn, Russell, *All Glory is Fleeting: Insights from the Second Lebanon War* (Santa Monica, CA: Rand Arroyo Centre, 2012).

Glenn, Russell, 'Megacities: the good, the bad and the ugly', in David Dilegge, Robert Bunker, John Sullivan and Alma Keshavarz (eds), *Blood and Concrete: 21st Century Conflict in Urban Centers and Megacities* (US: Xlibris, 2019), 350–69.

Glenn, Russell and Kingston, Gina, *Urban Command in the 21st Century* (Santa Monica, CA: Rand Arroyo Centre, 2005).

Glenny, Misha, *Nemesis: One Man and the Battle for Rio* (London: Bodley Head, 2015).

Goldstein, Donna, *Laughter Out of Place: Race, Class, Violence and Sexuality in a Rio Shantytown* (Berkeley: University of California Press, 2003).

Graham, Stephen, 'Vertical geographies: Baghdad and after', *Antipode*, 36(1) (2004), 12–23.

Graham, Stephen (ed.) *Cities, War and Terrorism* (London: Verso, 2000).

Graham, Stephen, *Cities under Siege: The New Military Urbanism* (London: Verso, 2010).

Graham, Stephen, *Vertical: The City from Satellite to Bunkers* (London: Verso, 2018).

Grau, Lester, 'Changing Russian urban tactics: the aftermath of the battle from Grozny', *INSS Strategic Forum*, 28 July 1995.

Grillo, Ioan, *Gangster Warlords: Drug Dollars, Killing Fields, and the New Politics of Latin America* (London: Bloomsbury, 2017).

Guevara, Ernesto Che, *Guerrilla Warfare* (BN Publishing, 2007).

Hack, Karl, 'The Malayan Emergency as Counter–Insurgency Paradigm', *Journal of Strategic Studies*, 32(3) 2009, 383–414.

Hall, Peter, *Cities in Civilization* (London: Weidenfeld and Nicolson 1998).

Haltiner, Karl, 'The definite end of the mass army in Western Europe?' *Armed Forces and Society*, 25(1) (1998), 7–36.

Harel, Amos and Avi Issacharoff, Avi, *34 Days: Israel, Hezbollah and the War in Lebanon* (London: Palgrave Macmillan, 2008).

Harris, Arthur, *Bomber Offensive* (London: Collins, 1947).

Harvey, David, *Social Justice and the City* (London: Edward Arnold, 1973).

Harvey, David, 'Cities or urbanization?' in N. Brenner (ed.), *Implosions/ Explosions* (Berlin: Jovis, 2014), 52–66.

Head, William, 'The battles of Al–Fallujah: urban warfare and the growth of air power', *Air Power History* (2013), 32–51.

Headquarters, Department of the Army, FM 31-50, *Combat in Fortified and Built-Up Areas* (Washington, DC: US Government Printing Office, 1964).

Headquarters, Department of the Army, FM 3-21.8, *The Infantry Rifle, Platoon and Squad* (Washington, DC: US Government Printing Office, 2007).

Headquarters, Department of the Army, FM 90-10-1, *An Infantryman's Guide to Urban Combat 1982* (Amsterdam: Fredonia, 2003).

Headquarters, Department of the Army, FM 90-10, *Military Operations on Urbanized Terrain* (Washington, DC: US Government Printing Office, 1979).

Headquarters, Department of the Army, FM 3-06, *Urban Operations* (Washington, DC: US Government Printing Office, 2006).

Hedges, William, 'An analytic framework for operations in dense urban areas', *Small Wars Journal*: https://smallwarsjournal.com/jrnl/art/an–analytic–framework–for–operations–in–dense–urban–areas.

Hills, Alice, 'Fear and loathing in Fallujah', *Armed Forces & Society*, 32(4) (2006), 623–39

Hills, Alice, *Future Wars in Cities: Re-thinking a Liberal Dilemma* (London: Frank Cass, 2004)

Hills, Alice, 'Continuity and discontinuity: the grammar of urban military operations', in Stephen Graham (ed.), *Cities, War and Terrorism* (London: Verso, 2004), 231–46.

Hills, Alice, 'Can we fight in cities?', *RUSI Journal*, 146(5) (2001), 6–10.

Hippler, Thomas, *Governing from the Skies: A Global History of Aerial Bombing* (London: Verso, 2017).

Hippler, Thomas, *Bombing the People: Giulio Douhet and the Foundation of Air-Power Strategy, 1884–1939* (Cambridge: Cambridge University Press, 2013).

Hirst, Paul, *Space and Power* (Cambridge: Polity, 2005).

Hodges, David, *The Philosophy of the Urban Guerrilla: The Revolutionary Writings of Abraham Guillén* (New York: William Morrow and Company, 1973).

Hoffman, Frank, 'Complex irregular warfare: the next revolution in military affairs', *Orbis*, 50(3) (Summer 2006), 395–411.

Horne, Alastair, *The Fall of Paris* (London: Macmillan, 1965).

Hosler, John, *The Siege of Acre: 1189–1191* (New Haven, CT: Yale University Press, 2018).

House, Jonathan, *Combined Arms Warfare in the Twentieth Century* (Lawrence, KS: University of Kansas Press, 2006).

Howard, Michael, *War in the European History* (Oxford: Oxford University Press, 2000).

Howcroft, J., 2019. 'Intelligence challenges in urban operations', in David Dilegge, Robert Bunker, John Sullivan and Alma Keshavarz (eds), *Blood and Concrete: 21st Century Conflict in Urban Centers and Megacities* (US: Xlibris, 2019), 225–36.

Huesing, Scott, *Echo in Ramadi* (Washington, DC: Regnery, 2018).

International Institute for Strategic Studies, *The Military Balance 1991* (London: IISS, 1991).

International Institute for Strategic Studies, *The Military Balance 2019* (London: IISS, 2020).

Joes, Anthony James, *Urban Guerrilla Warfare* (Lexington: University Press of Kentucky, 2007).

Johnson, David, *Hard Fighting: Israel in Lebanon and Gaza* (Santa Monica, CA: Rand Arroyo Centre, 2011).

Johnson, David, Markel, Wade M. and Shannon, Brian, *The 2008 Battle for Sadr City: Reimagining Urban Combat* (Santa Monica, CA: Rand Arroyo Centre 2013).

Josephus, *The Jewish War* (Harmondsworth: Penguin, 1967).

Kern, Paul Bentley, *Ancient Siege Warfare* (London: Souvenir, 1999).

Kilcullen, David, *Out of the Mountains: The Coming of Age of the Urban Guerrilla* (London: Hurst and Company, 2013).

King, Anthony, 'Close-quarters battle: urban combat and "special forcification"', *Armed Forces & Society*, 42(2) (2016), 276–300.

King, Anthony, *The Combat Soldier: Infantry Tactics and Cohesion in the Twentieth and Twenty-first Centuries* (Oxford: Oxford University Press, 2013).

Knight, Charles and Theodarakis, Katja, *Special Report: The Marawi Crisis – Urban Conflict and Information Operations* (Barton, ACT: Australian Strategic Policy Institute Ltd, 2019).

Kofman, Michael, Migacheva, Katya, Nichiporuk, Brian, Radin, Andrew, Tkacheva, Olesya and Oberholtzer, Jenny, *Lessons from Russia's Operations in Crimea and Eastern Ukraine* (Santa Monica, CA: Rand Arroyo Centre, 2017).

Koonings, Kees and Kruijt, Dirk (eds), *Fractured Cities: Social Exclusion, Urban Violence and Contested Spaces in Latin America* (London: Zed, 2007).

Koonings, Kees and Kruijt, Dirk (eds), *Megacities: The Politics of Urban Exclusion and Violence in the Global South* (London: Zed Books, 2009).

Koonings, Kees and Kruijt, Dirk, 'The rise of megacities and the urbanization of informality, exclusion and violence', in Kees Koonings and Dirk Kruijt (eds), *Megacities: The Politics of Urban Exclusion and Violence in the Global South* (London: Zed Books, 2009), 8–28.

Krieg, Andreas and Rickli, Jean-Marc, *Surrogate Warfare* (Washington, DC: Georgetown University Press, 2019).

Krohley, Nicholas, *The Death of the Mehdi Army: The Rise, Fall and Revival of Iraq's Most Dangerous Militia* (London: Hurst and Co., 2015).

Kumer, Peter and Krevs, Marco, 'Understanding the implications of spatial segregation in Belfast, Northern Ireland', *Geografski vestnik*, 87(2) (2015): https://doi.org/10.3986/GV87204.

Lambeth, Benjamin, 'Israel's war in Gaza: a paradigm of effective military learning and adaptation', *International Security*, 37(2) (2012), 81–118.

Lefebvre, Henri, *Writing on Cities* (Oxford: Blackwell, 2004).

Lefebvre, Henri, *The Urban Revolution* (Minneapolis: University of Minnesota Press, 2002).

Lee, Wayne, *Waging War: Conflict, Culture and Innovation in World History* (Oxford: Oxford University Press, 2016).

Leeds, Elizabeth, 'Cocaine and parallel polities in the Brazilian urban periphery', *Latin American Research Review*, 31(3) (1996), 47–83.

Leenders, Reinoud, 'Collective action and mobilization in Dar'a: anatomy of the onset of Syria's popular uprising', *Mobilization*, 17(4) (2012), 419–34.

Lewis, James, 'The battle of Marawi: small team lessons learned from the close fight', *The Cove*, 26 November 2018.

Lewis, S. J., 'The battle of Stalingrad', in William Robertson (ed.), *Block by Block: The Challenges of Urban Operations* (Ft Leavenworth, KS: US ACGS College Press, 2003).

Liddell Hart, Basil, *Paris: The Future of War* (London: Kegan, Paul, Trench, Trubner and Co., 1923).

Little, Jonathan, *Syrian Notebook: Inside the Homs Uprising* (London: Verso, 2015).

Livingston, Gary, *An-Nasiriyah: The Fight for the Bridges* (Open Library: Caisson Press, 2017).

Lowe, Keith, *Inferno: The Devastation of Hamburg* (London: Hamburg, 2007).

Macgregor, Dan, *Breaking the Phalanx* (London: Praeger, 1997).

Mahan, John, 'MOUT: the quiet imperative', *Military Review*, 64(7) (1984), 43–59.

Malkesian, Carter, *Illusions of Victory* (Oxford: Oxford University Press, 2017).

Mallory, Kevin and Ottar, Arvid, *Architecture and Aggression: A History of Military Architecture in North West Europe, 1900–1945* (Wallop: Architectural Press, 1973).

Manaugh, Geoff, *The Burglar's Guide to the City* (FSG Originals, 2016).

Mansoor, Peter, *Surge* (New Haven, CT: Yale University Press, 2014).

Mansoor, Peter, *Baghdad at Sunrise* (New Haven, CT: Yale University Press, 2008).

Marcus, Raphael, 'Learning "under fire": Israel's improvised military adaptation to Hamas tunnel warfare', *Journal of Strategic Studies*, 42(3–4) 2019, 344–70.

Marcuse, Peter, 'The "war on terrorism" and life in cities after September 11, 2001', in Stephen Graham (ed.), *Cities, War and Terrorism* (London: Verso 2004), 263–74.

Marighella, Carlos, *Minimanual of the Urban Guerrilla* (Spade, 1969).

Mark, James, *Island of Fire* (Sydney: Leaping Horseman Books, 2006).

Marshall, S. L. A., 'Notes on urban warfare', Army Material Systems Analysis Agency, Aberdeen Proving Ground, Maryland (April 1973), 8–11.

Matlary, Janne and Heier, Tormod (eds), *Ukraine and Beyond: Russian's Strategic Security Challenge to Europe* (London: Palgrave Macmillan, 2010).

Matthews, Matt, *We Were Caught Unprepared: The 2006 Hezbollah–Israel War* (Ft Leavenworth, KS: US Army Combined Arms Centre, Combat Studies Institute, 2008).

McKenna, Justin, 'Towards the army of the future: domestic politics and the end of conscription in France', *West European Politics*, 20(4) (October 1997), 125–45

McKee, Alexander, *Caen: Anvil of Victory* (London: Souvenir, 1984).

Mearsheimer, John, 'Maneuvre, mobile defence and the NATO central front', *International Security*, 6(3) (1982), 104–22.

Mearsheimer, John, 'Why the Soviets can't win quickly in Central Europe', *International Security*, 7(1) (1982), 3–39.

Middlebrook, Martin, *The Battle of Hamburg* (London: Cassell and Co., 1980).

Moss, Robert, *The War for the Cities* (New York: Coward, McCann, and Geoghegan, 1972).

Mosul Study Group 2017, *What the Battle for Mosul Teaches the Force*, US Army: https://www.armyupress.army.mil/Portals/7/Primer–on–Urban–Operation/Documents/Mosul–Public–Release1.pdf.

Murray, William, *The Age of the Titans: The Rise and Fall of the Great Hellenistic Navies* (Oxford: Oxford University Press, 2012).

NATO, *Allied Tactical Publication 9–9 Urban Tactics* (February 2017).

Newman, Oscar, *Defensible Space: People and Design in the Violent City* (London: Architectural Press, 1972).

Nikolsky, Alexey, 'Little, green and polite: the creation of Russian special operations forces', in Colby Howard and Ruslan Pukhov (eds), *Brothers Armed: Military Aspects of the Crisis in Ukraine* (Minneapolis, MN: East View Press, 2014), 124–34.

Norton, Richard, 'Feral cities', *Naval War College Review*, 56(4) (2003), 1–10.

Overy, Richard, *The Bombing War* (London: Penguin, 2014).

Pape, Robert, *Bombing to Win* (Ithaca, NY: Cornell University Press, 1996).

Park, Robert, *The Crowd and the Public* (Chicago: University of Chicago Press, 1972).

Park, Robert, *Human Communities* (Glencoe, IL: Free Press, 1972).

Parkinson, Alan, *1972 and the Ulster Troubles: 'A Very Bad Year'* (Portland, OR: Four Courts Press, 2010).

Patrikarakos, David, *War in 140 Characters* (New York: Basic Books, 2017).

Peddie, John, *The Roman War Machine* (Bodmin: Alan Sutton, 1994).

Perry, Walter L., Darilek, Richard E., Rohn, Laurinda L. and Sollinger, Jerry M. (eds), *Decisive War, Elusive Peace* (Santa Monica, CA: Rand Arroyo Centre, 2014).

Perlman, Janice, *Favela* (Oxford: Oxford University Press, 2010).

Peters, Ralph, 'Our soldier, their cities', *Parameters*, 26(1) (1996), 43–50.

Peters, Ralph, 'The future of armored warfare', *Parameters*, 27(3) (1997), 50–59.

Peters, Ralph, 'The human terrain of urban operations', *Parameters*, 30(1) (2000), 4–12.

Phillips, Christopher, *The Battle for Syria: International Rivalry in the New Middle East* (New Haven, CT: Yale University Press, 2018).

Pollak, Martha, *Cities at War in Early Modern Europe* (Cambridge: Cambridge University Press, 2010).

Posen, Barry, 'Urban operations: tactical realities and strategic ambiguities', in Michael C. Desch (ed.), *Soldiers in Cities: Military Operations on Urban Terrain* (Carlisle, PA: Strategic Studies Institute, 2001), 149–66.

Postings, Robert, 'A guide to the Islamic State's way of urban warfare',

Modern War Institute, 9 July 2018: https://mwi.usma.edu/guide–islamic–states–way–urban–warfare/.

Postings, Robert, 'An analysis of the Islamic State: SVBIED use in Raqqa', *International Review*, 11 May 2018: https://international-review.org/an–analysis–of–islamic–states–svbied–use–in–raqqa/.

Quinn-Judge, Paul, 'Ukraine's meat grinder is back in business', *Foreign Policy*, 12 April 2016.

Prier, Jarrad, 'Commanding the trend: social media as information warfare', *Strategic Studies Quarterly*, 11(4) (2017), 50–85.

Pritchard, Tim, *Ambush Alley* (Novato, CA: Presidio, 2007).

Pullan, Wendy and Baillie, Britt (eds), *Locating Urban Conflicts* (London: Palgrave Macmillan, 2013).

Radden Keefe, Patrick, *Say Nothing: A True Story of Murder and Memory in Northern Ireland* (London: William Collins, 2018).

Rapaport, Anatol, *The IDF and the Lessons of the Second Lebanon War* (Begin-Sadat Center for Strategic Studies, Bar Ilan University, Middle East Security Policy Studies No. 85, 2010).

Richemond-Barak, Daphné, *Underground Warfare* (Oxford: Oxford University Press, 2018).

Ripley, Tim, *Operation Telic: The British Campaign in Iraq 2003–2009* (Lancaster: Telic–Herrick Publications, 2016).

Ripley, Tim, *Operation Aleppo: Russia's War in Syria* (Lancaster: Telic–Herrick Publications, 2018).

Robertson, William (ed.), *Block by Block: The Challenges of Urban Operations* (Ft Leavenworth, KS: US ACGS College Press, 2003).

Runkle, Benjamin, 'Jaffa, 1948', in John Antal and Bradley Gericke, *City Fights: Selected Histories of Urban Combat from World War II to Vietnam* (New York: Ballantine, 2003), 289–313.

Russell, James, *Innovation, Transformation, and War: Counterinsurgency Operations in Anbar and Ninewa Provinces, Iraq, 2005–2007* (Stanford, CA: Stanford University Press, 2010).

Russell, James, 'Innovation in war: counterinsurgency operations in Anbar and Ninewa Provinces, Iraq, 2005–2007', *Journal of Strategic Studies*, 33(4) (2010), 595–624.

Sampaio, Antônio, 'Out of control: criminal gangs fight back in Rio's favelas', *Jane's Intelligence Review* (December 2014), 44–8.

Sampaio, Antonio, *Illicit Order: The Military Logic of Organized Crime and Urban Security in Rio de Janeiro* (London: IISS, 2019).

Sanders, Andrew, 'Operation Motorman (1972) and the search for a coherent British counter-insurgency strategy in Northern Ireland', *Small Wars and Insurgencies*, 24(3) (2013), 465–92.

Sassen, Saskia, 'When the city itself becomes a technology of war', *Theory, Culture and Society*, 27(6) (2010), 35–50.

Sassen, Saskia, *The Global City* (Princeton: Princeton University Press, 1991).

Sawyer, Ralph, *Fire and Water: The Art of Incendiary and Aquatic Warfare in China* (Cambridge, MA: Westview Press, 2004).

Scales, Robert, *Yellow Smoke* (London: Rowman & Littlefield, 2003).

Scott, James, *Against the Grain: A Deep History of the Earliest States* (New Haven, CT: Yale University Press, 2017).

Serrati, John, 'The Hellenistic world at war: stagnation and development', in Brian Campbell and Lawrence Tritle (eds), *The Oxford Handbook of Warfare in the Classical World* (Oxford: Oxford University Press, 2013), 461–97.

Sharre, Paul, *Army of None: Autonomous Weapons and the Future of War* (New York: W. W. Norton and Company, 2019).

Schneider, Jane and Susser, Ida, *Wounded Cities* (Oxford: Berg, 2003).

Shunk, David, 'Megacities, ungoverned areas, and the challenge of army urban combat operations in 2030–2040', in David Dilegge, Robert Bunker, John Sullivan and Alma Keshavarz (eds), *Blood and Concrete: 21st Century Conflict in Urban Centers and Megacities* (US: Xlibris, 2019), 173–82.

Singer, Peter and Brooking, Emerson, *LikeWar: The Weaponization of Social Media* (Boston, MA: Houghton Mifflin Harcourt, 2019).

Sloterdijk, Peter, *Terror from the Air* (Boston, MA: MIT Press, 2009).

Smith, M. L. R., *Fighting for Ireland: The Military Strategy of the Irish Republican Movement* (London: Routledge, 1995).

Smith, M. L. R and Neumann, Peter, 'Motorman's long journey', *British Contemporary History*, 19(4) (2005), 413–35.

Smith, Ray and West, Bing, *The March Up* (London: Pimlico, 2003).

Soja, Edward, *Postmetropolis* (Oxford: Blackwell, 2000).

Spencer, John, 'The most effective mechanism on the modern battlefield is concrete', Modern Warfare Institute, 14 November 2016: https://mwi.usma.edu/effective–weapon–modern–battlefield–concrete/.

Spencer, John and Amble, John, 'A better approach to urban operations: treat cities like human bodies', Modern Warfare Institute, 13 September 2017: https://mwi.usma.edu/better–approach–urban–operations–treat–cities–like–human–bodies/.

Spencer, John, 'Stealing the enemy's urban advantage: the battle of Sadr City', Modern War Institute, 31 January 2019: https://mwi.usma.edu/stealing–enemys–urban–advantage–battle–sadr–city/.

Spencer, John, 'The city is not neutral: why urban warfare is so hard', Modern Warfare Institute, 4 March 2020: https://mwi.usma.edu/city–not–neutral–urban–warfare–hard/.

Spiller, Roger, *Sharp Corners: Urban Operations at the Century's End* (Ft Leavenworth, KS: US Army Command and General Staff College Press, 2001).

Stern, Jessica and Berger, J. M., *ISIS: The State of Terror* (London: HarperCollins, 2016).

Strauss, Barry, 'Naval battle and sieges', in Philip Sabin, Hans van Wees and Michael M. Whitby (eds), *The Cambridge History of Greek and Roman Warfare, Volume 1* (Cambridge: Cambridge University Press, 2007), 223–47.

Starr, Stephen, *Revolt in Syria: Eye-witness to the Uprising* (London: Hurst and Co, 2015).

Sullivan, John and Elkus Adam, 'Command of the cities: towards a theory of urban strategies', in David Dilegge, Robert Bunker, John Sullivan and Alma Keshavarz (eds), *Blood and Concrete: 21st Century Conflict in Urban Centers and Megacities* (US: Xlibris, 2019), 84–101.

Sullivan, John and Elkus, Adam, 'Postcard from Mumbai: modern urban siege', in David Dilegge, Robert Bunker, John Sullivan and Alma Keshavarz (eds), *Blood and Concrete: 21st Century Conflict in Urban Centers and Megacities* (US: Xlibris, 2019), 32–53.

The Sunday Times Insight Team, *Ulster* (Harmondsworth: Penguin, 1972).

Taber, Robert, *War of the Flea: A Study of Guerrilla Warfare Theory and Practice* (Washington, DC: Potomac Books, 2002).

Tamari, Dov, 'Military operations in urban environments: the case of Lebanon, 1982', in Michael C. Desch (ed.), *Soldiers in Cities: Military Operations on Urban Terrain* (Carlisle, PA: Strategic Studies Institute, 2001), 29–56.

Therborn, Goran, *Cities of Power* (London: Verso, 2017).

Thomas, Timothy, 'The 31 December 1994–8 February 1995 Battle for Grozny', in William Robertson (ed.), *Block by Block: The Challenges of Urban Operations* (Ft Leavenworth, KS: US ACGS College Press, 2003),

Thompson, Robert, *Defeating Communist Insurgency: Experiences from Malaya and Vietnam* (London: Chatto & Windus, 1974).

Thornton, Rod, 'Getting it wrong: the crucial mistakes made in the early stages of the British Army's deployment to Northern Ireland', *Journal of Strategic Studies*, 30(1) (2007), 73–107.

Thucydides, *The Peloponnesian War* (Harmondsworth: Penguin, 1967).

Toomey, Charles Lane, *XVIII Airborne Corps in Desert Storm: From Planning to Victory* (Central Point, OR: Hellgate 2004).

Tracy, James D. (ed.), *City Walls: The Urban Enceinte in Global Perspective* (Cambridge: Cambridge University Press, 2000).

van Dam, Nicholas, *Destroying a Nation: The Civil War in Syria* (London: I. B. Tauris, 2017).

van der Bijl, Nick, *Operation Banner: The British Army in Northern Ireland 1969–2007* (Barnsley: Pen and Sword, 2017).

van Riper, Lieutenant General Paul, *A Concept for Future Military Operations on Urbanized Terrain* (Quantico, VA: Department of the Navy, Marine Corps Combat Development, 1997).

Venkatesh, Sudhir, *American Project* (Cambridge, MA: Harvard University Press, 2000).

Virgil, *The Aeneid*, trans. David West (London: Penguin 2003).

Verini, James, *They Will Have to Die Now: Mosul and the Fall of the Caliphate* (London: Oneworld, 2019).

Virilio, Paul, 'The state of emergency', in James Der Derian (ed.), *The Virilio Reader* (Oxford, Blackwell, 1998), 48–57.

Virilio, Paul, *Bunker Archaeology* (New York: Princeton Architectural Review, 2008).

Virilio, Paul and Lotrine, Sylvère, *Pure War* (New York: Semiotext(e), 1997).

Wahlman, Alec, *Storming the City* (Denton: University of North Texas Press, 2015).

War Department, FM 31–50, *Attack on a Fortified Position and Combat in Towns* (Washington, DC: US Government Printing Office, 1944).

Warfare Branch, Headquarters Field Army, *Operations in the Urban Environment* (Warminster: Land Warfare Development Centre, Doctrine Note 15/13).

Warfare Branch, *Urban Tactical Handbook* (Warminster: Land Warfare Centre, 2013).

Watson, Alexander, *The Fortress: The Great Siege of Przemyśl* (London: Allen Lane, 2019).

Webb, Patrick, 'The battles for Divis Flats: a study in community power', PhD thesis, Ulster University, 2016.

Weiss, Michael and Hassan, Hassan, *ISIS: Inside the Army of Terror* (New York: Regan Arts, 2016)

Weizman, Eyal, 'Strategic points, flexible lines, tense surfaces and political volumes: Ariel Sharon and the geometry of occupation', in Stephen Graham (ed.), *Cities, War and Terrorism* (London: Verso, 2004), 171–92.

Weizman, Eyal, 'The politics of verticality', Open Democracy, 2002: http://www.opendemocracy.net/ecology–politicsverticality/article_801.jsp).

Weizman, Eyal, *Hollow Land: Israel's Architecture of Occupation* (London: Verso, 2007).

White, Robert and Falkenberg White, Terry, 'Revolutionary in the city: on the resources of urban guerrillas', *Terrorism and Political Violence*, 3(4) (1991), 100–32.

White, Robert, 'From peaceful protest to guerrilla war: micromobilization of the Provisional Irish Republican Army', *American Journal of Sociology*, 94(6) (1989), 1277–302.

Whiteside, Craig and Mironova, Vera, 'Adaptation and innovation with an urban twist: changes to suicide tactics in the battle for Mosul', *Military Review*, November/December 2017, 78–85.

Winton, Doug, 'Is urban combat a great equalizer?', PhD thesis, John Hopkins University, 2018.

Wirth, Louis, *The Ghetto* (Chicago, IL: Chicago University Press, 1956).

Wirth, Louis, *On Cities and City Life: Selected Papers* (Chicago, IL: Chicago University Press, 1964).

Wolman, Abel, 'The metabolism of cities', *Scientific American*, 213 (1956), 179–90.

Wood, Kevin, *The Mother of All Battles* (Annapolis, MD: Naval Institute Press, 2008).

Yassin-Kassab, Robin and Al-Shami, Leila, *Burning Country: Syrians in Revolution and War* (London: Pluto Press, 2016).

Ydstebo, Palle, 'Russian operations: continuity, novelties and adaptation', in Janne Matlary and Tormod Heier (eds), *Ukraine and Beyond: Russian's Strategic Security Challenge to Europe* (London: Palgrave Macmillan, 2010), 153–61.

Zucchino, David, *Thunder Run: The Armored Strike to Capture Baghdad* (London: Atlantic Books, 2004).

Index

civilians (*cont.*)
  force ratios 57
  as hostages 149–50
  Houthis in Yemen 132
  influencing 182–4
  Iraq 116
  ISIS information operations
      191–7
  LA's homeless 69
  modern suffering of 12–13
  Mosul 4, 196
  Mumbai hotel attacks 8
  murder rates and 21–2
  outnumber military forces 183–4
  as partners 169
  rich and poor areas 69
  Sabra and Shatila 170–1
  Sarajevo 5–6
  social media mobilizes 189–91
  Syrians under Assad 132–3
  winning over 184–7
The Clanging of the Sword (ISIS videos)
      192
Clausewitz, Carl von, *On War* 20–1,
      26
close-quarters battle (CQB) 149–53,
      152
  five-step entry 151, *152*, 153
  hostage situations 149–50
  risks of 161–2
  room clearance 150–1
  stacks 161
Cluseret, Gustave Paul 91
Cold War
  air power and 115
  decline of mass armies following
      27–8
  insurgencies 42
  tanks 163
Colombia, FARC and 62
Comando Vermelho 61–4, 99, 139
The Combat Soldier (King) ix
Command of the Air (Douhet) 116
Commissar's House, assault on *see*
      Stalingrad, Russia
communication *see* information and
      intelligence; social media
concrete *see* walls
The Condition of the English Working Class
      (Engels) 69
conflict, definition of 21
Corregidor, Camp 175
  see also Ramadi, Iraq
Counter-Terrorist Service 159

COVID-19 pandemic 206–7
crime
  Brazilian supergangs 61–4
  compared to war 21–2
  drug cartels 62
  police in Ramadi 173
cyber operations 17
Cyprus
  EOKA 43
  force ratios 59
  insurgency 42, 43–4

Davis, Mike 68
Deane, Lt. Colonel Tony 173
Debord, Guy 144
Debray, Régis 61
  The Revolution in the Revolution? 46
Defensible Space (Newman) 96
Delbrück, Hans 25, 32
Deleuze, Gilles 144
Demosthenes, *Philippics* 169
desert combat 38
  see also Iraq
Dick, Philip K., *Do Androids Dream of
      Electric Sheep?* 210
Discourses (Machiavelli) 87
Do Androids Dream of Electric Sheep?
      (Dick) 210
Donbas war
  battle of Avdiivka 8
  civil and interstate war 32–3, 39
  proxy forces for Russia 180, 181
  Russian troops 204
  social media and 186
  urban infrastructure and 39
  see also Donetsk; Luhansk; Russia/
      Soviet Union; Ukraine
Donetsk 8
  concrete walls 86
  length of battle 157
  People's Army 39
Douhet, Giulio 210
  Command of the Air 109–10, 116
drones
  Fallujah model 117–21
  mapping and 128
  smart warfare and 211
  tactical 119
Dubai, Burj Khalifa in 68
Dubrovnik, Croatia 85
Dudayev, Dzhokhar 5, 135
Duffy, Christopher 25–6, 27–8, 32–3,
      38
Dürer, Albrecht 87

Printed in the USA
CPSIA information can be obtained
at www.ICGtesting.com
LVHW082241211123
764609LV00005B/89